DADS and DAUGHTERS

JOE KELLY

A Lark Production

BROADWAY BOOKS
NEW YORK

DADS and DAUGHTERS

How to Inspire, Understand, and
Support Your Daughter When
She's Growing Up So Fast

BROADWAY

A hardcover edition of this book was published in 2002
by Broadway Books.

For permissions credits, see p. 253

PRINTED IN THE UNITED STATES OF AMERICA

BROADWAY BOOKS and its logo, a letter B bisected on the diagonal, are
trademarks of Random House, Inc.

Visit our website at www.broadwaybooks.com

First trade paperback edition published 2003

The Library of Congress has cataloged the hardcover edition as follows:
Kelly, Joe, 1954–
Dads and daughters : how to inspire, understand, and support your
daughter when she's growing up so fast / Joe Kelly.—1st ed.
          p.   cm.
          1. Fathers and daughters. I. Title.
          HQ755.85   .K445   2002
          306.874'2—dc21   2002018526

ISBN 0-7679-0834-1

*For Mavis Gruver, Nia Kelly, and Nancy Gruver,
the women who made me a dad*

CONTENTS

INTRODUCTION

Every father can make a huge difference in his daughter's life. A father is the first man his daughter knows. With that potent position of "first man" comes the ability to set the norm of manliness for her—a norm that ultimately can be stronger than what anyone else tells her. When we truly listen to our daughters, we help reduce the odds that our girls will be caught in a cultural straitjacket that limits their options and behavior because of their gender. We can fight the effects of the gender straitjacket by never requiring or expecting our daughters to wear it when they are with us—thus helping them feel a freedom they may not have elsewhere.

By reading these words, you've already begun to do more than pay lip service to becoming the best possible father you can be. Many wonderful doors open when we explore why a father-daughter relationship matters so much, as you'll discover in the coming pages.

My own journey with daughters began in 1980, when my wife Nancy Gruver and I had twin girls.

In 1992, that journey accelerated when Nancy and our daughters, Nia and Mavis, decided to launch an alternative magazine to counter the lousy content of mainstream girls' magazines like *Seventeen, YM, Teen,* and the like. The result was *New Moon: The Magazine for Girls and Their Dreams,* an international, ad-free bimonthly that is edited by girls between the ages of eight and fourteen. As things turned out, I became *New Moon's* first employee; answering phones, entering subscriptions, copyediting, occasionally vacuuming, and working closely with the fifteen or so girls who edit *New Moon.* Every other Sunday afternoon, these girls (including our daughters) met in our living room to decide everything about each issue of the magazine: its theme, cover art, feature stories, choice of authors and letters to the editor, and more. In between meetings, while the girl editors were in school, I worked to carry out their instructions. Our editorial meetings bubbled with vigorous discussion in which girls shared their insights, opinions, concerns, and dreams. They didn't tolerate overbearing adult behavior, and I worked to be a partner, not a boss. I learned a ton about what it's like to be a girl in today's world.

For seven years, I also edited *New Moon Network: For Adults Who Care About Girls,* a newsletter gathering the experiences of parents, stepparents, teachers, coaches, researchers, clergy, counselors, relatives, and other adults concerned about rearing healthy, confident girls. Today, I am publisher of the national newsletter *Daughters: For Parents of Girls.* All of this gives me the chance to talk with dads of daughters all the time. While *New Moon* is still going strong, my work with fathers and daughters took another path in 1999.

That's when northern California father and *New Moon* subscriber Michael Kieschnick e-mailed us about an idea he had: a national organization for fathers and daughters aimed at helping fathers better understand the issues daughters face, and better understand the positive influence we can have on those issues. Soon thereafter, Michael created the national nonprofit called Dads and Daughters, and hired me to run it. Dads and Daughters (DADs) is a membership organization that, through education and advocacy, provides tools to strengthen father-daughter relationships and to transform the pervasive cultural messages that value girls more for how they look than for who they are. DADs uses *Daughters* (which DADs owns), biweekly e-mail newsletters, monthly member activism, an extensive Web site, media interviews, educational materials, radio programs, an online fathers discussion group, and presentations around the country to accomplish that mission. Through DADs, I've met thousands more fathers.

Over the last ten years while writing, traveling, and speaking about daughters and dads, I've been thinking about the need for this book. I have written it to challenge you, not only to reassure you; to raise questions we can begin to answer together, not to placate any father. There are critical issues our daughters need us to address and we cannot rise to the occasion without taking a critical look at ourselves. My goal is that, after reading this book, you see your relationship with your daughter more clearly, appreciate your own importance in her life, start to listen to her with a sharper sense of hearing, and share your experience, strength, and hope with her and with other dads.

No girl's life will be free of problems. Whether those problems are large or small, a father's involvement can be key. That fact underlies everything in this book and should underlie everything we do as fathers of daughters. In these pages, you'll gain a greater awareness of the confusing world girls face today. You'll understand how you can be a positive influence in every part of that world. Plus, you'll learn ways to help reduce the number and severity of problems for your daughter and for other girls.

Each chapter lays out an issue, exploring some of its complexity. All of it is in plain English, easy to understand and work into your life. You'll read about how fathers:

- successfully listen to girls
- overcome fathering hurdles
- nurture a daughter's emerging sexuality
- encourage athletics and physical activity
- support good body image
- fight cultural limitations placed on girls (and boys)
- deal with serious problems like alcohol abuse
- strengthen a daughter's confidence and savvy
- build a lifelong father-daughter relationship.

To help accomplish all this, the book has plenty of practical tools. After all, what dad doesn't like a nicely stocked toolbox? There are tips, resources, and ideas to help you figure out where you are and where you'd like to go in your relationship with your daughter. These tools provide ways to have fun with our daughters, communicate better with them, and help them succeed.

While writing this book, I tape-recorded extended conversations with more than 125 fathers of daughters in Nebraska, New Mexico, Arizona, Oklahoma, California, Oregon, Montana, Minnesota, New York, New Jersey, the District of Columbia, Maryland, Virginia, Pennsylvania, Wisconsin, Illinois, and Massachusetts. These men are grandfathers, stepfathers, biological fathers, married, divorced, raising a second family, widowed, and never married. They come from a wide range of socioeconomic classes, family situations, and ethnicity. In about a quarter of the interviews, I also talked with the father's daughter or stepdaughter. This book also draws on thousands of submissions to the DADs online discussion group. I make no claim that these interviews and comments add up to a scientific sample. These are simply conversations between fathers.

Fair warning: you may get angry, inspired, upset, encouraged, or all of the above. That's OK—even good. But you'll also get involved and smarter and learn how to make changes. You'll see that when we expand opportunities for girls, we expand them for boys, too.

Fathers influence how daughters see themselves. With a father's positive words and support, a daughter can be safe and healthy, and can thrive no matter where life takes her. A girl whose father listens to and respects her will *expect* her life partner to listen to her and treat her well. That's why it's so important for us to show and tell our daughters that we believe they are capable of anything! Fathering a daughter with love and respect ensures she will choose people and situations that nourish her long after she's left our house. There's no greater legacy for us to leave our daughters.

Note to reader: The indented and italicized portions of the text are words drawn from interviews with and writing by real fathers (and a few daughters). Some people's names have been changed in order to respect their privacy.

DADS and DAUGHTERS

1.

"I DON'T KNOW WHAT SHE WANTS FROM ME.": BUILDING A FATHER-DAUGHTER RELATIONSHIP

Perhaps every father should be issued a football mouthguard when his daughter is born, since he's liable to spend the next few decades biting his tongue.

When my daughter Nia was thirteen, she announced that she was going to dye her hair orange. In the following split second, a volcano of emotions and objections exploded in my gut. If, at the last possible instant, I hadn't bitten my tongue, here's what I would have blurted out:

1. Oh no, you don't! No daughter of mine is going to look like a freak or a punk!
2. What is wrong with you?
3. You're so pretty; don't mess it up.
4. For years I've been working so hard to instill in you that your appearance doesn't matter as much as what's inside. And this is how you repay me? First, you start wearing a little makeup

(without telling me) and now you want to dye your hair? And dye it *orange*?!?

5. I'm a failure as a father. You have completely caved in to seventh-grade peer pressure.
6. How dare you dye your hair without asking my permission first?
7. What's happening to my little girl?

Fortunately for me (and both of my daughters), another, louder voice caught my internal ear just before I opened my mouth to let her have it. That voice cried: *Pick your battles!* I thought to myself, *It's only her hair. How much energy did my father and I waste arguing about the length of my hair at thirteen? What real difference does it make? At least she told me and didn't just show up with an orange fait accompli.*

And then, finally, my teeth freed my tongue and out came a sparkling, insightful response.

"Oh," I said. "When?"

"We're gonna do it tomorrow night after school."

"Oh," I said (repeating my eloquence while scrambling for what to say next). "What are you using?"

"Stuff from Walgreen's. It washes out after seven showers or something."

"Oh," I replied (Tip #1: Once you discover a good fathering phrase, keep using it), "okay."

I still wasn't happy about the idea of orange hair, but I decided not to raise a stink. I also decided not to be terrifically supportive—or even hang around the house—when the deed was done. The next day after school, though, my curiosity won out. I went to the bathroom to watch as Nia sat on the edge on the tub with an old towel draped over her shoulders. Her sister, Mavis, donned clear plastic gloves, squeezed some garish goo out of a tube, and started working it into Nia's wet hair. The whole scene looked a bit wild and ridiculous. Again I had to bite my tongue, this time to keep from giggling.

The girls were having fun, but also taking the task quite seriously. In addition, they kept their antennae up for objections or snide comments from Mom or Dad. Since it was their first time mounting such an elaborate home beauty salon, there were false starts and several "Oops! Gotta try it again" moments. Soon, all four of us were giggling and I goofily stuck my head over to see if they'd put some dye in my thinning hair. That's the moment when Mom snapped a photograph that I now have framed on my bookshelf.

In the years since, this photo has accompanied numerous media stories about my work and me. Magazines and newspapers choose it because it's a funny, animated image. But it's important to me because it captures a significant moment in my development as the father of daughters. In twenty-four hours, I'd journeyed from wanting to angrily reject Nia's decision to accepting—and even enjoying—her choice. Dyeing hair in the bathroom may not seem like a major turning point in anyone's life, but in that minor moment, I discovered a major capacity to accept how Nia's journey is different than mine—because she is a girl.

My daughters' concern with their appearance was not as intense as many of their peers, but it was real and important to them. Even though I didn't really understand why they cared so much about how they looked—and passionately wished that they would care not at all—I needed to accept that they cared in order to accept them.

Even better, while participating in the silly bathroom scene, I began to *celebrate* how my daughters and their journeys are their own, not mine. Freed from my initial, enraged knee-jerk reaction, I saw that Nia's orange-dye decision sprang less from peer pressure than from experimenting with who she wants to be. I was proud of how womanly the girls acted by doing all the dyeing themselves—and was also secretly happy when Nia's dark brown hair so overpowered the orange dye that it required a little white lie to say, "Oh, of course I can see it!"

Today I treasure this snapshot because it shows my girls' independence, my faith in their judgment, and how much I enjoy being their father. I also treasure it because it reminds me how different it is to be a girl.

FATHERING A DAUGHTER

I'm really struggling with the fact that I don't think that I verbalize how wonderful my daughters are often enough. I do tell them, but it does not flow spontaneously from my being. I don't have the training or the modeling for it. I'll say, "Good job!" But I also don't want it to be a "job." You know—the idea that you have value because you did something. That has been my toughest thing. Maybe just sitting with them with my arm around them, maybe that's telling them how special they are to me. I'm not sure. I have very little confidence about myself.

Henry

Our impact as fathers on our daughters is astounding. We may sense this truth, but not fully understand it. Often, we can't understand our daughters at all. Having grown up as boys, we are in the dark about what it's like to be a girl. Fathers ask me this question all the time: *Do you ever feel like you don't know why these girls are acting the way they are? I feel like I'm living on another planet.*

Sure, most of us spend a lot of time with females: colleagues, mothers, sisters, girlfriends, aunts, wives, and partners. But daughters affect us with greater intensity than any other female in our lives. We might be able to articulate a little bit how our life has changed (should anyone bother to ask), but the picture is often fuzzy. We worry that we're not doing things right, not preparing her well enough, not getting through to her, and that's scary.

> *The other night, my sixteen-year-old daughter was in a lot of pain. She pulled something playing hockey and the doctor gave her a shot of cortisone. She had a bad reaction to it, and was getting almost hysterical, hyperventilating. Her mother couldn't deal with it, so I tried to calm her down. I told her to breathe into a paper bag, to slow her breathing, to relax. No matter what I said, it seemed to make the situation worse. She accused me of yelling at her, told me to leave, she only wanted her mother. Finally, we took her to the emergency room, where the doctor instantly got her to breathe into a paper bag. It was so frustrating. Why couldn't I get her to listen? Am I not sensitive enough? I feel as if no matter what I do, it's not the right thing. I'm worried that she's starting to flounder. Getting hurt and quitting hockey is not a good sign. I think she's scared of all the decisions she's going to have to start making, and I'm scared that I haven't prepared her well enough. Have I not given her the right tools to make her way in life? What am I supposed to be giving her? I don't know what she wants from me.*
>
> *Randall*

In these intense emotional moments—whether fear or joyous pride—we know that our life has been fundamentally changed because we're raising (or have raised) a child who is female.

Throughout this book, the voices of many fathers' experiences show that none of us fathers is alone. These voices illustrate the immense power of the daughter-father relationship, how influential this relationship is from the very beginning of a girl's life, and the influence a father-daughter pair can have on everyone around them.

We don't hear much talk about the influence of fathers on daughters. It's much more common to hear about how girls are influenced by their mothers. But all it takes is a moment's reflection to start realizing the huge impact we fathers have on every one of our daughters. To find the roots of a father's influence, think of your own daughter. It's normal and natural that she wants to know what's interesting to, or gets the attention of, members of the opposite sex. That's important knowledge for her to have even if she never dates a boy or marries a man, because she lives in a world half full of boys and men.

Where will she turn first for this information? Most often, she'll turn to the first member of the opposite sex she gets to know: Dad. Even a stepfather, while not always the first male a girl knows, has a huge influence because he spends so much time with her. So the way we act toward our daughters and the other females in her life is what she will expect from boys and men. The same is true for our attitudes, words, and beliefs. In all of these, we represent to her the richness, honor, and value of being a man. When we are true to her and true to the best in our masculine heritage, she will learn to respect men and treat them as equals. She will learn to gravitate toward men who respect her and treat her as an equal, while turning away from men who threaten, violate, and abuse. That's good for both a daughter and her father. Perhaps that's what's behind the old saying: *When a girl grows up, she marries her father.* Her life partner is very likely to reflect her dad's characteristics. As one woman put it:

> *My father is my one role model as far as male, human behavior. And I really compare all other men in the world to my father. He is the most loving, the most accepting, the most honorable, the most responsible, the most nurturing—one of the greatest humanitarians I've ever known. He is the model that I judge all other men by—fair or not fair. Having this kind of relationship*

with him has given me a lot of trust, and it's given me a lot of
nurturing and guidance. That love and support and encourage-
ment I had through those years, and continue to have, has made
me a much stronger person.

Julia

We have great influence on our daughters and many choices about how to use it. We can send our daughters down their life roads with clear and healthy expectations for men, or leave our daughters lost in tangled underbrush, confused about what to accept from men. They will probably be drawn toward men who choose paths similar to the ones we tread as men and fathers. What does that mean for us? At minimum, it means being an integral part of our daughters' lives, not abandoning them to wander into the world of boys and men without our example of strong, supportive, and nurturing masculinity. Our example is the road map our daughters use to discover relationships (romantic or not) with boys and men we'd be proud to have as sons and brothers.

Fatherly influence reaches many parts of a daughter's life. Research demonstrates how important fathers are in the career and academic success of girls. Involved fathers show daughters ways to navigate the world outside the family, are role models of independence and competency, and are a moral anchor for them. We affect our daughters in thousands of ways, and we'll talk about many of them during the course of the book.

When we first reflect on the enormity of this influence and responsibility, it can seem overwhelming—even oppressive. As one dad told me, "If I screw up, that means she's going to spend the rest of her life with a screw-up. I don't want that!" Well, don't despair and don't give up. We can do the job well, even if we sometimes feel like we're completely in the dark. There's no magic formula for fathers to follow, but talking to each other sheds light on how to proceed—recognizing that fathering is far more art than it is science.

My own daughter recently recalled an example of a fathering moment in which I got to practice what I preach:

> *One of my earliest memories is of you sewing new backing on our baby blankets. We couldn't have been more than two years old. And that backing held up for the next nineteen years. But last year you were in a hurry, and accidentally grabbed my blanky and packed it off to a garage sale. When I discovered it was missing, I was very upset, even though I did my best to not make you feel bad about it—mistakes happen. But then, a couple weeks later, I got a box in the mail at college. Inside was a new blanky. You picked out the fabric, and pieced it all together, and learned to use the sewing machine to make it for me. And it's beautiful! But what really makes it special is that you stopped kicking yourself about making that mistake, and instead set about doing something special to make me happy and let me know how much you love me.*
>
> *Mavis*

True fathering is a unique and powerful contribution to a daughter—one that Will Glennon, in his book *The Collected Wisdom of Fathers*, describes as a miracle.

> *True fathering is not the physical act of planting a seed, it is the conscious decision to tend and nourish the seedling. Real fathering is not biological—it is the conscious choice to build an unconditional and unbreakable connection to another human being. Once that choice is made, it cannot be unmade.*

WHAT I'VE LEARNED

Fathers are most successful when we view the influence we have on our daughters as an opportunity as well as an obligation. But many of us don't see the opportunity or can't figure out how to use it wisely through the daily confusion clouding who our daughters are and what's going on with them.

Fathers with daughters have a wildly contradictory set of visceral feelings about raising girls.

- We want to protect our daughter more than anyone else who has ever been part of our lives. Yet we often feel as if there's no way that we can.
- We want our daughter to be attractive but not to sexually attract anyone. We pray she'll someday be happily married, but we don't want any boys coming around. We're scared stiff of her becoming a sexual being, but don't have anyone to talk with about it.
- We're baffled by and terrified of our daughters' messy emotions and messy bodies.
- We want to connect with her so that we become as special in her life as she is in ours. But some days she'll have nothing to do with us. Other days, our connection sparkles and we feel the power of our love for each other; maybe the most unconditional love we've ever experienced.
- We want to build her up, but instead our words sometimes seem to knock her down.
- We want to communicate, but we don't know when, where, whether, or how to begin talking with her about sexuality, body image, self-worth, careers, money, school, relationships, parenting, sports . . . you name it.
- We can't seem to hit the right note in listening so she'll talk, or in talking so she'll listen. We might easily banter with and tease a son, yet be totally unable to predict how a conversation with a daughter will go—or if there will even be one.
- We're proud of what she accomplishes independently in school, onstage, or in sports. Yet we're apprehensive about her independence and not sure how to let her go.

If anything on this list sounds familiar to you, it's no surprise. We've all ridden at least one loop of this roller-coaster. When my daughters were teenagers, they'd swing back and forth from snuggling and sharing secrets with me to storming off and slamming doors should I even dare to open my mouth. I couldn't make any sense of it either.

I had sisters who were younger than I was, and I've been married twice now, and neither of those experiences taught me very much about girls or women; not as much as seeing my daughters from the start and trying to figure out how they work. My girls in different ways reflect me, but they're still so different. I thought I would know better. I still don't understand a lot about girls or women.

Herb

FIVE HURDLES FOR FATHERS

I'm not sure what a father to a daughter is supposed to be, since I was a son.

Jerry

When we start fathering a daughter, the obstacles may seem insurmountable. The hurdles spring up from our own attitudes and ideas, and the attitudes and ideas of people around us.

Hurdle #1: We grew up as boys.

We simply have no experience in what it's like to grow up a girl.

My teenage girlfriends were sometimes moody and mysterious; but when I was sixteen, it felt like I could understand *them.* It was much harder to understand my own daughters when they were sixteen. No wonder we feel in the dark.

*I know that my daughters treat me differently than they treat
their mother. And I don't know if that's because of the way I
treat them or the way I learned how to be around girls from my
father. They tend to confide in their mother more than they do
me. It would be nice if that were a little bit different. But they
get embarrassed talking about certain things in front of me, and
not embarrassed in front of their mother.*

Victor

No matter how much we love them and how much we want to connect, our growing daughters are sometimes a complete mystery to
us, just because they're females. From a daughter's earliest days, we
ask ourselves "What is she thinking?" Believe it or not, we *can* begin
finding out what's on her mind, open up communication, and improve the connection, but that requires asking for information and
guidance. That leads to our second hurdle.

> ***Hurdle #2: There's no one to talk to.*** Who can we talk to
> about raising a girl (or even about being a father, period)?
> Women talk about mothering all the time with their daugh-
> ters and mothers, with each other, around the water cooler,
> with relatives, at parties. They always seem to find a place to
> talk about—and to—their kids.

So where can we get the tools and insight we need? Not many
places immediately spring to mind. We're afraid that if we ask our
daughters' mothers a basic question, we may get a roll of the eyes
that leaves us feeling like dolts. It's embarrassing to ask our own
mothers for advice, and our dads seem to know as little as we do. We
fathers are more likely to talk with each other about the complexities
of baseball free-agency than the complexities of fatherhood.
Without fathering conversations, dads don't get much information
from each other; and we can't really rely on osmosis.

Osmosis would be great if it worked, because other fathers have lots of parenting expertise. Robert, who lives across the street from me, has two daughters like I do. George lives next door on one side and John on the other; they have three kids each. Add up the ages of all our kids, and within twenty yards of my front door are three other fathers and together we have more than 160 years' experience raising daughters (and twenty-five years raising sons).

But how many of us actually talk to another father about things? "Yikes, no way. Guys don't do that sort of thing. What would the neighbors think?" We end up not really knowing what our role is.

> *Hurdle #3: We're Stereotyped.* One minute, fathers are seen as second-class parents—invisible or incompetent. The next moment, we're cast as all-knowing superheroes. Which role do we take on?

Most folks (including dads) think that Mom is best suited to be the primary and most influential parent. That mindset manifests itself everywhere from the school nurse to family court. How often has the school nurse called you at work to come pick up your sick kid? Does she even have your work number? It's not hard to find signs that fathers are seen as irrelevant, if they're even noticed at all. Watch the sitcom daddy who doesn't know which end of the baby to put the bottle in, or who gags when changing a diaper. That's the stereotype of Daddy as a dummy.

The opposite stereotype pops up on TV, too. A great example is *The Cosby Show,* the most popular sitcom of the 1980s and still in reruns on cable. Bill Cosby's character, Dr. Heathcliff Huxtable, has a wife, kids, a beautiful house, and the rich lifestyle of a high-salary OB/GYN physician. It's a wonderful, funny show with fabulous examples of family respect and support. The only thing is, Cliff never seems to go to work or have outside stresses. He's always available; the perfect parent wisely, lovingly, and humorously raising wonderful children.

No real man gets to live a fantasy fatherhood like Cliff Huxtable. Ours is a less handsome reality where being a provider means actually spending time at work.

> *I guess my model of a perfect dad is a "Father Knows Best," or a Bill Cosby, or someone who always has the solution: mild-mannered, who can calm the troubled storm with a few words. I haven't figured out how to do that yet. I guess to a certain degree that's why I feel inadequate. Because I think [what I'm doing] is not how it's supposed to be. This is not how I'm supposed to act. And I guess I'm basing that on what the ideal TV father is supposed to be like. But in real life, we have a lot more problems than they have on TV.*
>
> Rob

Hurdle #4: The Provider Predicament. Growing up, we learned that a father's primary role is to provide for his family. That's a true and good thing for us to learn. But too many of us equate the key word—provide—with our wallets.

We expect ourselves (and others expect us) to spend more time at a paying job than Mom, so that we fulfill our role as provider for our kids. This often makes practical financial sense since men still earn more, on average, than women do (an ugly reality we'll look at later). So, a father believes, *If I'm the one doing most of the paid work, my family will have more money and be better off.*

However, this way of thinking requires a significant trade-off that we seldom address squarely. To meet that relentless economic provider expectation, we spend more time, energy, and attention away from home (and our kids) than mothers do.

> *I realize that I don't have that much of a relationship with Amelia on an internal level a lot of times, because I work. That's sad, because there's always something you miss. You have regret*

*because you don't communicate like you should. You're always off
doing something and you're separated from each other. I don't
know if that's natural, but I have a lot of regret that I haven't
done enough for her and her brother. I haven't been there all the
times I should've been there.*

Daniel

Our fatherly impact is in the details of life. Think of all the looks exchanged and words we speak every time we change a diaper; the affection we show when we walk the midnight floor calming a colicky baby; or the pride we convey by listening to our daughter read her first books. Our greatest opportunity to deepen and strengthen our relationships with our children lies in the never-ending, mundane (often boring and monotonous) daily caring for those children.

*About five years ago, my wife went back to school. Two of her
six-week internships were out of town. It was very hard to work
and manage the household. I have all the respect in the world for
parents who do this year after year without someone coming back
after six weeks. But I am also forever grateful for that time with
Kris and Lindsay, because I got closer to them than I ever had
before. I think that dads are cheating themselves if they aren't actively involved in fathering their children.*

David

Some folks use the term *second shift* to describe the unpaid work at home that parents (mostly moms) do after getting home from their jobs. Younger fathers seem to be doing more second-shift work than we older dads; but very few of us pull as much child-rearing duty as the mothers of our children do. Sometimes, if we try to do more, mothers resist, criticizing how we handle things. They may be hesitant to share influence within one of the few realms in which women traditionally hold sway—the home. It's hard to stay motivated when we feel defensive or put down. But these are not good reasons to pull back; they are opportunities to communicate about parenting and learn from women who may have been told lots more about the job than we were.

The more we buy into the strict expectations of a narrow, money-based definition of the father-provider role, the more time we spend away from our kids and the more we miss out on being a dad. But it's hard to know what other route to take, since few of us got the clearest road maps from our own fathers.

> *Hurdle #5: The Silence of Our Dads.* How much second-shift work did your father do? Probably not much. How much did he tell you about how to be a father and why it matters so much? Ditto.

If your dad was like mine, he said little (if anything) to you about fatherhood. He probably showed by example that a father works to bring in money and is the final judge when it comes to laying down the law at home—even if he doesn't spend enough time at home to know much about what's going on there.

> *The first time I heard my father's voice coming out of my mouth was when my daughter was very young and I got angry about her making some noise. I had this feeling that my father didn't have to put up with that racket. He just had this patriarchal entitlement; the feeling of coming home from work and having everything taken care of: "Do it because I said so." I didn't want to be that way, but there was my father's attitude coming out of my mouth. [From that] I learned a whole lot about the importance of process and staying in touch. I really think the fundamental job of being a parent is just being present.*
>
> *Peter*

Many of our fathers were withdrawn and distant from others in the family, absorbed in work or booze or exhaustion—if they even stayed around through all of our childhood. Withdrawal, abandonment, and laying down the law leave little room for father-son conversation or questions about being a dad. So, compared to what moms usually learn from their mothers and their kin, we're flying deaf, mute, and blind.

We seldom share this insecurity with other fathers; hence, we often feel alone, our confidence shaken, and we learn little from each other. Meanwhile, the way our fathers did things sometimes doesn't seem to make sense today.

Hey, how do I do this? There isn't anyone here to show me what to do and the roles are all different now—both their mother and I work full time. Am I being too wimpy? Too rigid? Am I just trying to win the argument or do the kids really need to know that parents do sometimes know what's best? How are they going to make it unless I lay down the rules? But laying down the rules doesn't really teach them to think. It's part of the old way, where Dad is "in charge" and the kids better know it. For me, the first hurdle is to accept freedom to change the father role to whatever makes sense, no matter how it was done before.

Dave

There are two wonderful things about all this uncertainty. One is that we can create new ways to father. The other is that we can break the Silence of the Dads and start talking to our kids and to each other about how we're playing this gig. This is actually fun and exciting to do!

FATHERING YOUR WAY

More fathers are accepting the freedom to change the father role to whatever makes sense for them, no matter how it was done before.

Younger dads seems to be developing some vocabulary to surmount the classic silence of generations before us. A year 2000 study by the Radcliffe Institute at Harvard finds that 79 percent of men between age forty and forty-nine said challenging work and career advancement were more important than additional family time. But 82 percent of men between age twenty and thirty-nine put having more family time *ahead* of work and career advancement. Seventy-one percent of the younger men said they would give up some pay for more family time.

Several professional athletes put faces to these statistics. In the midst of the 2000 Olympics, basketball player Alonzo Mourning flew halfway around the world, from Australia to Miami, to participate in the birth of his daughter (named, appropriately enough, Sydney). Mourning missed three games of the U.S. team's gold-medal run, and seemed bemused by the media fuss made over his decision. "What else would I do?" he said, a bit baffled as to why anyone would ask why he skipped playing ball to help his daughter be born.

Professional golfer Phil Mickelson led the prestigious 1999 U.S. Open in Pinehurst, North Carolina, when back home in Scottsdale, Arizona, his pregnant wife, Amy, was trying to delay the onset of labor. After Saturday's round, reporters asked Mickelson what would happen if his wife went into labor before the tournament ended—say, at the sixteenth hole of Sunday's final round, battling Payne Stewart and Tiger Woods down the stretch. Mickelson said that if his caddy's beeper sent word that Amy's labor was under way, he would leave immediately for Arizona. "But how could you give up the rare chance to win a major?" reporters pressed. "It's not worth the tournament," Mickelson replied. "Come the middle of June next year, we're going to have another U.S. Open. This is the birth of my first child."

As it turned out, the Mickelsons' daughter, Amanda, was born on Monday, the day after Mickelson lost by one stroke to Stewart at the eighteenth green—on Father's Day. As the competitors embraced, Stewart (whose own children lost him in a plane crash weeks later) told Mickelson, "There's nothing like being a father."

Mourning and Mickelson each recognized that his daughter's birth was something that simply could not be duplicated. The same holds true for the rest of her life, too. My daughter's entire childhood happens as often as her birth: exactly *once*. I can't be satisfied with just being a Lamaze coach or a breadwinner.

The challenge (and the freedom) for fathers today is to carry our delivery-room intensity into the rest of our children's lives. Yes, it's an enormous obligation; it is also an exhilarating opportunity. Our daughters don't get second shots at having their childhood with us as their fathers, either—and girls like the following teenager know it, too.

> *So many parents of my friends are split up, and they come to school saying, "I hate my dad so much. I hate him." And I think, "How could you hate your dad?" I can't understand how they could just never want to be around him. My friend repeatedly asks her dad to come to her games, repeatedly asks him to come to her choir concerts. And he'll say, "Yeah, I'll come." And he'll never show. She is so enraged at him right now. And that's scary. I couldn't live with that.*
>
> *Ana*

In fact, a daughter's childhood is so fascinating that we seldom lack for motivation to be part of it. That's true even if, because of divorce, separation, or other difficulties, we live away from our daughter. If we're willing to look, there are effective, loving, and supportive ways to be a vital part of our daughters' growing up, regardless of where we live.

> *DEAN: I have this theory, right or wrong, that there's got to be some sort of normalcy during the time we're together. It's hard to have*

normalcy, 'cause we can't always meet in the same city, but anyway,
the normal thing for the two of us is that we both like to read. We'll
normally go to a bookstore, we'll buy a bunch of stuff, go back to the
hotel room, read, watch a little television, order food, and act like it's
our world. We don't do "Disneyland Dad" weekends because that
isn't real.

LIZ: Yeah. When we read books, we just totally click. We're in our
own separate world together. We don't really pay attention to the
outside the two or three days we're together.

The payoff for a daughter is easy to hear in how lovingly Liz remembers details of hanging around a hotel room with her dad—
just being together. Listen to how huge the payoff is for fathers who
successfully parent across a distance, too.

For me the most moving moment was about six years ago, when
my daughter was eleven. I had been divorced within that year.
We'd stopped at an Arby's to have lunch on our way to her
grandfolks', and I distinctly remember having this wonderful
conversation with her one on one. Before then it seemed like we
were always in groups going somewhere, or doing something. But
this moment was so rewarding. I felt like I knew from that point
on that I was going to be a big factor in her life. Up until then,
I was worried that with the divorce I would lose that relation-
ship. It really started something for me in my development as a
better father.

Andy

Of course, we have to take the simple step of making time for this
special relationship—even if it's just driving somewhere in the car.
Then, we have to keep our eyes and ears open if we hope to figure
out what comes next.

LISTEN TO GIRLS

Girls tend to be a riddle to fathers. Like any mystery, our relationships with our daughters can be frightening, exciting, entertaining, baffling, enlightening, or leave us completely in the dark; sometimes all at once.

If we want to unravel this mystery, we have to pay attention, even in the most ordinary moments. If we want to figure it out, we have to listen even before our daughters can speak.

> *At three days old, she had jaundice, and they were giving her the foot prick to get a blood sample. The person giving it asked me to give her a pacifier or hold her but I told her, "That's your business, you are the one who wants the blood, I don't need the blood. You prick her and she is going to be mad, because it hurts like hell. Let her scream; let her have those feelings." At that moment I realized that everyone is going to try to snuff her feelings. It starts that early—from the very beginning. Stick something in her mouth and say, "Don't feel this, it's O.K." Well, I don't believe that, and as a result I think she is a lot better off.*
>
> *Jeff*

Why is it so important for us to listen to girls? Because a girl's voice may be the most valuable and most threatened resource she has. Her voice is the conduit for her heart, brains, and spirit. When she speaks boldly and clearly—literally and metaphorically—then she is much safer and surer. We have to nurture these qualities.

Dr. Mary Pipher's best-seller, *Reviving Ophelia: Saving the Selves of Adolescent Girls*, is the most widely known of a cadre of books and studies documenting the silencing of girls' voices in our culture during the pivotal adolescent years. Research into the development of girls shows that the norm for girls is to be loud, opinionated, and physically confident until age twelve or so. But then a typical girl will begin, in several important ways, to silence her voice and herself.

The sassy, tree-climbing ten-year old (with feet spread wide, chest puffed out, and an opinionated answer for every question) expects justice from the world for everyone, including herself. She assumes she will be taken seriously when she shouts, "That's not fair!" But then this strutting child often turns into a soft-spoken, passive thirteen-year old (with timid stance, shoulders hunched to hide her chest, and answers of "I don't know" to even the most basic questions), who may still demand justice from the world—but, strangely, not for herself.

Granted, the energy and rough edges of the ten-year-old can be a little tough to live with, but there seem to be few signs in the thirteen-year-old that her younger self ever existed. Where did she go? Underground? Why does she feel the need to silence her voice?

My wife, Nancy Gruver, writes a lot about this question. She says, "A girl silences herself because she encounters a culture that still encourages her, in ways both subtle and blatant, to put her own needs second. A culture that is extraordinarily uncomfortable with girls who know what they want and expect to get it. A culture that labels girls' complaints as whining and their pursuit of their desires as bitchiness and self-centered."

A girl feels good about herself when she is loud and bold. Then she runs into the notion (sometimes reinforced by Dad) that loud behavior is not ladylike. She hears that it's unattractive to recognize your own needs and speak up openly for them. People (sometimes within her family) begin seeing her as a sexual object rather than as a person. She begins to wear the gender straitjacket that squeezes out her breath while rewarding her more for her looks, passivity, and being soft-spoken than for her passions, insights, and beliefs.

A girl also gets strong messages that silencing herself is the only way to maintain her relationships with girlfriends, boyfriends, family, and anyone who is important to her. She learns the myth that loudness and friction will threaten the survival of relationships—

and that a relationship will not continue if she demands that it meet her needs. It's not a pretty picture in which to imagine our daughters. Many adult women spend years trying to emerge from this underground and reconnect with that spunky ten-year-old.

Fortunately, we can help address many of these problems. Since the father-daughter relationship is one of her most important ones, we are in a unique position to counter these negative cultural messages by encouraging our daughters to speak up and rewarding them when they do. The best way of doing this is to actively listen to our daughters.

When we turn our attention to what a daughter says, does, and cares about, we show her that a crucial man in her life—her father—cares about who she is, above all else. When we respect what our daughters' voices say, we build up their inner strength.

> *RIK: I'm proud of the fact that she'll include me in things that I need to be concerned about. I don't expect her to tell me every little thing. But I think the trust is the thing that I'm the proudest about. I'm a single dad and the laundry guy, so I go through her pockets to try to keep the stuff from destroying the washer. And I'll find notes from her friends at school. I never read them, but the fact that she doesn't hide them from me means a lot to me. In a sense that ensures her privacy. Being able to communicate, that's the key thing. She isn't afraid to share things with me or get my opinion, but she'll also share her creative ideas with me, and her takes on things: how she reads something. We have a lot of fun with that.*
>
> *I see other kids who don't talk to their parents that way. And it's sad because I think a big reason is that a lot of guys don't really try to extract what's important to their kids from their kids. They're missing out.*
>
> *ERIKA: The thing I love most is the way I can tell him things that normal parents would get really, really upset about. And he's just really laid back about it. I can talk to him about my problems or*

something that I did. He wouldn't freak out, he would just tell me. Trust. That's it right there. The trust that I could leave stuff in my pockets and he won't read them when he does the laundry. Even though I wouldn't mind if he did; of course some of my letters, I don't want him to read. I have my private life, but if I want to open that up to him, I do.

RIK: I don't doubt for one minute that she values her relationship with me as much as I value my relationship with her. It's extraordinary. We have kids over to our house and you can just tell that there's an uneasiness in them. But she is so grounded, and so well adjusted and involved that I sense it's because we do have such a good relationship. Frankly, I hope that a by-product of our relationship is that she will understand men better, so she will have a little less difficulty in her boy/girl relationships.

Listening—really paying attention—gives our daughters great confidence and strength. But listening to girls is not always easy. It can stir up the emotional dust always underfoot on the father-daughter journey so we feel as if we're being blinded and led off track. Paradoxically, unless we do our part to stir things up, our daughters will have trouble finding their way, and so will we.

HOW TO LISTEN

Listening to girls is fairly simple to do, as long as we practice. Here are a few things a father needs to know in order to listen to his girl:

1. There is a reason why I have twice as many ears as I do mouths; don't interrupt or talk more than she does.
2. Don't try to fix it before I ask if she wants solutions and ask what she wants from me in the conversation.
3. She is different from me; respect the difference.

4. Trust what she knows about herself and her world.

5. Trust her strengths and her ability to learn from mistakes.

6. Hear what she says, not what I think she'll say.

7. Ask questions that can't be answered yes or no.

8. Listen to what she "says" without words—her body language and tone of voice.

9. Give my mind and heart; don't let my attention wander.

10. Learn from her.

When our daughters talk to us about problems or difficulties, many of us are quick to jump in with solutions. Those solutions are often really good—but beside the point. Our daughters come talk to us because we are important to them, not necessarily because they want us to fix their problems. They want to know that who they are and what they say is important to Dad. Because these conversations regularly involve emotions and a girl's experience in the world, we are often in unfamiliar and uncomfortable territory.

> *When she cries or doesn't feel good about something, I want to bypass that and go on to the next stage. She's let me know that I have to allow her time for her feelings. She's said, "Hey, Dad, it takes me some time to process this whole thing."*
>
> *Now, I try to get her to talk about how she feels, and just tell me what she thinks. I've learned to not say anything about how she feels, just let her say it. When she's basically through with that, I explain where I'm at on the same issue. So I have tried to become more of a listener and not a teacher.*
>
> *Louis*

It is hard to just sit there and listen to our daughters' feelings. As boys and men, we're often trained to set aside our feelings; deny or run from them. We're usually not big on "processing." If we encounter conflict or difficulty, we're taught to plow through and get it over with as soon as possible. So, we have to keep remembering that our daughters are different from us and approach these things quite differently.

> *I've always been sort of a fixer. A rescuer. Someone who leaps into the breach and uses all his energy to make everything better. Well, it's hard to make things better with people like my daughters. You have to let them sort of make things better with themselves. You can give them guidance if they want it. For whatever it's worth; it might be right, might be wrong. But what I've had to learn is that when daughters come and talk to you, they want you just to listen to them. And if they want something else, they'll ask.*
>
> *Rob*

Fathers take deep pride in their ability to be fixers. Our pride can get hurt when we don't get to bring our expertise into play. Almost every time I played Mr. Fix-It in conversation with my daughters, they were frustrated and I got burned.

When Mavis was fourteen, she quit ballet after taking it for eight years. She's a physically active person and soon missed having something athletic like ballet to do. One night, she came into our bedroom confused and crying, going round and round about the whole thing, citing reasons why every idea she'd had for a new sport or physical activity wouldn't work for her schedule and tastes.

I reached over to the nightstand and pulled out the Yellow Pages. "Remember we suggested tae kwon do a few weeks ago? I'll look up some tae kwon do clubs for you to check out."

Mavis was pissed. The look she gave me was about the nastiest she'd ever sent my way. In sharp anger, she told me: "I didn't come in here to have you solve my problem or try to get me to stop feeling bad. I don't care if you don't like it when I'm feeling bad, that's your problem." Clearly, when I jumped in with lists and phone numbers, she felt that I was discounting and disrespecting what was going on with and in her. And she was right; I was uncomfortable when she felt bad—I don't want her to hurt!

I was taken aback by the intensity of her reaction; after all, wasn't it a good idea to call some places? But I think she'd accumulated the annoyance she felt the last dozen or so times I'd donned my Mr. Handyman garb without her invitation. Needless to say, we didn't use the Yellow Pages that night.

Eventually, Mavis and Nia learned more cordial (but still firm) ways to tell me to knock off my fix-it-first instinct: "I don't want a solution, Dad. I just need to vent." A few years later, it occurred to me that in our conversations *I* could ask *them* what they wanted me to do. It's not complicated: I say, "Do you want my advice or ideas? Or do you want me to just listen?" They tell me what they want from me. When I ask what they want, they are much more open to any advice I eventually give. The bottom line is, you don't have to give up completely on being Mr. Fix-It; just delay it a bit.

It's also hard on our pride when we don't instinctively know what our daughters are trying to tell us or when we feel disrespected by how they communicate. When my daughters were teenagers, we had emotionally charged conversations that sometimes resulted in one of them angrily and emotionally (or actually) slamming a door and shutting me out. Sometimes, my feelings got hurt and my reaction was, "OK, if you're gonna be like that, I'll blow you off, too!"

Fortunately, my wife (a former teen girl herself—and thus a valuable source of information) assured me that such eruptions are normal for adolescent girls as they try to discover and hang on to who they are. My girls needed to have me hear them out, and they also needed to find safe ways to push away from me. My job was not to drown in my wounded pride and say, "I'll show you; I'm taking my marbles and going home." Instead, it was to remain outside that slammed door so that when my daughters eventually emerged from their explosions and snits (which they always did), they knew that I was still there and still loved them. It is tough to stand there waiting and to open yourself back up when your feelings might once again be hurt. After all, if your daughter is a teenager, there are surely more slammed doors in your future. But it is worth it.

A daughter needs us to acknowledge and affirm what she is feeling and going through. She may think, "If Dad doesn't hear what I'm feeling, maybe what I'm feeling and what I'm going through is not important." But her experiences *are* important. We must show her that we believe this; and never belittle or dismiss her or her world. In other words, we have to trust her. When we trust what our daughter feels, she learns to trust herself now and later in life.

Much of a girl's strength is in her voice. By listening to her, you are being true to her voice. That will help her get through difficulties and give her courage. When you provide your ears and your presence, you amplify your daughter's voice and strengthen her belief in herself. It can be painful to listen when she is feeling sad or angry. But you have to have the courage to listen, and the courage to not prevent, deny, or abruptly try to end her painful experiences.

Our cat Pineapple just died. We decided to let him die at home. He laid down in the yard and I sat in a lawn chair for hours, and when Katie came home from school, she sat in that chair and just watched him and then read a James Herriot book to him. When I came back, she was bent over crying and Pineapple was still alive, barely. She said he was such a wonderful cat and she was going to miss him.

She has a real heart for animals and she relates to them in a whole different way than I do. I'm the giant stomping through the house telling the cats to get down off the counter, but they see her as a loving presence. It makes my heart feel good that I've got a child that is so connected to her world around her; the real world, as I like to think it is. She has a real capacity for love.

I wanted her to have this experience with Pineapple. I didn't want to make it better, but I wanted to be there with her, too. So

I put my hand on her. I asked her a couple of questions and lis-
tened to her. And then I backed up and went away and let her
be with it. I wanted her to know that she wasn't alone, but I also
wanted her to know that being alone is part of what happens in
the world. You can't have somebody take care of you all the time.
Sometimes life just hurts like hell.

Bill

Sometimes, a daughter will hurt no matter how much we try to shelter and protect her. It's hard to accept, but that pain is important to her. It takes courage to love a daughter by listening closely to what she says, even when those words express pain. It takes patience and wisdom to understand that listening to her is more than hearing the words she says; it also means watching and, like Bill did, sometimes stepping back to let her be alone.

But listening may be the single most important thing we fathers can do.

Listening to girls does not come without risk. They will say disruptive things and challenge both the world and us to be better. There is no question, however, that the risk is worth it. None of us want our daughter to be disrespected. We want our daughters to be heard and taken seriously. We start by listening ourselves, an act of genuine courage in a world where girls are silenced.

It's no surprise that when we truly listen to our daughters, one of the things they begin to talk about is their fathers—what they value in us, what they think of what we do and who we are. In these conversations, we are very likely to learn some important things about ourselves.

My stepdaughter says it seems that I'm angrier now than when
she first met me. In a way that feels bad to me, but in a way it
feels good. I do express my emotions more now. I've bottled up a
lot of anger for a lot of years being Mr. Patient, nice-guy. So def-

initely, because of Chloe, I'm getting more real. You can't bullshit
a kid. They know what you're feeling or where you're at. And you
see it reflected in their face. You can't pretend. Kids remember,
too. But I have also learned that I can love her as a daughter. I
really have a father's love for her. Her being in my life has
brought that out.

Andy

The father-daughter relationship is seldom easy, but it's always important. The rewards are huge for your daughter—as they are for
you. To earn the full measure of those rewards, a dad has to start the
challenging task of understanding in detail some of the challenges
girls face nowadays when it comes to body image, sexuality, drugs
and alcohol, cultural attitudes, and the everyday issues of life. The
more you understand the lives of girls, the clearer it becomes what
your daughter truly does need from you—and how you can provide it.

TOOLS

HOW WELL AM I DOING AS MY DAUGHTER'S FATHER?

Here is a short Dads and Daughters self-assessment quiz. It's a
quick way to get a sense of how well you're doing as your daughter's
father. Answer honestly and add up your score before peeking at the
scoring key.

	Often	Sometimes	Hardly Ever
1. I can name her 3 best friends	3	2	1

	Often	Sometimes	Hardly Ever
2. I know my daughter's goals	3	2	1
3. I comment on my wife/partner's weight	1	2	3
4. I'm physically active with my daughter (shoot hoops, jog, etc.)	3	2	1
5. I make dinner for my family	3	2	1
6. I talk with my daughter about managing money	3	2	1
7. I spend 1/2 hour, one-on-one with my daughter, doing something we both enjoy	3	2	1
8. I talk to other fathers about raising kids	3	2	1
9. I talk to other fathers about raising daughters	3	2	1
10. I restrict her activities more than I do/would for a son	1	2	3
11. I talk to my daughter about advertising	3	2	1
12. I tell my daughter what her strengths are	3	2	1
13. I comment on my daughter's weight	1	2	3
14. I know what school project she's working on	3	2	1
15. I protest negative media portrayals of girls	3	2	1
16. I view pornographic material	1	2	3

	Often	Sometimes	Hardly Ever
17. I participate in parenting organizations	3	2	1
18. I yell at my daughter's mother	1	2	3
19. I suggest my daughter go on a diet	1	2	3
20. I object when others suggest that she go on a diet	3	2	1
21. I converse with my daughter, and she does most of the talking	3	2	1
22. I know what my daughter is concerned about today	3	2	1
23. I know how many student government officers at her school are girls	3	2	1
24. I have read her school's sexual harassment policy	3	2	1
25. I help boys learn to respect girls	3	2	1
26. I tell my daughter stories about my own youth	3	2	1

For dads who live AWAY from their daughters

	Often	Sometimes	Hardly Ever
27. I initiate contact with her at least 5 times a week	3	2	1
28. I ask how she feels transitioning to and from my home	3	2	1
29. I demonstrate respect for her mother and stepparent(s)	3	2	1
30. I fulfill my visitation and support commitments	3	2	1

	Often	Sometimes	Hardly Ever
For dads who live WITH their daughters (extra credit for live-away dads)			
31. I volunteer to help with her extracurricular activities	3	2	1
32. I take my daughter to school	3	2	1
33. I visit my daughter's school during the school day	3	2	1
34. I take my daughter to work with me	3	2	1

Total Points:

Scoring Key

Over 72: *Your relationship with your daughter looks like it's on very solid ground.*

58–71: *You appear to have a good foundation, but there are places to improve.*

48–57: *You probably need active steps to reexamine your attitudes and learn ways to build deeper respect for each other.*

Under 47: *It's time to consider a serious change. Your actions and attitudes may be undermining your daughter.*

Here's a variation to try: Give your daughter a copy of this quiz, but don't show her your answers yet. Ask her to use the quiz to assess how *she* thinks you're doing as her dad. When she's done, trade copies. She reads your answers and you read hers. After you've read them, take a half hour alone together to talk about what you learned from each other's assessment.

"CHILDREN SHOULD BE SEEN AND NOT HEARD"

Among the biggest barriers to our ability to listen to girls are our assumptions about what roles daughters and adults are supposed to play in a relationship. In a workshop called "Share the Power," New Moon Publishing distributes a list (compiled by girls) of what kids think of as the unspoken rules operating in adult-child interactions.

The Usual Rules Between Adults and Girls

- Don't be honest with girls—they can't handle it.
- Girls can't understand adult feelings and experiences.
- Don't let girls challenge adults.
- Don't challenge girls.
- Girls need to be taken care of by adults.
- Girls need to be left alone by adults.
- Girls don't have anything important to say.
- Girls don't understand their own experience.
- Girls can't handle complexity.
- Girls don't know what real life (and real disappointment) is.
- Girls aren't interested in talking with adults.
- Girls don't listen.
- Girls are irresponsible, frivolous, and petty, absorbed in childish pursuits.

We've all had some of these attitudes toward girls sometimes. The New Moon girls offer an alternative list of rules that they think provide more respect.

The New Rules: Share the Power

- Everyone is responsible for a common goal. Therefore, everyone shares the meaningful work.
- Have a real interest in the task. Be committed to it and to each other.
- Listening comes first for the adults, and talking comes first for the girls.
- Not talking is okay, but not listening is not okay.
- Actively seek and encourage girls' opinions.
- Welcome disagreement but end in compromise.
- Discuss—don't force—ideas. Be willing to be persuaded by others in discussion.
- Express your deep feelings passionately, and if something isn't too important to you personally, defer to someone who does have very strong feelings.
- No one knows all the answers.
- Be open to learning from each other.
- Make decisions with girls, not for them. This takes more time!
- Be honest and build trust. Respect each other and each other's opinions.
- Don't be condescending.
- Be supportive, encouraging, positive, realistic, and patient.
- Be responsive and aware of nonverbal cues.
- Respect girls' commitments (like school).
- Sit so that no one is in a position of power—in a circle, on the same level.
- Make time for girls to take a break (or snacks, physical activity, etc.).
- Allow social time.
- Have fun together.

2.

"DADDY, DO YOU THINK I LOOK FAT?": THE BODY WARS*

A few years ago, Michael Kieschnick's nine-year-old daughter asked him, "Daddy, do you think I look fat?" Michael is a successful businessperson and his wife is a minister; they volunteer in the community, are involved in the kids' school and outside activities, and provide a healthy atmosphere at home. It never occurred to him that his little girl would ask this question because she never heard comments about her body shape at home. So when she did ask, he was stunned and almost speechless. What could he say to his daughter?

Michael could honestly have said "No," because she was a slender child, but that answer seemed like it would confirm that she should be worried about her body shape. What if she *was* chubby? An honest "Yes" answer might very well devastate her self-worth. Besides, why is the word "fat" considered such an insult?

*All statistics in this chapter come from studies gathered by the National Eating Disorders Association over the last ten years.

The more he thought about it, the more Michael believed that neither answer was "right." He decided that what was really wrong was the question itself. What did her question mean and why did she ask it?

Another dad might have dropped the issue after a few minutes of pondering, but this incident sparked Michael to found a non-profit organization, Dads and Daughters, to explore this question and more. Michael gained three key lessons from his daughter's question that now fuel DADs' mission.

1. It's significant that his daughter asked that question of her father, rather than her mother.
2. Raising children with your values at home is necessary, but not sufficient. The outside world influences them, and so we need to influence it.
3. In today's world, body image is a central issue for girls and women.

But what exactly is body image? Body image includes an individual's perception and judgment of the size, shape, weight, and any other aspect of the body—from hairstyle and makeup to skin tone and clothing—that relates to body appearance. Notice there's no innate negative connotation in this "official" definition. Yet, when asked to describe their bodies, the vast majority of girls translate *body image* into self-denigrating girlspeak such as "My nose is too big." "My breasts are too small." "I hate my thighs." "I have fat ankles." "My arms are too hairy." "I wish I were thinner."

It's all too often that a girl judges and perceives her body as flawed and bad. Study after study, statistic after statistic mirror the nearly universal truth that our daughters are unhappy with their bodies. A few of the facts:

- In a study of children aged eight to ten, half of the girls said they were dissatisfied with their size. Girls wanted to be thinner.

- One out of every four college-aged women engages in disordered eating behaviors, like binging and purging. In the United States alone, 5 to 10 million women and girls have active, destructive eating disorders.
- More than 50 percent of adolescent girls from diverse racial and economic backgrounds in the United States say they are overweight and dieting.

Think about what these numbers tell us: in the United States, a girl who *likes* her body is abnormal.

WHEN PEANUT BUTTER BECOMES THE ENEMY

Many fathers describe their daughters beginning to worry—at very young ages—about how they look. One dad told me that his daughter came home from day one of first grade to announce that, according to girls on the playground, she could no longer eat peanut butter because it would make her fat. What can we say in response to such statements?

> *My daughter has made comments that she has to go on a diet because she's getting fat. She's not fat in the slightest; she's as fit as she could possibly be. I explained to her that even if she were fat, I'd love her just the same. I asked her if someone had made a comment about her appearance, or if something else was wrong. She said someone was teasing a fat girl at school. I told her that that was an opportunity to give the girl a kind word that she might need, or even to stick up for her.*
>
> Scott

Throughout our culture, we are overly concerned with how we look and harmfully judgmental about how others look. We don't recognize how, and how often, we use someone's appearance to prejudge her or his worthiness, health, or morality (a phenomenon some call "look-ism"). In addition, it's often hard for fathers to understand how deeply a daughter's perception of her own appearance influences her perception of her own worthiness, health, or morality.

Of course, obesity (in kids and adults) is a public health problem because, as a rule, we eat too much junk food and are too sedentary for our own good. Our daughters' weight and body shape *may* be signs of health concerns—but, most of the time, our families and culture make weight the primary or *only* sign of health.

I know three fifteen-year-old girls, all about five feet tall. One weighs about 80 pounds, the second weighs around 160, and the third about 120. Which one do you think is the healthiest? Which one is in great cardio-vascular condition and eats a well-balanced diet? Which one is self-disciplined? Which has the best physical endurance and strength?

Most of us would guess it has to be either girl number one or number three. We'd be wrong—it's the "fat" girl at 160 pounds. She's the athlete of the group (varsity in two sports), regularly eating and training for physical strength and endurance. She's also the one whose parents and grandparents are tall, large, and generally athletic.

In other words, it's usually a fool's game to use a person's shape to judge his or her health, self-discipline, or other moral qualities. But we do it all the time, ignoring the immutable forces of genetic ancestry, internal metabolism, body chemistry . . . the list goes on. Unless we're physicians or nutritionists who observe these three girls over a period of time, we can't know for sure whether their health is good or bad. Nevertheless, we continue to judge people (including our own kids) as "good" or "bad" according to the shape of their bodies.

Pile all this on top of a girl's need to feel acceptable and desirable, particularly to members of the opposite sex, and we can begin to understand the intensity she feels about her appearance. As the first men in our daughters' lives, however, we can have a lot of influence over this thought process.

The toughest concept for a father to wrap his mind around in raising daughters is their obsession with body image. After all, if we believe that our daughters are amazing, wonderful, and fun creatures, how could *they* be so caught up in their looks? Nevertheless, our daughters unduly worry about their looks for significant periods of their lives. Body image concerns consume our daughters' energy and resources in attempts to do something that, A: can't be done (i.e., permanently change how one looks), and B: shouldn't matter. Our world continues to measure much of a girl's "success" by how much male attention she attracts to her body—and that's a poor reflection on us and our culture.

Dr. Joan Jacobs Brumberg's fascinating book *The Body Project* illustrates the intensity of modern girls' appearance obsession. Jacobs Brumberg studied a hundred years of girls' diaries and found that post-Victorian girls used their diaries for self-reflection, usually writing about improving their character and increasing their charitable contribution to the community. Granted, girls of that era too often subjugated their own needs and personality in order to please others, but at least they were focused on better behavior and altruism.

By the last half of the twentieth century, however, diary entries revealed that girls were more concerned about improving their *appearance* than their character. Girls' New Year's resolutions to lose weight and get makeovers far outnumbered resolutions to volunteer or improve academic performance. Unlike girls a century ago, who made their *lives* into projects, Jacobs Brumberg writes, girls today make their *bodies* into projects.

YOU WANT TO WEAR WHAT?

When I talk about body image, some fathers say, "But outward appearance does matter. People can't get away with going to work looking like slobs!"

It is true that outer appearance matters, and that can be a good thing. It can be invigorating to get dressed up or take pride in how we look. Alternately, it can suck the life out of us to be identified, categorized, and valued or devalued by our appearance rather than by who we are.

> *Recently my daughters came home with huge shopping bags filled with new clothes because everything was 70 percent off. They came prancing into the living room that evening and showed off the mini-skirts and other "womanly" clothes they bought. They were so wound up and excited. But the next morning, Meghan called and said, "Dad, I'm in the nurse's office. I'm sick. Can you come pick me up?" In every class, kids had made fun of her and her clothing. I felt incredibly awful, partly because there was nothing I could do about it. I felt so bad about her incredible excitement over this outfit, about how good she looked, and about how excited she was until she went to school and people made fun of her.*
>
> *Jerry*

Maybe this is just standard-issue classroom cruelty, terrible as it might be. But such school savagery usually hangs its hat on the hook of appearance. Think a kid looks trashy or nerdy? Then mock her or dis him. The word for behavior and attitudes like this is prejudice, as virulent as racism or sexism.

But girls continue to be prejudged on their looks. Even when they are excited about their clothes, makeup, or hair, cultural prejudice and media-driven insecurity can wash away that innate pride in their appearance. These are tough truths to acknowledge and address as a father.

> *I ask "why do we desire to be something we are not?" when I*
> *open the lofty "mind and body" section of our newspaper and see*
> *half a dozen breast augmentation and cosmetic surgery advertise-*
> *ments. I wonder how to explain these things to our daughter*
> *when the time comes. Hopefully by then we will have been able*
> *to instill in her that her value is largely derived from or reflected*
> *in greater constants. That her value is greater than the sum of*
> *her appearance, intelligence, material wealth, skills, or even the*
> *opinion of others. Without this perspective I think it is easy to*
> *fall prey to what the world says is true. It's not so easy even with*
> *that healthy perspective, but it gives you a rock to stand on—*
> *otherwise, your own two feet are firmly planted in mid-air.*
>
> *Tom*

Sometimes it feels like there's nothing solid on which to stand in the fight to help our daughters hang on to their well-being. Nevertheless, we have to realize that this is a fight—even a life-and-death fight for some daughters.

In her excellent book, of the same title, author Dr. Margo Maine calls this struggle "Body Wars." Girls and women battle their own natures because they learn early and often that they don't look or act like they're "supposed to." Maine says that, for a female nowadays, loving one's body is actually a revolutionary act! We can see effects of the body wars in the vast amounts of time, resources, and energy girls and women spend working on how they look. They wouldn't do that if their appearance wasn't a major concern.

Consider this: Has your male self-confidence at the start of a workday ever been affected by how successfully you'd applied your makeup that morning? No; for most men in our culture, this question falls in the "absurd" category. Now, ask a woman: Has your self-confidence at the start of a workday ever been affected by how successfully you'd applied your makeup that morning? Odds are she'll say yes.

We may think that a woman worrying about her makeup is silly, or we may think it's important for women to pay attention to "putting on her best face." But no matter what our opinion on the value of cosmetics, when we put our daughters' faces in the picture, different questions arise.

Is there any good, justifiable reason why my daughter's makeup should matter to her or anyone else when she's at work or school? What if she doesn't want to wear makeup; should her career opportunities suffer? Why does she seem to hold herself to a different, more time-consuming appearance standard than the guy at the next desk? Do I want it to matter that much to her?

> *My daughter needs to recognize her own beauty—whatever it is—as well as the fact that others will face greater challenges. Not only will the less "conventionally attractive" girls have harder times getting dates, but the very attractive girls will have a harder time being appreciated as anything but sex objects. All these things are best made clear at the outset, so that she can find her own value and set her own goals. Otherwise, pretty or unattractive, she will be burdened with labels before she has even come to understand who she is.*
>
> *Bob*

Positive father perspective can counterbalance a lot of the appearance-first nonsense our daughters internalize. In fact, that perspective is far more valuable to our daughters than any rules about how, when, and where they can start wearing makeup, get their ears pierced, or dye their hair. The important battles are not over lipstick (or tattoos, jewelry, clothing, and the rest). Much more significant is our daughters' right and ability to set their own standards and direction; and not succumb to what's imposed by others.

We need to teach our daughters that their time and money are limited resources—and that their lives are richer when they invest those resources in their courage, brains, and heart. Investing an overabundance of time and money in pursuit of the latest fashion fad only plays into the hands of marketers willing to sacrifice a girl's confidence in order to make a buck.

Our daughters, of course, are not the only targets of what author Naomi Wolf calls "The Beauty Myth." We fathers also learn to believe that Cindy Crawford is more desirable than the longtime public officeholder Christie Whitman, even if the latter contributes far more to her community than the former. Odds are, more men know who Crawford is (supermodel) than know who Whitman is (former New Jersey governor, now head of the federal EPA). A failure to examine our belief in this narrow standard of beauty can have insidious side effects on our daughters. We can, without realizing it, assign too much value to our daughters' appearance.

Beauty myths can also make fathers go so far as to believe that a daughter's appearance and dress is the cause of violence or abuse she might encounter.

My daughter is sixteen and she claims she is a Christian and wants to wait until she is married to have sex. But she came home from a shopping trip with several summer shirts that are very sensual, definitely attention-getters. I want her to dress more conservatively, not like a nun, but less provocatively. I told her she had to take them back. It got so bad that I told her to move out if she wants to dress like a slut. My wife says the arguing could cause her to do exactly what I fear she will start to do. My wife says to choose my battles and this one shouldn't be a big one. But I think it is.

Jeff

Jeff's wife is right. Many of us fear the messages that might be sent by clothing we consider provocative. However, there is a very important distinction to make: clothing *does not* give anyone the right or permission to abuse or manipulate. Of course, just because it's not right does not eliminate the presence of those Neanderthal boys and men who view girls and women as objects (rather than people with souls). They feel free to harass or violate females, and then use "excuses" like, "She wore a tight shirt/short skirt/slinky top; she was asking for it."

While her wardrobe choices may set off alarms about dangers she faces out in the world, you have to keep your eye on the nature of that risk. When your daughter brings home body-hugging clothes, she needs to hear two essential ideas from you (things she needs to hear from you no matter what she wears):

1. Some men and boys (Some! Not all!) are jerks and will use almost any tactic or any excuse to "score" or to harass a girl. They will use the kind of clothing you wear as an excuse for their inexcusable behavior and attitudes. That is a sad and sick reality, but *it is not your fault.* However, I want you to be aware of this ugliness and have solid ways to resist it and protect yourself.

2. You are a good young woman and I am very proud of you. I know that you believe strongly in your faith and values. I honor and trust this in you. I know how difficult it is to remain true to those values and to yourself in today's world— and I admire the strength you show in staying true to what's most important. I know that this strength will be a potent weapon against the danger in the world from which I cannot fully protect you. I am here to help you with this in any way I can, any time you ask. Forever.

Wearing sexy clothing (like having orange hair) is a normal adolescent behavior. It can be a daughter's self-directed effort to define herself and experiment with who she might be. In the big picture, those are exactly the kinds of experiments to hope for, since they don't involve directly risky behavior. Our job as father is to remember that she will make mistakes, (good thing, too—mistakes are a wonderful way to learn) and to support what she needs to protect herself. Her most potent weapon is trust in herself, her values and judgment. The best way for you to help is to believe in her. Because if you trust her, she will learn that "trusting myself and my values is a very smart thing to do . . . otherwise, Daddy wouldn't do it!"

In addition, when that trust is nurtured, our daughters are more open to fatherly wisdom and experiences we have to share.

THE PRICE OF SEVENS AND TENS

A twenty-something female television reporter once interviewed me about a father's role in his daughter's body image, and while chatting afterward, she told me about a young man she'd been dating. One day he sat her down and said, "You know, I'm really having fun with you. No one I've dated has ever treated me nicer. But you're not pretty enough for me. You're only a seven or an eight and I need to be going out with a ten."

Put your daughter's face in that scenario. Can you feel the kick in the gut she feels?

But pause for a moment and shift the focus away from the hurt this man inflicted on his "girlfriend" to consider what he has done to himself. He is walking through life with a pornographic view of the world; he doesn't think he's reached relationship success unless he has a *Playboy* bunny on his arm or in his bed. This young man is missing the entire point of being human—making genuine connection. He's walking around with a huge void in the center of his life.

Most disturbing of all: *he doesn't even know it's there.*

This is pathetic and it's dangerous. That void in his life becomes a greater handicap and a deeper source of pain the longer it remains. We may not realize it, but we and our sons are harmed by lifelong messages like "a good woman is a ten; don't 'settle' for a seven" and our pornographic objectification of women. The narrow notion that men and boys must always put titillation before connection handicaps our ability to fully experience the depth and thrill of truly intimate relationships.

This is one reason why, as men, we have a huge stake in how our culture views and treats females. Even if we didn't have daughters, these views affect us *as men*. It's time to start recognizing and talking to each other about our own "body project"—the false notion that success means landing a female with a good-looking body.

The predominance of those messages limits our ability to naturally see women (including our daughters) as full people with whom we can connect and have rich relationships. It distorts how other males look at our daughters. Often, our first instinct is to look at females as objects. Seeing women as things, as opposed to people, opens the way for many men to be violent and abusive to women. We can't have rich relationships with objects, and it's hard to use violence on someone we respect.

Simply put, we men pay too high a price for the objectification of women. The way our culture views women warps what we expect from men. And it distorts the way we see ourselves as men.

Society is always telling our daughters that they are not beautiful. It is incumbent upon us to instill in our daughters the deepest sense that they are *beautiful. In so doing, we need to overcome our own socialization as males. If that means we need to be less than honest about what we, personally, find attractive, that's a white lie we ought to be ready to tell.*

Charles

When I met my wife in 1978, I was attracted to aspects of her physical appearance. No surprise; that's how lots of romantic relationships start. We were outwardly beautiful in one another's eyes. Today, after more than two decades of marriage, we're still physically attracted to each other. That's good and fun. However, it will come as no shock to learn that neither of us look much like we did back then! Heck, even Mel Gibson doesn't look like he did in 1978.

Ongoing physical attraction is a nice marital asset, but we all know that there is no way a relationship of more than twenty years can be based on outward appearance—on the size and shape of a spouse's body parts. But that's exactly what we tell our sons every day if we don't challenge messages declaring that the most important thing about a woman is the size of her cleavage or the shape of her legs. Such beliefs are a setup for failure in long-term relationships—and your daughter will probably be part of a long-term relationship some day.

DYING TO BE THIN

Dissatisfaction with one's size and shape are devastating to a girl's health. At the least, it leads to insidious erosion of self-esteem and positive self-image. This may affect young women in a variety of ways including the capacity to make positive life choices. The Melpomene Institute, which researches connections between female self-esteem and physicality, did a study of 3,800 girls aged eleven to seventeen. It showed that more girls with poor body image reported being teased, especially by family members; girls with poor self-esteem tended to compare themselves to others who had some element of "beauty" attached to them (models, movie stars, or other girls with traditionally "attractive" bodies).

Serious eating disorders, from bulimia to anorexia, are among this problem's worst manifestations and may end in permanent health damage or death. Eating disorders have one of the highest death rates of any mental illness. Up to ten percent of the nation's young women are diagnosed with anorexia, bulimia, or some other form of disordered eating. Sadly, I have a very human face to put on that cold statistic.

Age Twenty-Seven

When Michael Kieschnick and I began building the Dads and Daughters organization in 1999, we hired a smart, organized, creative, and determined young woman named Heather Henderson to help us launch it. Heather had edited and done marketing for national magazines; she'd been a newspaper reporter and coached gymnastics. This multitalented woman created the DADs' Web site and membership system from scratch, did reams of research, ran the office, did media interviews, and a thousand other things. She quickly established relationships with hundreds of activists around the country, sharing information and promoting DADs. Sometimes it seemed like she did the work of five people! All the while, she radiated her insight, affection, knowledge, determination, skill, and curiosity.

One Wednesday morning in the fall of 2000, Heather didn't come to work, which was very unlike such a punctual, responsible woman. I went up to her house to see if anything was wrong. I found Heather lying facedown on the kitchen floor of her house, dead of a heart attack at age twenty-seven.

After eleven years of struggling with anorexia and bulimia, this talented, lovable, and well-loved woman's heart gave out at a sinfully young age, three days before her sister's wedding and seven months before her own. Her death crushed her fiancé, family, and friends. Activists and professionals nationwide called and e-mailed our office in shock that such a young and talented person was gone. I get very angry remembering her lifeless body and thinking about how anorexia and bulimia snapped off her life—and how they take root so readily in our culture.

Just Look at the Numbers

Eating disorders are insidious and too often fatal phenomena that affect 10 percent of young women in the United States, and a growing number of young men. According to the National Eating Disorders Association, anorexia (the medical term is anorexia nervosa) manifests itself in an intense fear of gaining weight. The symptoms include self-starvation, excessive weight loss, obsession with food, and a distorted body image.

A young person with bulimia (bulimia nervosa) will binge eat in secret and then, also often in secret, purge herself of the food through self-induced vomiting, laxatives, diuretics, excessive exercise, or fasting. She feels out of control during a binge, diets frequently, binges and purges repeatedly, and is overly concerned with the shape and weight of her body.

Binge eating disorder is the third major eating disorder and the least common. Its primary symptoms are periods of continuous eating or compulsive gorging. There's no purging, but a binge eater may use repetitive diets or sporadic fasts. Binge eating disorder can lead to dangerous levels of obesity.

In all three kinds of eating disorders, nutrition and internal systems are thrown out of whack. Bulimia and anorexia disrupt menstrual cycles, electrolytes, hormones, and major organs. When someone continually denies herself the fuel she needs to survive, her body turns on its own internal organs for that fuel, leading to the deterioration of major muscles like the heart. That is how a twenty-seven-year-old athletic woman with anorexia and bulimia dies of heart failure.

Does Heather's death have any relation to Michael's story about his daughter? Absolutely. Both represent clear moments on the continuum of how girls perceive body image in this country. It's easy to see how eating disorders flourish in a culture that tells a girl over and over and over again that inner beauty only goes so far and that her appearance should be her primary concern.

Culture has a major impact on what we see as physically attractive or beautiful. Indeed, in some less affluent parts of the world, heavy women are often considered most desirable. Why? Because their weight signifies access to a precious commodity—food. But that can change quickly when different values infuse those cultures.

A 1990s Harvard study of teen girls in Tahiti showed that they considered big and heavy their ideal body shape—that is until U.S. cable television reached the island. Within two years, the study reported that the thin, waifish look prevalent on American TV had become the overwhelming ideal among Tahitian girls—and that problem eating began manifesting itself for the first time.

While eating disorders result from a complex confluence of causes—family, psychology, biology, and culture—women with eating disorders overwhelmingly report that media images and cultural messages helped spark and reinforce their disease.

The sheer number of statistics and studies is damning evidence that media is the primary source of this ideal body image that girls feel they can't measure up to. Consider the following:

- Twenty years ago, models weighed 8 percent less than the average woman. Today they weigh 23 percent less.
- "How I think I look compared with images in magazines, on TV, and in movies" was reported as one of the top influences on body image by girls in one study.
- Researchers estimate that 60 percent of Caucasian middle school girls read at least one fashion magazine regularly.
- A psychological study in 1995 found that three minutes spent looking at models in a fashion magazine caused 70 percent of women to feel depressed, guilty, and full of shame.
- According to a recent survey of adolescent girls, the media is their main source of information about women's health issues. Another study of mass media magazines discovered that

women's magazines had 10.5 times more advertisements and articles promoting weight loss than men's magazines did.

- The average young adolescent watches three to four hours of TV per day.
- A study of 4,294 network television commercials revealed that 1 out of every 3.8 commercials sends some sort of "attractiveness message," telling viewers what is or is not attractive. Researchers estimate that the average adolescent sees over 5,260 "attractiveness messages" per year.

Another huge influence on body image is family attitude about food. In too many families, food becomes a moral issue: someone is "bad" because of eating a piece of cake or a bowl of ice cream and "good" because of eating broccoli. Lisa Sjostrom, director of the Full of Ourselves eating disorder project, explains, "Many girls go home from school to parents who judge them about their body size and shape, or a parent fretting about her own body." Dieting is the result of these messages, even though conventional dieting usually leads to eventual weight *gain*. Dr. Eric Stice of the University of Texas studied ninth grade girls from California who were dieting or using more radical weight-loss techniques like laxatives, vomiting, or appetite suppressants. He found that they were actually *more likely* to gain weight over the course of four years than those who weren't trying to lose. That's because dieting often leads to binge and other irregular eating that disrupt the natural balance of a body's metabolism.

When my friend Heather Henderson is repeatedly bombarded with the notion that how she looks is more important than who she is, should I be surprised if she takes drastic measures to control her appearance, even if they fly in the face of nature? If we repeatedly tell girls that their appearance is more important than their souls, then eating disorders are a logical result. Picture having a meal, getting up from the table, going into the bathroom, and putting your finger down your throat to throw up what you just ate. It's horrible to contemplate—especially if you imagine your daughter in that picture. If this is a logical result of our culture's influence on girls, then there's something very toxic at play in our cultural environment.

Eating disorders may be particularly horrific consequences of what we let our culture sell girls, but they are not the only ones. Distorted body image beliefs are common among girls who abuse alcohol or drugs, sexually act out, develop depression, drop out of school, and take up smoking. Body image issues also contribute to other serious problems that aren't so readily seen as critical: declining academic performance; self-selecting out of science, technology, and other "hard" subject areas; believing sports are not "ladylike"— to name just a few.

So what is a father to do?

WARNING SIGNS OF EATING DISORDERS

- Has she gained or lost a significant amount of weight lately?
- Does she avoid eating meals or snacks around you?
- Does she categorize foods as "good foods" or "bad foods"?
- Has she developed ritualized mealtime behavior, a preference for strange foods, secretive bingeing, or other abnormal eating behavior?
- Is she fasting or making herself vomit?
- Does she calculate the number of calories and fat grams in each bite?
- Does she talk or worry about her size and shape?
- Does she weigh herself often?
- Does she seem to feel isolated, depressed, or irritable?

- Does she exercise because she feels like she has to, not because she wants to?
- Is she regularly using laxatives, diet pills, or diet products without consulting a physician?

(Courtesy of the National Eating Disorders Association)

How to Respond if You Suspect an Eating Disorder

If you suspect that your daughter has or could develop an eating disorder, express your concern to her in a supportive, calm, caring, and firm way. Most important, get professional help for both you *and* your daughter. (Success rates in eating disorders treatment are higher when the patient's *father* participates in the treatment.)

- Use "I" statements like, "I'm concerned about you because you refuse to eat breakfast or lunch."
- Don't accuse. Avoid statements like "You have to eat! You must be crazy!"
- Recognize that simplistic, rigid solutions don't work. Avoid strategies like "I'm going to make you eat. If you'd just eat, everything would be fine."
- Visit the National Eating Disorders Association Web site at www.nationaleatingdisorders.org or call NEDA's hotline at (800) 931–2237.

WHAT YOU CAN DO

As entrenched as beauty myths and body image problems are, they can be countered with tangible tools. Fathers can work and play with their daughters to protect and build their self-esteem. That self-esteem, no matter its source, is a girl's most potent immunization against eating disorders, dieting, and distorted body image.

A New Mirror

Fathers can teach daughters the most important lessons in seemingly offhand ways. In casual day-to-day conversation, you can make observations and provide an antidote to unrealistic portrayals of physical beauty.

> I tell them things like, "Do you see the person on the cover of this magazine? Do you know that very few people in this world look like this?" I figured that a lot of girls and women obsess over how they look, and especially how they look compared to other girls and women, including supermodels and magazine cover models. My girls need to know early on that, even if my wife and I were the right "build," most likely they will not look like the magazine model. How many supermodels are there anyway? Eight in the whole world? May as well get over it now that they do not look like these women on magazine covers and move on to what is more important.
>
> Dan

Conversely, you can consistently point out characteristics you find appealing, especially when they belie the cultural standard of female "perfection": her grandmother's lovely laugh lines, the distinctive nose on a teacher, or the great quadriceps of a track star. Once you start looking, you'll soon discover there are alternative role models everywhere you—and your daughter—look. We can combine our family history with our "first man" influence to combat warped media messages and to keep our daughters in touch with reality.

When my daughter said she was tired of being teased because she had so many freckles, I said, "Let's get out Grandpa's old slides. Look at all these freckles; everywhere you look, our relatives have freckles. Here's a real strawberry face—your great-great-aunt Catherine, who was married less than a year before her husband ran off. Know what she did? Went to work for a big New York restaurant chain and worked her way up to become an executive—quite a feat for a woman in the 1950s!"

Matt

In a quick and natural turn of conversation, this dad showed his daughter that freckles are "the way it is" in her clan, that her foremothers were women of accomplishment, and that there are plenty of colorful, fascinating stories in her very own family—stories more interesting than anything in *Seventeen*. He put her in touch with important truths about who she is and where she comes from. These *real* role models make excellent alternatives to Britney Spears or the celebrity-du-jour.

Need more examples? Go a bit further afield and look around your own neighborhood. You're likely to find a woman who is president of her synagogue; a mother who volunteers at her kids' school every week; a grandmother who heads the local Nature Conservancy chapter; along with the woman who heads the region's agency on aging and runs a girls' group at her mosque. No matter what our circumstances, our community is filled with good role models for our kids. Best of all, they are real people, not some airbrushed cartoon of a manufactured megastar. When dads point out real "sheroes," daughters pay attention.

Next, take a more global approach and use national leaders to make your case for the beauty in real power, which is more powerful than mere beauty. We're fortunate to be living during a time in history that offers plenty of strong, well-known women who have risen to the tops of their fields. Help these women help raise your daughter upward by praising their accomplishments—no matter how they look.

There will always be people who are more and less "beautiful" than each other. Fine features, but a bad attitude. Insightful mind, but not conventionally pretty. The more I think about it, the more what I'm calling "beauty" is turning out to really be "power." And teaching girls to use their power—and to be aware of the societal taboos against using their power—is probably really what I'm after.

Madeleine Albright and Janet Reno are not "conventionally pretty," but they obviously know how to exercise their own power. When Janet Reno made her surprise appearance on Saturday Night Live, *she showed the kind of beauty that I'm talking about—the beauty and courage to embrace those who had mocked her in front of the nation for a decade.*

Bob

THROWING LIKE A GIRL

In addition to helping your daughter find effective new role models, another great strategy is nurturing the transformation of her body image into a stronger, healthier, more active version. You might have to overcome a common misperception first, that of thinking of your daughter as delicate or fragile. Many dads I meet share this mistaken idea:

I've been very nervous ever since my daughter came into this world. I think I would know how to raise her better if she was a son. I think that girls are more delicate and precious. I feel that she is like a very fragile vase sitting at the edge of the table waiting for someone to carelessly knock it down. And once it falls,

there is no way to keep it from breaking. I'm afraid that I will
turn out to be a very strict and restricting father.

Dean

A daughter is not a fragile vase. Ironically, the more you treat her like one, the more fragile she will be. Think about how different things would look if this father changed the image of his daughter from porcelain vase to a lithe, flexible, warm, powerful, living, breathing being. Suddenly, fathering a daughter becomes a lot more fun! He's in a position to substitute an obsession with how her body looks with an appreciation for what it can do. He can run around with his daughter, play catch, dance, have a good time.

When we stop treating our daughters like fragile vases, amazing potential and strength are released. We lay a foundation for them to become wonderful women—more solid than tottering porcelain on a pedestal. As boys, many of us grew up challenging and pushing each other physically. We grew up loving to wrestle, work, play catch, build things, play cards, shoot hoops, and make puns. We learned much of this love of using our bodies and brains in fun ways from our fathers, big brothers, uncles, grandfathers, and older cousins. This love of physicality is one of the most valuable gifts we fathers give our daughters.

My dad makes me very competitive in everything. It's a really
good thing, 'cause I love sports. As far as I can remember, he's al-
ways been there saying, "Go! Go!" If I'm not doing well, then
he'll be the one to tell me. He'll tell me the truth. And he'll say
"go out there and play how you know how to play, and do what
you know how to do, and beat them. Don't quit. You can't just
quit because you're tired." It's a lot of competitiveness. But it's
good, because it gets me places.

Maria

What motivates girls to take up sports and physical activity? Research by the Melpomene Institute shows that the most influential factor is a *father* who plays with his daughter when she is young. When a father bounces his one-year-old on his knee, horseplays with his three-year-old, kicks a ball around with his five-year-old, plays catch with his seven-year-old, and shoots baskets with his twelve-year-old, he increases the odds that she'll get and stay involved in physical activity as a teen. This substantially lowers the odds that his daughter will get in trouble during adolescence. Among older teen girls, those who engage in sports and other physical activities are least likely to drop out of school, get pregnant, develop eating disorders, put up with abusive relationships, smoke, drink, do drugs—or develop breast cancer as adults. They are also the ones most likely to have a dad who was physically active with them when they were young.

> *She and I took swim lessons when she was three months old. It was a delight having her get used to going all the way underneath the water. It was at a local YMCA, and I was the only dad. I liked that kind of oddness about being the only dad there with my daughter. I would say that, sixteen years later, activities continue to be a place where we can enjoy one another's company.*
>
> *Larry*

We fathers are often more willing to let our children (girls and boys) take physical risks than moms are. That's good! It stretches our kids, helps them deal with fear, and makes them feel more competent. So, for goodness' sake (and for hers), wrestle with her, play word games with her, run and build things together, toss the football, listen to her, and treat her as a whole person . . . not as a vase poised to fall and break.

We want our daughters to learn that they have their bodies not for how they look, but for what they can do. What they can do with their bodies includes what they can do with their brain, heart, and creativity. Every day has opportunities for Dad to draw attention to his daughter's multiple dimensions.

> *I was putting some flooring in, and she wanted to be with me.*
> *She was only three. The big sixteen-ounce hammer was too*
> *much for her, so she went into the house and got her mother's*
> *seven-ounce hammer and came out and sat there next to me,*
> *pounding on a nail forever. Absolutely forever. Every so often*
> *I would reach over and hit it a little bit. But she'd keep pound-*
> *ing. And she was putting little dimples in the floor all over the*
> *place. I'm a perfectionist, so ordinarily that should affect me.*
> *But I was getting a kick out of it, watching her. I'll bet she*
> *was twenty minutes doing it while I was putting down some*
> *other boards. And finally she turned to me and said, "Dad, I*
> *hit it six hundred times, and it still didn't go in." She probably*
> *had kept count, knowing her. She's very persistent and very*
> *articulate.*
>
> *Miguel*

Our daughters' age and ability don't have to be barriers to the benefits of physical activity, unless we hold them to some outside measure of performance. Remember that girls are continually being measured by someone else's standards in this culture. The wonder of physicality is its potential to teach girls how to measure themselves by their own, internal, self-developed standards. We fathers have to keep our "competitive" instincts in control so that our daughters learn this important lesson—rather than learning that they are failing to measure up to our expectations of their performance.

Maintaining a connection with our daughters is a big challenge as they get older. Sports and physical activity can be a natural way for dads to meet that challenge, especially because our daughters need healthy and affectionate physical touching from us.

We always had these little tickling sessions where we try to get each other giggling and laughing, but unfortunately those don't happen so often anymore. So, when we go on a trip, I always try to get a hotel with a heated pool. We'll all jump in the pool and horseplay around and it's a chance for me to make a lot of contact. Even though we kiss every night and morning, say we love each other and hug, there's not a lot of cuddling time. In the pool, though, I'm carrying them around and throwing them, and they're holding on to me. And that won't be for much longer, either. I want that time with them. We come up with all these goofy games in the pool. It's a real fun, silly time. It's a chance for me to hold my kids and still play with them at the same time.

Bill

Playing with our kids seems like such an obvious thing to do. But when we start understanding the continuous pressure our daughters face around their body image, our play takes on great significance. Remember, the underlying message girls get is that they have to make their bodies into projects (and often go to war with their own bodies) in order to win a male's attention and affection. Dad, her first male, blasts away at that destructive message whenever he plays a sport with his daughter, drives her to practice, attends her recital, applauds her physical persistence, and cheers on her brains and commitment. Plus, he gets to have fun while he's at it.

Sometimes, of course, we try to live vicariously through our daughters or get caught up in the idea that they *must* participate in organized sports. Sport can be wonderful, but it is not the only path in combating the body wars. Shared athletic activity can create special "alone time" for fathers and daughters. Girls cherish these times together, especially if the activities still have the reputation of being "guy things."

ANA: My favorite time would probably be when just Dad and I went duck hunting. When we got out to the duck shack, we went wandering around and looked at where the lake was and where the ducks were and where some good spots to shoot the next day were. It was a really nice night, good wildlife, and lots of ducks, which we didn't seem to find the next day. But it was fun anyway. It was cool just doing stuff, being there. Getting to know what hunting was like, and not having my brother around. Me and Dad.

PETER: *Duck hunting is my passion. It's such a neat thing for you to be able to show your daughter something that she's really going to love. I think that's what brings you the closest. And it's always this great, secret fun.*

Our love for this secret fun—the fun of doing physical things that connect us with our bodies and the natural world—can be infectious. It doesn't even matter if we're any good at the physical activity itself.

I haven't played an organized sport since running cross-country in my sophomore year of high school. I like riding my bike and occasionally shooting at the eight-foot-high basketball hoop on our garage. But when my daughter was nineteen, she told me something I'll never forget. After riding her bicycle more than halfway around Lake Superior (750 miles), she said that she got interested in biking, ballet, tae kwon do, and other physical activity because I liked sports; and because I sometimes shot hoops or rode bikes with her. I was stunned; the guy who gets winded after three flights of stairs influenced her physicality? Yes.

She liked that I stood out back repeatedly rebounding the basketball when her little girl shots seldom made it up to the rim. She liked that I kept playing outdoor games with her, even though she never liked playing catch as much as I wanted her to. She loves bragging about the day she first out-rode me on the long bike trail. She likes going to baseball games with me and still sits and listens to a Twins game on the radio with me, and that's one of the sweetest thrills of my fatherhood—like we're sharing a secret.

I never thought of these times as "sports moments" or even as conscious efforts to encourage physical activity. I thought of them as just things we did together occasionally. But these are all significant memories for her. So, depending on how old your daughter is, go grab a ball, or racket, or a stopwatch and start making memories based on her knowledge that she has a body designed to throw, jump, and run.

TOOLS

THE AIR DIET

Our bodies are genetically predisposed to be diverse sizes and shapes. If we eat healthy and stay physically active (not easy in a world of junk food and couch potatoes), we'll naturally fall into our healthy weight range.

In *Healthy Body Image: Teaching Kids to Eat and Love Their Bodies, Too!*, Kathy Kater exposes the myth that dieting is the cure for the "wrong" body. Kater's Air Diet demonstrates why.

- Get the family together and ask what things are necessary for human survival (air, water, shelter, food, and sleep).
- Ask "What happens when one of these basic needs is not met? How do you feel the day after you have to get along with 3 hours less sleep than usual? What happens if you have to give up that much sleep every night for a week or a month?" Of course, you will feel crabby, have difficulty concentrating, and crave sleep. Then ask, "what happens when you finally can sleep as long as you want?" Even children understand that they'll sleep long hours to make up for sleep deprivation, and it may take days or weeks to get back to normal.

- Then ask, "Do you think the same would happen if we didn't get enough air to breathe?" Explain that the newest "fashion" is ashen-colored skin, so each of us must now go on an air diet to reduce the oxygen in our blood that gives our cheeks that rosy glow—"It will be worth it to 'get the right look.' "
- Give these instructions: "Close your mouth and use your finger to close one of your nostrils, breathing only through the other." (You can also close both nostrils and breathe through a straw.) Once the air diet begins, explain that no laughing or talking is allowed, because that requires using the mouth to breathe. If she says she has a cold, tell her: "Tough luck." If she breaks her air diet, chastise her, "What's the matter, don't you have any willpower?"
- After 3 to 4 minutes, tell her she can "go off her diet." Listen closely to her gasping for air. Then ask how she felt while air dieting.
- Explain that the same thing happens when people restrict their hunger on weight loss diets. You may lose pounds at first, but you'll have trouble concentrating and tend to obsess about food. That naturally leads you to stuff yourself when the diet ends, usually regaining any lost weight, or even additional pounds. After all, your metabolism naturally slows down when your body goes hungry, so it can't burn up the post-diet calories as efficiently as before.

Adapted from Kathy Kater's *Healthy Body Image: Teaching Kids to Eat and Love Their Bodies, Too!* It contains many other fun exercises that build healthy body image. Available from NEDA, 603 Stewart Street, Suite 803, Seattle, WA 98101; phone: (206) 382-3587. For more ideas, visit Kater's Web site, www.bodyimagehealth.org.

JUST US TIME

Write and sign a contract with your daughter in which you agree to set aside a specific amount of time over the next three months to do something together you both enjoy. This will be your "Just Us Time" contract. Keep the original prominently displayed on the refrigerator or family bulletin board. And have fun keeping up your end of the agreement! Here's a sample contract:

Agreement entered into on this eighth day of August 2002, between Joe ("Dad") and Mavis ("Daughter"), in which Dad and Daughter agree to spend one hour per week playing Scrabble ("board game") together for the next three months. By mutual agreement only, Dad and Daughter may elect to play an alternative board game, so long as the time requirements herein are adhered to by both parties, with no alterations, revisions, or other lame excuses permitted..

Agreed and accepted:

Dad: _____

Daughter: _____

YOUR DAUGHTER'S FAMILY TREE

Our society puts so much pressure on women to fit in a narrow definition of "beauty" that by around age ten or so, you may hear your daughter complain about the things she thinks are wrong with her body or face. You can help her accept who she is by showing her where she came from. Look through old photograph albums and find family members who share her features. *Aunt Jane has freckles, too? That's grandmother's pug nose—and look, your cousins have it also!* When she sees the resemblance, your daughter might appreciate the features that run in the family of which she is proud to be a part.

To take this activity a step farther, have your daughter "grow" her own family tree using pictures or images of as many members of the family as the two of you can find. If she is artistic, she can draw or paint the tree. Keep the finished family tree near at hand or consider framing it as a loving reminder of where the freckles, curls, and dimpled chin came from.

GET A KICK OUT OF SPORTS

Research shows that fathers are the biggest influence in motivating their daughters to get and stay involved in sports and other physical activities. So get out and kick a ball around with her, shoot hoops, play catch, jump rope, or toss a Frisbee. Sign up to be line referee or assistant coach on her soccer team. Take her sledding, skating, or skiing. Go to swim practice with her before the next big meet. Your daughter will cherish that special time with you, and in the meantime you'll be laying the groundwork for a healthy and strong young woman.

3.

"MY DAUGHTER'S FACE HERE": MEDIA MADNESS

As fathers, we like to think that what we do at home is more important than what our daughters see on TV, in movies, or out on the streets. Most of the time, we do carry more weight. But those other, outside images and messages relentlessly influence girls, and often in ways that fathers don't recognize—because we're guys. This chapter shows how to open our eyes to the way media and general culture affect our daughters.

CULTURE AND THE GENDER STRAITJACKET

Nia always loved to organize things, make lists, and tell me in detail about them (she still does). The night before starting seventh grade, she recited all the things she'd put in her knapsack for the beginning of school. She said in passing she wasn't sure about including a new pencil box she'd just received for her birthday from a friend. "It has these hearts and stuff on it," she said. "I don't really like it. Actually, I *do* like it, but it's too girly-girl to take to school."

This seemingly insignificant remark about a minor decision stuck in my mind. I later realized that her words were perceptive and chillingly honest. She was observing that, in some important ways, the school culture was not an entirely safe place to express herself. She didn't feel safe liking her pencil box at school. Its "girly-girl" qualities would open her up to teasing or ridicule—hassles she didn't want to deal with.

The year before, she never worried about her girlness, if she even reflected on it. Now, being that same person—a girl who delights in being a girl—made her vulnerable.

I was sad that Nia felt that she had to hide her preference for girly things in order to establish herself in the middle school social scene. I was sad because it looked like she was denying part of herself and avoiding close identification with being a young girl. I was frustrated because there seemed to be nothing I could do about it. I wished she'd adopt an in-your-face "I'm using this pencil box and I don't care what you think" attitude toward her classmates. But I didn't want to criticize *her* for not bringing the pencil box; the school yard hassling and bullying wasn't her fault, and she was making a savvy decision in the face of an unpleasant reality. Thank goodness that she was doing what felt safe to her and not relying on what I thought *should* be safe in an ideal world.

I was grateful that she still revealed her vulnerability to me in offhand remarks; she didn't feel the need to hide herself from me yet. But her words and that small pencil box decision brought home the wide array of ways girls feel forced to separate themselves from their girlness in order to feel safe in a culture where being a girl is less than OK—and sometimes even dangerous.

Our culture is our collective way of life, all the ideas, objects, and ways of doing things created by the group. It includes arts, beliefs, customs, institutions, inventions, language, media, technology, and traditions. We make the culture and it makes us (especially as kids). We shape our culture together, each one of us, through the attitudes and behaviors we encourage—and those we allow to pass unchallenged.

With subtle and overt means, our culture communicates to a thirteen-year-old girl that it isn't smart or safe to flash a pencil box covered with hearts and flowers (images the culture identifies as girlish) at school. If this strikes you as a trivial example, stop and think about what our culture would communicate to your thirteen-year-old son if he brought a cherished pencil box covered with hearts and flowers to school.

The girl will be subject to teasing or ridicule. Your son will be subject to ridicule or getting the stuffing beaten out of him. When it comes to middle-schoolers who show a preference for flowery pencil boxes, our sexist culture is dangerous to girls *and* boys—substantially more so for boys.

These school yard reactions lay out (sometimes violently) what's expected of and permitted to individuals based upon their gender. Youthful peer behavior reflects other cultural restrictions that keep many of us (including our children) in a gender straitjacket.

> *I'm hypersensitive to what's going on around her, how gender issues are dealt with, what we have around the house: movies, books, and how we talk about stuff. It's one of the lenses I see the world through now because I have a daughter.*
>
> *Phil*

We have a responsibility to recognize how cultural influences play out in our daughters' lives. Our daughters and our sons need us to keep watch on how sexist gender expectations limit and harm them—and how easy they are for us fathers to reinforce. It harms a child when she (or he) has to hide parts of who she (or he) is in a gender straitjacket for fear of bringing cultural sanctions on her (or his) head. None of this is abstract; if we look, we can see ways it happens to our children every day. When thinking about these ideas, put your child's face in the picture. We can't ignore culture's profound impact on how our kids see themselves.

DO YOU SEE WHAT I SEE?

A few years ago, I was walking down a New York City street when I encountered a Maidenform advertisement on the side of a bus shelter. It showed a young woman in a bra looking dreamily up into a big blue sky. In large letters across the top, the ad read: Inner beauty only goes so far.

That slogan brought me up short. For a moment, I didn't know why. Inner beauty only goes so far?

Then I did something that I'd never done before, but that I've done many times since. I imagined my daughter's face in that ad. I instantly got angry and sick to my stomach. That strong reaction caught me by surprise. After all, I see and hear messages just like this every day, and most advertising is exaggerated. But with Mavis's face in the picture, I couldn't keep the slogan's meaning out of my mind. What if Mavis walked down the street in Manhattan and, every block, a guy approached and said, "You know, girl, inner beauty only goes so far." If I were walking with her, I'd want to slug that guy! I don't want anybody ever telling my daughter to believe such a lie as she moves through her life.

When I tell this story, women and girls often say, "Now you're seeing what we see all the time and getting a taste of how it feels to us."

Once I did begin to see it, my reaction was fierce because I don't believe that inner beauty only goes so far is one bit true for my daughter; and I don't think it's something any child—girl or boy—should believe.

I know the sexist sort of nature of the world. The violence
toward women and the manipulation of women as objects in

commercials. I think that bothers any father to differing degrees. I want to teach her that happiness flows from inside her mind, that it has nothing to do with the outside world at all. No matter what's going on around her, and what the world is constantly telling her, there's always this place she can tap into that will give her that happiness, the awe-inspiring perfectness of reality. When I look around at the media, it sure doesn't seem like she's going to find much of that out there.

Malcolm

Almost daily, our daughters get harmful, false messages from the culture and from the media. The six-word Maidenform slogan crystallizes the worst of them. There are three major problems with inner-beauty-only-goes-so-far messages, and their corollary, outer beauty is what counts most. First, they cloud our own vision and become cultural truisms. Second, these messages rain down on our daughters hundreds of times a day—on television, in school, movies, newspapers, magazines, billboards, computer games. Third, precious few parents give kids strong umbrellas to fight off the downpour.

The good news is that fathers have what it takes to provide a good umbrella—and even to stop some of the rain. We start by putting our daughter's face in the picture, learning to see the world through her eyes, and then testing how that feels.

Because I'm a man, I'm seldom conscious of—and don't have to deal with—the constant bombardment of inner-beauty-only-goes-so-far messages. But no matter how well we raise our daughters at home, they still live in a culture that has some very damaging values. This sort of thing doesn't strike men unless we actively pay attention.

If we are going to be fully effective fathers for our daughters, we have to raise our awareness of how our culture impacts our daughters—and respond accordingly. It's all right there in front of us—we just have to start looking more carefully.

BEYOND BLAMING

We are all intertwined: media, culture, and us. We can't make media into a big bad Other that is disconnected from us—at least not if we want to stay in touch with reality.

Mass media has been around for centuries and electronic media for more than eighty years. But there are far more media sources today than there were a generation ago. Think about it—how many television stations could you get when you were a kid? Growing up in 1960s southern New Jersey, I got more than most—four Philadelphia stations: ABC, CBS, NBC, and NET (now PBS). How many channels can your daughter access? If you have cable or satellite television, she can get fifty to five hundred or more.

Media takes up more space and time in our lives than ever before. Hence, the ways in which our media and our culture reflect and influence each other (and us) grow stronger every day.

The number of media outlets continues exploding, with mushrooming niche cable channels, on-demand movie services, DVDs, Web sites, music listening systems, radio stations, magazines, and more. One result is an increase in sensationalism as each media source battles aggressively against an expanding field of competitors to win our attention. As sensationalism grows, so grows the danger of desensitization. This hyperkinetic competition also tends to overwhelm our ability to separate fantasy from reality, while drowning out voices that reflect real-life truths and rhythms to our children and us.

I'm emphasizing media heavily because media is so potent in reinforcing the gender straitjacket. If you begin understanding how media does this, you can more easily recognize the messages harmful to your daughters—and do something constructive to counter them.

First, we must learn how to decipher the overt and subtle vernacular of media. It helps to think of media as a language, like

Spanish, English, or Japanese, that has both vocabulary and grammar. In media, the vocabulary is the words and images we see, while the grammar is how those words and images are put together to communicate a meaning and/or motivate us to buy or do something.

Our kids tend to absorb more media words and images than we do, and thus can recite more vocabulary. But very few adults or kids understand its grammar—how and why all those words and images get put together in ways aimed to influence us. This is a serious knowledge gap at a time when reams of research reveal connections between media consumption and child behavior.

MIND OVER MEDIA

Media disseminates messages about female roles beginning when girls are very young, and it happens in media environments we consider innocent and educational.

> *I was watching* Rugrats *with my six-year-old twin girls when the commercial for a local plastic surgeon came on. It showed pictures of school age girls while a girl's voice told how plastic surgery helps girls look better and feel better about themselves. On* Rugrats! *That's a show for preschoolers!*
>
> *David*

In her book *Can't Buy My Love: How Advertising Changes the Way We Think and Feel* (Touchstone, 2000), Dr. Jean Kilbourne explains how sexualized appearance-first messages infuse advertising for the most innocuous products, like shoes and cereal. That's easy to see once we start looking closely. For example, an ad for Doc Martens shoes shows a girl's legs (the rest of her body is missing) sitting on outdoor bleachers. The photo's focus is the pair of Doc Martens she is wearing. The ad copy reads, "The second thing guys look at."

The clear implication is that boys look first at her breasts, therefore both girl and boy should be concerned about her cup size. Not only is this message harmful to girls and boys—it's an insult to both sexes.

A teen magazine ad for Honeycomb cereal shows a photo of a girl's torso (again, the rest of her body is missing) with a bare midriff. Over her navel are diamonds patterned in the shape of a piece of Honeycomb cereal. In one corner is a tiny image of the Honeycomb cereal box. In this example, sexy imagery is used to sell cereal to kids. What's the connection between sex and cereal? I seriously doubt that Honeycomb is an aphrodisiac, and even if it was, using its sexual qualities would be an irresponsible way to market to kids.

In addition, there are other not-so-subtle messages communicated by images like the Honeycomb torso. In this and many other ads, you will see only part of a girl's or woman's body—often her legs, torso, and/or breasts. Missing are her head (home of her brain), hands (tools for her talents), and her feet (her method for moving herself where she wants to go). This portrayal of disembodied female body parts reinforces the notion that we should view female bodies in pieces, and as "pieces"—the objectifying slang term by which many boys and men refer to a woman or girl.

We've probably seen many ads like these, but they are so ubiquitous that we seldom notice all of what they communicate. When we stop to think about the messages, they are blatantly silly; but we're all busy and there are so many others just like them. However, the fact that we are seldom fully conscious of what they say does not mean that their messages leave our kids or us untouched.

Every day, we can find hundreds of examples of what the media is throwing at our daughters. Once we unlock the language in a few examples, we begin to broaden our perception of almost every media we absorb.

An effective trick is imagining boys or men in the media portrayals that girls and women usually are assigned.

For example, back when the U.S. women's soccer team won the Women's World Cup, *Sports Illustrated* did a cover story about them. I'd be proud to see this *cover* as a poster in my daughter's bedroom. But the article inside undermined the powerful message conveyed by the photograph. In a cloying piece, shot through with titillating comments about the athletes' bodies, *SI* wrote about the player's diets, boyfriends, children, and taste in clothes. *Sports Illustrated* shed little light on the way these women excel at their grueling sport.

Now flip-flop the genders. Imagine that, after winning another NBA title, *SI* features the Los Angeles Lakers on its cover. If *SI*'s cover story was similar to the women's soccer profile, it would tell us how Kobe Bryant stays so slim, what Phil Jackson makes his kids for breakfast, and how Shaquille O'Neal met his wife. Ridiculous, right? But this is the unfortunate reality for a professional woman athlete (or a girl who aspires to be one). Mainstream media more often goes for superficiality and titillation, while seldom acknowledging those female athletes' amazing accomplishments.

Another great place to start becoming literate in media is with the magazines our daughters already consume. For example, they are likely to read a top-selling girls magazine: *Seventeen, YM, Cosmo Girl, Teen People*. Despite the ages suggested by their titles, girls often start reading these magazines around age ten (seventeen-year-olds wouldn't be caught dead reading *Seventeen*; they've moved on to *Cosmopolitan* or *Glamour*). Together, you and she can use these magazines to learn the untruths you'll encounter and understand the ways (and reasons why) media regularly misrepresents reality.

For example, compare photographs of the same celebrity, someone like Britney Spears, on the covers of several different teen and women's magazines. You'll usually notice that her skin shade is different in each picture. You'll also notice that her breasts appear to be different sizes and shapes from photo to photo, as may her hands, hair, tummy, or legs. How can this be?

Simple: each magazine repeatedly runs its Britney image

through computer programs such as Photoshop for alterations. The goal is to achieve what that month's editors dictate is beautiful, even if it means changing how the same beautiful person looks from month to month.

> I've just read an article on the many ways magazine photos are altered. I think more young girls and women (and guys, too) should read about very superficial tricks used just to intimidate young women into feeling they look like junk. Let's face it, advertising agencies and magazines are trying to sell their product. Don't fall for one of the oldest tricks in the book. Being beautiful and looking good is a state of mind and not any kind of "buyable" product.
>
> *Randy*

The most telling thing about these images is how little use they are in identifying the celebrity should she happen to come through your front door. Perhaps you remember the famous poster of Richard Gere and Julia Roberts for their movie *Pretty Woman*. That's megastar and sex symbol Julia Roberts's face you see, but not her body. *Pretty Woman*'s promoters decided that Roberts's own body wasn't pretty enough, so they pasted a photo of someone else's body to a photo of Roberts's head. This kind of image manipulation is so normal in media that the pictures we see frequently don't look like the actual person. No matter how beautiful a model or movie star may be, marketers resort to special effects to alter her image.

Why does it matter? It matters because we and our daughters are continually consuming images that don't represent any knowable reality. These images can be no more representative of a person than a cartoon character is.

Of course, there's nothing inherently wrong with make-believe; we use both nonfiction and fairy tales to teach our daughters how to read. But at some point, we also teach the difference between the two so they can master the English language and make their way sensibly through the world. This is a key concept as fathers and daughters decipher media, too; learning to understand what's real, what's make-believe, and how to tell the difference.

It's often hard to find reality in media aimed at girls. For example, here are the headlines (what magazines call teases) that highlight the top stories inside one issue of *Seventeen*:

- The Boys of Buffy [TV's Buffy, the Vampire Slayer], Unzipped
- How Far Would You Go for Him?
- Hair Goo, What Works for Your Do
- '*N Sync* on Love. This One Girl Broke My Heart
- The Club Drug That Kills
- Your Summer Check List: The Most Bathing Suits Ever, Body Tone-up Tips, Bare-it-all Beauty

Half of these six teases are about boys, despite the fact that it's a girls' magazine. Of the three about girls, two are about outward appearance. The one other, The Club Drug That Kills, describes a date rape drug. Put your daughter's face in that picture and remember that *Seventeen*'s readership includes many ten-year-old daughters.

Our daughters do care about appearance and getting boys to notice them. That's fine! Wanting to look nice, feel attractive, and attract people we like can be a valuable and healthy part of being a girl. But it's a fraction of our daughters' life, while most girls' media presents it as the sum total. Why? The idea behind *Cosmo Girl* magazine's articles and ads is to make readers feel insecure about themselves, how they look and how they act. Breeding that insecurity creates more willing consumers. With the turn of each page, our daughters grow less sure that they are good enough—good enough to fit in, to be cool, to get a boy's attention, to be admired.

In these magazines, a girl also finds scores of advertisers marketing products and services as the solution to one or all of her insecurities. The advertisers know that exacerbating a girl's anxieties tends to make her more motivated to buy. This knowledge sets up a symbiotic relationship between advertisers and many girls' magazines because advertising is those magazines' primary source of income. If you take away all its subscription revenue, *Cosmo Girl* would probably still be profitable; but if you take away just half of its ad revenue, *Cosmo Girl* would go out of business. If advertisers play on a girl's fear and insecurity to sell their products, then fear and insecurity are what the publishers and editors deliver to readers. The symbiotic relationship between magazines and marketers harms girls because it attacks their sense of self-worth. It's sad that magazines and marketers seem willing to undercut our daughters' well-being just to make a buck. What's even sadder is that this formula has worked for generations, in large part because we haven't exposed the formula for the scam it is.

MTV, MOVIES, AND MEDIA MAGIC

It's not just magazines that reinforce the corrosive "inner beauty only goes so far" lie. Sit through an hour of music videos and count how many times the girls and women appear in scant clothing, acting as little more than sexualized props—objects included for their ability to titillate and nothing more. Men and boys are very seldom portrayed the same way on MTV or VH1.

Watching music video channels is another good way to absorb current pop song lyrics, where girls and women also are regularly assigned the role of sexual objects. Check out the lyrics of female vocalists like Lil' Kim ("What's on your mind when you fuck me from behind . . . It was a trick when I sucked his dick.") and you hear that even female artists reinforce the idea that a girl's primary purpose is to focus on providing a male his sexual pleasure.

These are the most obviously outrageous messages and images aimed at our daughters. Much of the other television they watch has more subtle, but no more encouraging, tales to tell. From cartoons to Disney Channel live-action programs, very young girls consistently see more male characters. In the majority of shows, the male characters make the decisions and do the physical actions that move the story along and lead to resolution, while the female characters offer support or act as fretting, fearful obstacles to problem solving.

There is progress of a sort in recent years' teen action-adventure series starring strong female characters. However, in most of these shows—*Xena: Warrior Princess, Dark Angel, Sheena*—there is as much attention paid to exposing the star's cleavage as there is to her being an action hero. For example, the star of *Sheena* was the featured pictorial in the November 2001 *Playboy*.

Lead characters like *Star Trek: Voyager*'s Captain Kathryn Janeway and Dr. Quinn in *Dr. Quinn: Medicine Woman* stand out as positive exceptions; although neither show remains in production, they are on syndicated reruns. In both shows, the female lead relies on savvy, knowledge, and courage (rather than sex appeal) to overcome obstacles and lead the show's other characters to safety each week. The producers of *Voyager,* in particular, did an excellent job showing Janeway lead a Starfleet crew that collaborates well, but also gives respect and allegiance to the captain without regard to her gender.

Turn to the various manifestations of Reality TV—up there with the most mindless television—and you'll see more reinforcement for narrow gender roles. Fox's *Temptation Island* is a good example. Most of the dynamics feature a woman trying to lure a man, while the men make the substantive decisions about the relationship. The participants' bodies are continually objectified in the shameless titillation for which Fox is infamously known, but female cleavage always gets far more airtime than male washboard abs do.

The Reality TV of celebrity news and daytime talk shows does no better. Dozens of programs like *Entertainment Tonight, Access Hollywood,* and their clones tell as much about a celebrity's fashion choices as they do about her next movie role. Another regular feature is almost continuous tracking of female (not male) stars' weight. Meanwhile, even the most influential talk show host ever, Oprah Winfrey, makes almost daily reference to her weight control struggles—a topic also getting maximum coverage in the celebrity press.

The movie scene presents another troubling message about what girls should expect to be and have done to them in our culture. Teens make up more than a quarter of the moviegoing audience, so they are the biggest target for new films. Sit down and watch a couple of popular movie thrillers with your daughter. No matter what slasher flick is hot today, you're likely to find a pattern that's been around for years in teen classics like *Halloween*, *Scream*, and *I Know What You Did Last Summer*. The girl (or girls) are the vast majority of the victims: raped, stabbed, degraded, mutilated, terrorized.

This sensibility is becoming more mainstreamed in advertising and other media. For example, a notorious 2000 Nike TV ad showed a masked man with a chain saw (typical slasher-flick fare) chasing Olympic runner Suzy Hamilton through the darkened streets of a town. After Hamilton outruns her attacker—leaving him to find another victim, one supposes—the ad asks, "Why do sport? You'll live longer." Nike insisted the ad was a joke, but after viewer complaints, networks stopped running the spot.

If there were just one or two of these kill-the-girls movies, maybe we could chalk them up as nothing to worry about. But the continuing parade of entertainment built on terrorizing girls sends a very disturbing message about what we and our kids consume for amusement. It also sends a clear message to our daughters about how females are valued in our culture.

Teen-oriented comedy films, most following the tired tradition of *Animal House*, routinely build their humor on boys' grotesque comments and behaviors about sex, girl characters used as large-breasted props, and scripts that don't bother to portray females as even two-dimensional. An effective (and fun) way to uncover and blast apart these cinema stereotypes is to grab your daughter and watch good satires of teen flicks—movies like *Clueless* or *Romy and Michele's High School Reunion.*

Video games generally follow the same constricted model of gender roles as that found in TV and movies. One of the most popular video games, Lara Croft, puts as much emphasis on Lara's breasts as it does on her brains; the same pattern you'll see in TV's *Xena.* In a CD-ROM game called Panty Raider, boys strip supermodels down to their underwear, then provide photographs of them to aliens who wore out their one lingerie catalog—or else the aliens' hormone-driven anger will destroy the earth. Among the gamers' tools to induce the undressing: "Lures—items such as tiny mints (lunch!) and credit cards. No self-respecting supermodel can resist these items." From making fun of anorexia, objectifying girls, and stereotyping them as obsessed with shopping to assuming that boys just want titillation from computer games, Panty Raider is a disgrace.

Narrow gender expectations often infuse computer products aimed at very young girls, too. When Mattel released its Barbie PC computer (done in pink) and its Hot Wheels PC (done in blue), the company made a striking revelation of how it perceives girls. The Barbie PC came *without* software programs—Logical Journey of the Zoombinis, Compton's Complete Reference Collection, Body Works, ClueFinders Math, and Kid Pix Studio—that Mattel included on the Hot Wheels PC. Instead, Mattel loaded the Barbie Fashion Designer program and defended the decision by saying that's what girls want on a computer. The message: boys deserve mental stimulation, while girls deserve new outfits. This was an amazing marketing choice for the nation's leading toy maker in light of ongoing trends showing that girls continue to steer away from interest in computers, math, science, and technology—the skills of the future.

You may be surprised to learn that there's an upside in all this. When it comes to media and culture, fathers are ideally positioned to develop their daughters' ability to see media with a critical eye—and improve our own critical vision in the bargain. Plus, today's intense media competition can work to our advantage if we decide to become active consumers by influencing existing media and creating positive alternatives.

That's where we dads come in.

> *I think my daughters are very much reflective of the society today. And my ability to help them cope is a big issue. I have to spend more time being conscious about the things that I say and do, that I'm not trying to reinforce what the media is trying to throw at them. [I have to] portray them as individuals and being unique, as opposed to what the media hype and the rest of the world is trying to throw against girls their age. I want to show them the benefit of their being individuals as opposed to trying to mirror how other people perceive them.*
>
> *Anthony*

BRINGING THE MESSAGE HOME

So, now that you see more clearly how today's media culture tends to convey unhealthy, destructive values to your daughter, what can you do? First and foremost, you can speak up. Communicate your own girl-friendly values to her, starting at an early age. If you are silent about the things your kids hear from media and culture, then those things gain an authority that they do not deserve. Your silence can leave your daughter feeling adrift and uncertain. The way to clear up the confusion is to speak up about how your personal and family values compare to values in the media. When we teach our daughters from an early age how to interpret and analyze elements of the media—whether it's a movie, fashion photo, headline, music video, or advertisement—we help them separate reality from fantasyland, especially in the crucial arena of what guys want. Since we are guys, we have a big influence in this arena. But first, we have to give our daughters credit for their taste in media.

When I was a kid, I used to say that I didn't like asparagus. One day, my aunt Peggy asked if I'd ever tasted it. I said no. "Then how can you know that you don't like it?" she asked. I did finally try it, and I didn't like it (still don't). But my opinion now has the legitimacy of being based on experience. By sitting down with your daughter and an open mind to sample the media she enjoys, your insights will be greater and *your* opinion about that media will carry more weight with her. Watch, read, and listen to media with your daughter. Sure, her taste in music may elude you, but your willingness to at least listen to that music tells her that you respect her opinion. Teach her that we have a choice about how—and even whether—to consume the media sent our way every day.

> She doesn't have a TV in her room. We feel that that really kind of invites isolation within the family unit. We struggle as parents with finding a balance. You don't want to be overprotective where you just shut your child completely out of the culture. And we do hear her say, "So-and-so gets to do this." It's a constant process of trying to find balance. We want her to be safe and healthy, but we also want her to be able to experience life and be able to make choices.
>
> Sandy

While my daughters were growing up, one choice I made was to comment on the television or movies we watched: Look at how sexist that story is; I don't like how they're treating that woman and stereotyping that man or I love this character because she reminds me of you/your mother/your aunt.

Sometimes the girls would join in the spirit of media-literate, analytical viewing. Other times they'd get annoyed and say, "Will you stop being so critical all the time? Just shut up and watch the movie!" Those sharp responses sometimes upset me, but at least I knew the girls were hearing me and what I value. Still, there may be unexpected sacrifices required, at least temporarily, to get our point across.

Last summer we turned the TV off. And we'll do it again this summer. But what that means is, when the TV's off, the parents work harder. So whether it's over a card game or during a walk, we get into some pretty interesting family discussions.

Harry

Turning off the TV is just one way to convey our values about the media our daughters consume. We can also talk with them about music, the Internet—even good old-fashioned books. When we're tuned in to what they get from those media, we're in a much better position to help create alternative messages.

I'm afraid this damsel in distress mentality starts very early. My two-and-a-half-year-old already loves the Cinderella, Snow White, *and* Sleeping Beauty *stories. In each, the heroine must wait for the prince to kiss her, wake her, or bring the shoe. A message like that is very easy to learn when your child likes a story and wants to read it over and over again. And since it is so hard to find alternative stories to counter these messages, I do role-playing and pretending our own different endings and different stories with these characters. My daughter loves to role-play with her dolls and Little People, reenacting situations, but also exploring variations in the characters' behavior.*

Walt

Ironically, role-playing and pretending may keep a daughter better grounded in reality than the media can. Her pretending is more likely to reflect her experience and personality than corporately produced media does. She'll have access to our experience, too, if we join in the play.

Another alternative to TV are quality kids' magazines like *Cricket, Cobblestone, American Girl, Stone Soup, Muse,* and *New Moon: The Magazine for Girls and Their Dreams,* none of which carry advertising. *Cricket* and its companion publications (*Ladybug* and *Spider*) are well established, high-quality literary magazines for school-age girls and boys. In the same age range, *Cobblestone* focuses on U.S. history while *Stone Soup* carries only articles and artwork created by kids. *American Girl* centers on upbeat stories, historical fiction, and activities aimed at extending the shelter of childhood a bit longer for girls. Published by Mattel, *AG* also features the company's American Girl books and doll collection. Some publications with advertising, like *Teen Ink* (primarily writing by teens) and *Teen Voices* (aimed at urban teen girls), are also good.

New Moon is especially helpful for girls on and around the cusp of adolescence. Eight- to fourteen-year-old girls edit it, and most of its content is written by girls. These girls talk about their entire lives, their inner life, what they're doing in the world, the impact they're having in their families and in their communities. They talk about appearance and boys, too, but in amounts that put them in perspective relative to the rest of a girl's life. How many of these magazines have you heard of or seen? Which are or have been in your house? These alternative publications are sometimes harder to find because they don't have big ad revenue to do marketing like that which brings *Seventeen*'s offer of twelve issues for $9.99 to my mailbox. Alternative magazines like *Stone Soup* and *Teen Voices* are more expensive. Parents regularly tell me that they get *YM* or *Seventeen* for their daughter because it's cheaper than *New Moon* or *American Girl. New Moon* only comes out six times a year and it costs twenty-nine bucks, compared to *YM,* which cost fifteen bucks for twelve issues!

Which one is cheaper? It depends on how you are paying—with your checkbook or with your daughter's self-worth. The advertising that makes *YM* so cheap to a subscriber also eats away at that reader's sense of herself. Which model of feeding your daughter's brain and heart do you want to support?

On the other hand, I do not think it's wise to forbid daughters to read *YM*, *Seventeen*, and its sisters. Censorship is not a good solution and seldom works.

> *The idea is not to ban* Seventeen *from my house. The idea is to read it. If we don't have it in our house, and my daughter wants to read it, she'll get it somewhere else—from her friends or she'll sneak around to read it. Better we should both be reading it so I can tell her what I think.*
>
> *Bobby*

What you think matters because, in the end, your values will have enormous sway—but only if you consciously convey them to your daughter. Let your daughter know what your values are and that you value her for who she is and not for her resemblance to some silly stereotype.

Regular conversations about media and culture can build up your daughter's resistance to the negative media messages that intensify serious adolescent problems like chemical abuse or sexual acting-out. But it doesn't make her immune. While our daughters can bypass the worst of what can befall teen girls, they still do battle with the media. My daughter Nia talks about it:

> *I've almost stopped reading popular media because it makes me feel bad about myself, even with my heightened sense of the manipulation that's at work and the sense that I know that I'm a good person and I know that I'm doing what I ought to be doing and that I shouldn't be giving into these pressures. When there's so*

*much of it, it's really hard, so I try to distance myself from that,
except to look at it and critique it. I try to just stay away from
the stuff that I know will be a negative influence. Because otherwise, when you've got it around all the time, it's really hard to
stand up to it.*

Even if our daughters are doing well, they still do battle with the
narrow cultural vision often offered by the media. They need us as
their allies in that fight.

In addition to communicating your values to your daughter at
an early age and explicitly commenting on media as she encounters
it, there is a third way to balance the media message: create alternatives that help both of you be more active participants in life.

REACHING FOR REALITY

We are usually passive when we consume media; we're absorbing
someone or something else's ideas and imagery. It seems like common sense, therefore, that the best antidote to a media overdose is
to become more directly engaged with the world.

When you encourage and get involved in your daughter's extracurricular activities, that helps her discover who she is through
what she enjoys or doesn't enjoy about the school newspaper,
French club, soccer squad, or the debate team. She gains an appreciation for the richness of possibilities when she ventures beyond
the artificial—and adult-driven—environment of most media. As
our daughters move toward tangible personal activities that reveal
important truths, they will be better prepared for their future—in
real life, not la-la land.

When you expose your daughter to other forms of culture—
theater, concerts, exhibits—you help her learn that creating her
own video, song, or dance is more fulfilling and fun than sitting at

home watching MTV. Taking her to see live performances might be just the creative kick she needs to get her going. Depending on her talents and interests, you might suggest she sign up for dance lessons, audition for a local theater production, or simply start carrying a camera around to take photographs.

When you volunteer with your daughter, she learns that active participation—along with her enthusiasm and energy—can help make her world a better, if not Hollywood-picture-perfect, place to live. I'll talk about volunteerism in more depth in Chapter 7, but the point here is that it's a subtle counterweight to media overload. And opportunities to pitch in are literally everywhere you look, from your street corner—I know a dad and daughter who moved some rocks, cut the grass, and made a path on their corner so commuters had a better route to the train station—to global organizations.

When you travel with your daughter, she learns that seeing, touching, and smelling a national park or a big city is far more awesome than magazine photographs or a movie can be. Can you take her on your next business trip? Would she consider an exchange program in another country? Does your faith community offer youth weekends? Not only does travel in and of itself help your daughter grow and stretch, it teaches her that media varies all over the world. One region's version of ideal beauty is very different from another's. By observing these innate variations, your daughter will begin to understand the arbitrary quality of media standards.

DEAR MR. CEO, ARE YOU A DAD?

It's hard to identify the biggest media offenders when it comes to undermining our daughters—because there are so many. Beyond fighting back at home with media literacy, we can get at the root of the problem by becoming media activists.

About once a month, the Dads and Daughters organization encourages our members to e-mail, write, or call companies that advertise and market in ways that affect girls. It only takes a few dads speaking out to have a big impact because fathers have more clout than most of us realize. Why?

Because men (many of them fathers) head nearly all media, marketing, and advertising companies in the United States. As of this writing, only four of the Fortune 500's largest U.S. corporations are led by women. The other 496 CEOs are men—most of them fathers and/or grandfathers. Fathers like us are the ones who run these organizations and so we can talk to CEOs father-to-father about the messages they send our kids.

If I (as a father) ask a CEO (as a father) to put his daughter's or granddaughter's face into the picture of what he's selling and how he's selling it, my question might carry special legitimacy and weight with him.

For example, Sun-In, a long-established hair-bleaching product, once ran a troubling ad in *Teen People* magazine. (I'd never heard of Sun-In, but women often say, Oh sure, I used it when I was a girl.) The ad's copy reads: "Four of five girls you hate ask for it by name. Stop hating them. Start *being* them with Sun-In, the original."

In response, DADs' members wrote to Zan Guerry, CEO of Chattem, Inc., the multinational manufacturer of Sun-In, Ban deodorant, pHisoderm skin cleaner, Dexatrim diet pills, and dozens of other products. We asked, Do you want your children to hate others? If they did have that corrosive feeling, would you encourage them to start *being* the people they hate? We assume that your answer to these two questions, like the answers of any responsible parent, is a strong "No!" Then we asked him to have Chattem stop running the ad.

A couple of weeks later, Guerry himself wrote to say he'd been on vacation with his family when our letters arrived, but upon his return, the ad was the first topic he took up with his marketing managers.

In my twenty plus years at Chattem, I am aware of no similar
problem with any of our ads. We certainly always intend to mar-
ket our products with good taste and sensitivity. Unfortunately it
is apparent that this ad has been misunderstood, for which we
take full responsibility.

The purpose of communication is not to communicate so you
can be understood, but so you can't be misunderstood. Clearly, we
failed in this measure.

Guerry went on to say that Chattem was pulling this Sun-In ad; it
never ran again. Speaking father-to-father, a few dozen DADs'
members got our message through.

When Campbell's soup created a thirty-second TV commercial
pitching soup to prepubescent girls as a diet aid, it aired during
after-school programs like *The Rosie O'Donnell Show.* Puberty is the
time when nature adds body fat to females so they can bear children
and lactate. You can't fool Mother Nature; marketing diet aids to a
prepubescent is insane.

Once again, Dads and Daughters wrote a father-to-father letter
to the CEO. Two days later, Campbell's vice-president John
Faulkner called DADs to say, we've pulled this ad. Faulkner explained that when creating the commercial, Campbell hadn't recognized the danger of the message, but it was clear after reading our
letter.

Thirty-second national TV commercials are not cheap to make
or air. Campbell's was willing to kiss that money good-bye in response to letters from one small organization because competition
for consumer attention and loyalty is greater than it's ever been. To
succeed, companies must be agile and respond quickly to what consumers say. For example, NBC used to have only two competitors
for TV advertising revenue: CBS and ABC. Now it has more than
five hundred. Each one of those five hundred has a big stake in listening closely to what viewers—us—tell them.

We can use that leverage to point out examples of good advertising, too, just as we try to catch our children being good and reward positive behavior.

You may have seen a Chevrolet Truck TV commercial that showed a lifelong father-daughter relationship in which Dad consistently supports Daughter's dream of being a ski racer. As a young woman, she wins a race and is surrounded by cheering female coaches and teammates. Through congratulatory hugs, she searches for Dad in the crowd. Their eyes meet and they give each other an excited thumbs-up. Then the announcer's deep male voice says, "Year after year, it's good to have someone to depend on. Chevy. The most dependable, longest-lasting trucks on the road."

To draw attention to this positive portrayal of a father-daughter relationship, we mobilized DADs' members to write letters of thanks and encouragement to both Chevrolet and Campbell-Ewald, its Michigan ad agency. We gave both companies a Father's Day award.

That's not to say that we get what we want every time we speak up (kind of like being a dad). Sometimes, companies don't respond to DADs' actions at all. But even then, there's a benefit in the enthusiastic fatherly teamwork—we feel less overwhelmed by the wide reach of the media. When DADs raises a ruckus, we bat around .300 in getting the outcome we want. Still, we're setting a great example for our kids with our willingness to speak up and put ourselves out there.

Taking risks is a big part of being a father. In the next chapter, we discuss perhaps the biggest risk a father takes—trusting his daughter as she becomes a woman.

TOOLS

WRITE A LETTER TOGETHER

If you see an ad that portrays women negatively, talk about your reaction to it with your daughter. Then write a letter together to the
company responsible for the ad or product—the broadcaster, the
publisher, the ad agency, the food or clothing company, the manufacturer. State your objections to the harmful messages and ask that
they halt the campaign or discontinue selling the product. Be specific. Present your own background, and express your concern as a
father and your concern for our society.

If you see an ad that sends a positive and affirming message to
girls, don't hesitate to send that advertiser a congratulatory letter
thanking the company for the job well done.

Here is a sample letter template written by DADs in response to
an advertising campaign:

Douglas A. Conant
President and CEO
Campbell Soup Company
Campbell Place
Camden, NJ 08103-1799

Dear Mr. Conant:
On behalf of fathers across the country, please stop running your
current television commercial that promotes Campbell's Soup to
young children, especially girls, as a way to watch their weight.
[DESCRIBE OFFENDING MEDIA]

There is not a single thing "M'm! M'm Good!" about
encouraging eleven- and twelve-year-olds to diet, and marketing
soup to girls as a weight-loss tool. In fact, this is a dangerous

message to send to children this age. Your latest TV commercial is irresponsible and should stop immediately.

[CONTINUE EXPLANATION OF WHY THE AD IS HARMFUL]

Your commercial appears to play on these disturbing realities in order to sell more soup, especially as we have observed it airing during shows with large girl viewership like *The Rosie O'Donnell Show.* Dads and Daughters is the national nonprofit for fathers and daughters. DADs helps strengthen father-daughter relationships, acts against marketers who undermine girls to sell products, and applauds those who don't.

We have asked the members of Dads and Daughters and our friends to contact you, express their concerns, and demand that Campbell's immediately stop running this commercial. We look forward to a prompt response.

Sincerely,

Joe Kelly

Note: In response to this letter, Campbell's Soup actually pulled this ad off the air! Voicing our opinion really works.

WRITE A LETTER TO THE EDITOR

Sending a letter to the editor of your local newspaper or even a national magazine is another way dads and daughters can make themselves heard on the issue of women in advertising and media. Here are tips on how to get your letter published:

- Be topical. Use recent news and events as the reason to send a letter. If possible, refer to an earlier story or letter in the newspaper. Stick to one issue in your letter.

- Keep it short and simple. Editors prefer letters between two hundred and three hundred words, which is about one typed page.
- Think local. Say how the issues affect your local community.
- Make it personal. If possible, show how an issue might affect an editor personally.
- Sign it. Include your name, address, and telephone number. A newspaper may need to contact you before printing your letter (and they won't print it if you don't provide your name and address).
- Look for national opportunities to have your voice heard. Most popular news programs on radio and television invite listeners or viewers to submit their views by e-mail. These e-mails are often read on the air.
- Avoid form letters. A custom letter is more effective because it shows more personal effort.
- Don't be discouraged if your letter is not printed. Each time you submit a letter, you educate the editorial board of your paper and pave the way for future letters to be printed. Keep trying.

DESIGN YOUR OWN AD

With your daughter, look through a selection of magazines and find an ad that the two of you think is harmful or offensive to girls. Then, each of you design and write your own ad countering the negative messages of the original. You can cut out images and words from old magazines, or use any art form to create your ad. Your slogan might be, Outer Beauty Only Goes So Far and you could include a collage of positive images of women—engaging in sports, reading to a child, wearing a doctor's uniform, carrying a briefcase, climbing a mountain, etc.

When each of you are done, show each other your creation and talk about what you were trying to accomplish, and what methods you used to do it. The goal is media literacy: you and your daughter will begin to understand how ads are constructed and how they manipulate viewers.

TEN FAMOUS WOMEN

Have you and your daughter list ten famous women *without naming models, rock stars, or movie stars.* It may be harder than you think. If either of you can't think of ten, then it's time to do some research. If she easily comes up with them, ask her to name a few more. Think about what it is that makes women on your lists famous. What is your reaction to this? Your daughter's? Why do you think we didn't want you to use models or actresses in your list? How are models, rock stars, or movie stars valued in society as opposed to the people on your list?

A BETTER VISION

Here is a list of movies that show girls and boys in a wider range of roles—and which offer a broader cultural vision.

For younger children there are all of the various Pippi
    Longstocking movies; great fun for the grownups, too.
Also for younger ones, the PBS-Wonderworks version of
    Ramona Quimby (from the Beverly Cleary books). Nicely
    done with realistic, affectionate, and very funny family
    portrayals

The six-hour PBS presentation of *Pride and Prejudice* by Jane
   Austen

The Secret of Roan Inish

Ever After, with Drew Barrymore, a modern-day retelling of the
   Cinderella tale

Fly Away Home

The BBC's version of *The Secret Garden*

Mary Poppins

Chicken Run (this is a mixed bag as the heroine is portrayed
   nicely but there is especially one female chicken that is very
   ditsy. Nothing harmful though, lots of fun)

Crouching Tiger, Hidden Dragon (A great Chinese film)

Billy Elliot (rated R, but may have been able to get by with PG-13—
   language, subtle homosexuality, and a bit of violence)

The Princess Bride

Little Women (1994)

For older, teen audiences:

Antonia's Line

The Joy-Luck Club

Contact

The River Wild

What's Love Got to Do with It?

Dead Man Walking

The Hiding Place

Fargo

The Borrowers

Sister Act (both I and II)

Mermaids

Princess Cariboo

Riding in Cars with Boys

TURN BEAUTY INSIDE OUT

Every girl is beautiful! That's the message of the nonprofit group Mind on the Media's annual Turn Beauty Inside Out (TBIO) campaign. Celebrating Inner Beauty, the TBIO campaign suggests many easy ways to make a difference individually or with a group. Held the third Wednesday in May, TBIO is a great counterbalance to all the pressure girls get to compare themselves to impossible beauty images in the media. Find out how you and your daughter can participate at www.motm.org.

4.

"NO DATING UNTIL YOU'RE THIRTY-FIVE!": NAVIGATING YOUR DAUGHTER'S ADOLESCENCE

*When I was holding her in the delivery room, she was so beauti-
ful. It was just amazing. The first thing I remember saying to
her was, "Noooo, sweetheart, no boy is ever gonna take you away
from Daddy."*

Jon

The most intense periods in fathering a daughter are her birth and
her adolescence, and many of us start thinking about the teen years
right there in the delivery room, if not before. The problem is that
adolescence lasts a lot longer than birth and tends to be much more
complicated—at least it seems to be for a dad.

Adolescence is a pivotal time in our daughters' lives. What may
be less obvious is how much our daughters' adolescence is a pivotal
time for our lives, too. Many a veteran father (and many an adult
daughter) judges his success by how he did during his daughter's
teen years. The way we respond to her adolescence (before, during,

and after) reflects and shapes our relationship in fundamental ways. Our best approach during this period in our daughters' lives is trust—in our daughters, ourselves, her peers, boys, family members, and the world. The quality of that trust colors our father-daughter relationships from start to finish.

CLEANING THE SHOTGUN

> *The first time a boy comes calling on my daughter, I'll be out on the front porch just casually cleaning my shotgun. Because I was his age once; I know what he's after and I want him to know it.*
>
> *Tony*

When a dad tells his newborn, "Daddy's not gonna let you date till you're thirty-five," we all know why. He's talking about sex. Even from day one our top worry is that she might have sex or that someone else will try to have it with her. Our reaction is sheer panic.

I've heard some variation of the shotgun story from fathers all over the country: laid-back Malibu, inner-city Oakland, Philadelphia's Main Line, conservative Phoenix, liberal Eugene, on two Indian reservations, and dozens of places in between. Dads from many racial, geographic, ethnic, political, and socioeconomic backgrounds tell some version of this story. If every dad got a "Bible of Fathering" at his daughter's birth, this would be the opening parable.

At first blush, the shotgun parable may seem (especially to women) like further evidence that all men are Neanderthals. Rest assured, it's not. I've yet to meet a father who has actually taken a weapon to the doorway of his apartment when his daughter's date first arrives. Few of us really plan to wave a pistol around or make the boy fill out one of those gag "applications to date my daughter" floating around the Internet that ask questions like "Where would you most like to be shot?" and have rules like "No looking below her shoulders." Instead, we e-mail the application to our friends as a joke. But the shotgun story reveals how even the most optimistic of us yearn for a surefire solution for our apprehension about our daughters' adolescence and sexuality.

> *I'm afraid of these next few years. Will some boy take advantage of her? Will some teacher or mentor take advantage of this sweet young thing with all this potential? She is vulnerable during this period of time. I want her to have boyfriends, go off to camp, have wonderful teachers, and travel as part of growing up and finding out who she really is. But all those things have risks and I fear those risks.*
>
> *Randy*

Fearing those risks, we long to engineer a single word or action powerful enough to protect our daughters. If only a shotgun could do the trick! Many of us wistfully imagine being the ultimate father-protector able to issue a foolproof warning to the boys audacious and foolhardy enough to call on his daughter.

> *When she starts going out with boys, I think, "I was a boy. I know what boys are like. I don't want her to be with people who are like me." And, toward the boy, my thoughts are, "It doesn't matter what you tell me. I know exactly what you're thinking."*
>
> *George*

THE SHOTGUN'S RANGE

When I tell the shotgun story in my talks, men and women always laugh in recognition. That's because, at some point in our lives, most of us have been one of the three characters in the story—the father, the daughter, and/or the boy who comes calling. If we look at the story as a parable (small "p"), we can start to uncover the message it conveys to each of its three "characters."

The Daughter

This shotgun parable tells the daughter: Daddy doesn't really trust me. He doesn't have faith in my choice of friends or in my ability to choose good friends. He doesn't believe there are any decent boys out there anyway. He doesn't think that I can stay out of harm's way, and he doesn't believe that I can get out of trouble should I get into it. As one woman told me:

> *In the way he behaved toward my boyfriends, my father's message to me was very clear. It was: "You can't be trusted and you're not smart enough. You can't be trusted to choose a boy who will treat you right; and you're not smart enough to recognize such a boy, even if there was one around."*
>
> *Michelle*

The memories of adult daughters like this one should give fathers serious pause. Our deep love and concern for our daughters can drive us to protect by hovering or threatening. But how do our daughters react to these attempts to protect them—during adolescence and through the rest of their lives? Often, they experience it as a lack of faith in their own judgment and abilities.

Don't get me wrong—I'm not advocating that we let eleven-year-olds wander the streets at night or let fourteen-year-olds hang out at keg parties. Our kids need some degree of parental protection, especially as youngsters. However—and this is true at every stage of childhood—we have to find the balance between safety and stifling. Fathers who fall into the overprotection trap can seriously undermine their adolescent daughters' ability to grow.

The Boyfriend

What does the parable's overprotective, "shotgun-wielding" dad tell the *boy* coming down the apartment hallway or marching up the front walk? The boy learns the following, disturbing lesson: this girl's father expects me to be a predator. Whether or not he knows me, if I am calling on his daughter, he sees me as a danger. He thinks that's how all boys are, and maybe how all boys should be. He's also telling me that the way to address fears or solve serious problems is with violence or the threat of violence.

The boy learns all this from a man in his community—a key influence on his understanding of what it means to be a man. Are these the messages we want to convey to the next generation of boys and men—the sons of our contemporaries? Is this how we want our fellow fathers treating our own sons? Many of us got that treatment from girls' fathers when we were boys—they gave us a new appreciation for the term "if looks could kill." That attitude never seemed fair to me. I used to think, "Cripes, her dad doesn't even know me! What's he looking at me like that for?"

A father might say it doesn't matter what the boy thinks, or that it's more important to keep his daughter safe: "I was a boy. I know what boys are like. I don't want her to be with people who are like me." But I think that we base this reaction on a very selective memory of our own adolescence. We're mining only a portion of own experience. In a knee-jerk way, we remember spending our teen years as hormonal boys relentlessly pursuing sex, with pressure from our peers to "score." But wasn't there more to it than that, even for us boys?

When I was a teenager and had girlfriends, I was looking for an emotional connection—exploring what it felt like to be in love and to have a "deep" relationship with someone outside my family. Yes, "making out" was exciting and fun (and harmless), once I had the courage to try it. Early on, I was so terrified of girls that I felt too intimidated to even reach "first base." But these feelings were lost on the hovering, suspicious fathers I usually encountered when calling on girls—not that I ever talked to them (or my own father) about it!

> *On a tenth-grade field trip, the guys gave me grief because I refused to engage in the debate they were having about every female within eyesight—how sexually desirable (that's wording it as nicely as I can) they were. Anyway, after a few hours of not participating, another guy wondered out loud, "What's wrong with you? Are you gay or something?" I wish I'd said, "No, but so what if I am?" but I just glared at him. On the way home, my nonparticipation came up again, and at least one guy seemed sincerely interested about why I didn't join in. I felt very self-conscious and somewhat foolish being a fifteen-year-old romantic, but managed to let them know it was because I wanted "to be in love." I was surprised when they told me they could relate! My friends wanted to be in love, too, but it wasn't cool to admit it.*
>
> *Jefferson*

Now, like any teenager, I had glaring areas of immaturity in my personality and behavior—in essence, I think that's what it means to be a teenager. But I didn't do things that threatened the girls I dated during adolescence. Raised without a single parental word spoken to me about sex, sexuality, or even—as I recall—romantic relationships, I believe I was too frightened to inflict much damage. So there I was—standing on a girl's front porch; just hoping that she'd like me as much as I liked her. Why was her father out there "waving his shotgun" at *me*? I didn't get it.

Now that I have daughters, I do understand what those dads back in South Jersey felt when I came calling on their daughters. I also understand that they probably longed for a strategy more effective than staring suspiciously at me and the other boyfriends who crossed their daughters' paths. Fathers today are still looking for that strategy. What can we do differently?

> *I wonder how I'm going to relate to my daughter's boyfriends. There must be some means of being somewhere between the hip dad and the stern dad. I don't know what it might be.*
>
> *Colin*

Believe it or not, there are helpful tactics that draw on what we know about our daughters and what we know about ourselves. To find out what they are, we first need to take a closer look at what the shotgun story has to say about the third and final character—Dad.

The Dad

With its image of a father with fire in his eyes and a trusty weapon in hand, the shotgun parable illustrates the depth and intensity of our paternal fear. We're afraid that our daughters will be hurt or violated in a way that we cannot fix. We fear that they will be raped, physically assaulted, manipulated, or persuaded to do things they don't want to do—or that we don't want them to do. We're afraid someone (her or her friends) will make a bad decision that leaves deep emotional or physical scars. We're afraid they'll get pregnant, start drugging, be duped, catch AIDS. We're afraid they'll die.

> *It's scary because I have this tremendous amount of overprotection for her now. I couldn't imagine not having her, or the possibility of her being injured.*
>
> *Gene*

These fatherly fears are not idle, foolish, or unjustified; they are based in reality. That may sound like a shocking and depressing admission in a book focused on positive fathering. On the one hand, it is shocking and depressing to see reasons for our fears in the facts of a kid's life nowadays—for example, one in three girls (and one in five boys) will be sexually abused by the time they are adults. Some adolescent girls will get pregnant, catch STDs, and encounter other difficulties that last a lifetime.

But the source of our fears is not the boy walking up the front steps, and the solution is not the shotgun. The culprit, I believe, is a culture that glorifies violence against women and girls, romanticizes rape, and counts the sexualization of children as an acceptable strategy for marketing products.

LAYING DOWN THE SHOTGUN

The shotgun on the front porch—and the overprotective approach it symbolizes—is completely inadequate when dealing with the culture we are discussing. Attempting to threaten one boy does nothing to address the cultural milieu (other than, perhaps, reinforcing one more boy's notion that violence is how to deal with females). The solution lies in laying down the shotgun, getting our butts off the front porch, and moving out into the culture to attack the true source of our fears.

I use the self-assessment quiz on page 31 often with groups of fathers, and sometimes dads will challenge its notion that overprotection of one's daughter is scored as a negative. "My daughter needs protection!" some fathers say, or "I'm not gonna let my ten-year-old daughter go wherever she wants whenever she wants!"

Younger children of either gender do need more of our physical protection. But as our daughters grow older, we're faced with some tough challenges. How much protection is enough? Do our "protection" decisions reinforce a double standard between boys and girls?

Of course, too much fearlessness in our sons would concern

us—we'd want more than a dash of street-smarts mixed in with their fearlessness. But are we more ready to accept and encourage fearlessness in our sons than in our daughters? Does it carry different risk?

It seems natural for many parents to allow their sons more autonomy and physical freedom than their daughters. "Girls are more vulnerable, more in jeopardy," as one dad told me. "My son can't get raped." Sadly, a son can be raped and boys are vulnerable to a range of threats, including sexual abuse, bullying, male-on-male violence, and the like. Still, we tend to think that girls are more threatened by the world around them. If they are more vulnerable (and there's a strong case to be made that they are), then we're confronted with serious problems if we're really listening to our daughters.

First, if we listen closely, we probably hear our daughters repeating some variation of the cry: "That's not fair!" Girls have a strong sense of justice about them; in their eyes, a double standard about what's safe for boys versus what's safe for girls is a deep, personal, and immediate injustice.

Second, if we agree that our daughters face threats that require more active parental protection than their brothers do, then we have to look at where those threats come from. We have to, along with our daughters and their brothers, confront the sexist, violent, unfair nature of the world. In other words, building up our daughters' sense of happiness, strength, and savvy is essential, but it is only part of our fatherly obligation and opportunity.

Imagine that there's a poorly managed toxic landfill in your neighborhood and, as a result, one of your children develops leukemia. There is no doubt that you'd do everything you had to do in order to get her the medical treatment that she needs. That might include battling HMOs, finding and using specialists (even if they are far away), and calling on friends and family for help. There is also little doubt that you'd raise hell from the city council to the EPA about why there's a toxic landfill so close to your house, or at the very least, why it's so poorly managed that children living nearby develop cancers. You'd instinctively know that it's not enough only to address the personal consequences of the threat—you must also try to remove the threat itself.

In the same way, when it comes to sexuality and the sexual safety of our children, we must simultaneously address the personal consequences of our culture's threats *and* try to remove those threats from the culture. For now, I'll stick primarily to aspects of the solution inside our homes, behind the front porch. It boils down to building up our daughters' strength, savvy, confidence, and understanding. These are the things most useful to girls as they try to make their way safely through adolescence and adulthood.

THE TWO EXTREMES OF FATHERING

A daughter's adolescence is tough on her dad. Sometimes you feel frightened by her vulnerability. Sometimes you feel terrified about all the consequences of her developing sexuality—including the pain of eventually becoming the number-two guy in her life.

We all feel this way. Successfully navigating your daughter's adolescence—and successfully helping her to navigate it—depends on avoiding two common and seductive roles fathers often play: Overprotective Dad or Absent Dad.

Overprotective Dad

As our daughters get older, it is less and less realistic for us to follow them everywhere they go, hovering nearby ready to ambush any threat that approaches. It's physically impossible and, even if we could follow them everywhere, it would be psychologically damaging. When we slip over the line from protecting to overprotecting, we've stopped doing our job as fathers.

Indeed, rather than helping our daughters, the overprotective shotgun strategy actually harms them, adding to the difficulties our daughters already face. Several of the young women I met while preparing this book told of fathers cross-examining them every day about the clothes and makeup they wore, sending the message that they should be attractive, but at the same time, never project any attitude or aura that might draw a boy's sexual attention.

These fathers insisted that their daughters never be alone with a boy, while simultaneously saying how much they looked forward to their daughters marrying educated, affluent husbands and having many children. It's as if these dads expected husbands and grand-children to appear miraculously without any trace of sexuality or desire marring the picture.

They told their daughters to be intelligent, but never to violate the standards of "femininity" by questioning any of the fathers' de-cisions or attitudes. These are impossible boundaries for a daughter to navigate, especially when a father's interpretation of where the boundaries lie can change from day to day. Most of these fathers probably think they are communicating the depth of their love to their daughters. What the daughters receive, however, is a commu-nication of mistrust, control, power, and the father's deep insecu-rity. Those aren't the elements of love.

Not surprisingly, such fatherly expectations often produce the very results the fathers were trying to "protect" their daughters from. With this much contradictory pressure bearing down on them, many of these daughters say, they rebelled by sneaking out and engaging in even more risky sexual behavior than they might have otherwise.

As one woman put it, this left both her and her father wracked with guilt, and confirmed for her that, paradoxically, her father ex-pected all along that she would respond to his pressure with this kind of "rebellion."

A metaphoric shotgun on the porch also indicates to a girl that she will be held responsible if she "allows" herself to be violated and may even risk harm at her father's hands. In the end, that response tells a daughter that her sexuality—a key part of the woman she is becoming—is evil, dangerous. That's a toxic concoction of emotions and attitudes.

Daughters are aware of the world's dangers, and not all of them have to do with sex. Girls are also conscious of our fears from an early age. Since my daughters' birth, I've wanted to lash out at people who I see as threats to them: an insensitive ballet instructor, hurtful friends, or a misguided schoolteacher. Angry over my daughter's pain, I would seethe or erupt in righteous (and vocal) indignation. In almost every case, my overprotective reaction only frustrated the daughter involved. She wanted me to support *her*, not to threaten those who caused her pain.

When we erupt, we forget that a key lesson of childhood is learning to cope with hurt. My outbursts only undermined my girls' ability to learn that lesson. My rage and veiled threats invaded their turf, the part of their lives for which they have greater personal responsibility as they get older. While girls may welcome a sympathetic ear, and occasionally some guidance, they primarily want to figure things out for themselves.

Clearly, a big part of the dating experience is learning to figure out for oneself the complexities of relationships, especially when the romance gets rocky. It's a skill my daughter will need for the rest of her life and long after I'm no longer able to hold a shotgun because I'm six feet under. She should start learning that skill now, and I should help instead of getting in the way.

We may justify our instinct to treat our daughters like Rapunzel by calling it paternal and protective, but it is really more paternalistic and poisonous. Not only does it weaken our daughters' sense of their own abilities, it also injures our relationships with them.

My daughter is in her twenties now. Looking back on the teenage years, I would tell her more how much I really do care for her, did care for her, still care for her. I thought we were doing it in actions, but I'd really take more time to tell her that the things

*we were arguing about didn't matter that much and maybe
apologize more, be more vulnerable earlier on. Now I realize
that I was trying to be the authoritarian dad. I never saw myself
as a real strict parent to start with, but when push came to shove,
she was supposed to obey. And I guess I'd probably give up some
of that to have had a better relationship with her.*

Tom

The bottom line is that overprotection is inadequate to keep our
daughters safe, and it harms the fundamental trust between daughter and father. Do your daughter and yourself a favor and let
Rapunzel out of the tower.

Absent Dad

It can sometimes be intense, painful, and confusing to father a
daughter through adolescence. We may feel like we just can't take it
anymore and want to bail out. But if Overprotective Dad is a harmful role to play, Absent Dad may be worse.

*When I was a girl, my father and I were super close; he was my
favorite. But then when I was about thirteen, it was like he disappeared. I mean, he was still there, but he all of a sudden got
cold and distant. I think about it now and figure he was terrified of me turning into a sexual creature. But back then, I was
crushed and I couldn't figure it out. I tried all kinds of things to
get his attention back; finally I started acting out sexually. None
of it worked; he just blew me off. I'm still really angry years later,
we're still not close, and now I guess I've pretty much blown
him off.*

Rebecca

A father's flight can take many forms, but all are hurtful. A father
might be so scared off by his daughter's adolescence that he clams

up and pulls away from her emotionally, no matter how close they were when she was younger. He may bury himself in work or other activities that physically distance him from his fear of his daughter's emerging sexuality. Sometimes he will physically leave the family through divorce. No matter how it happens, the worst injury we can inflict is to violate our special daughter-father bond by emotionally, physically, or affectionately abandoning our daughters.

> *As soon as I started developing breasts, my father stopped hugging me. I instinctively knew that that was why. I decided that if my breasts were going to get in the way, I'd try to make them stop— and try to make myself stop growing up—because I didn't want to lose him. So I stopped eating. And I ended up in the hospital with anorexia.*
>
> *Rita*

During your daughter's adolescence, there's a crosswind of emotion and uncertainty swirling through you both. These conflicting emotions about our daughters' developing sexuality may seem overwhelming and the urge to flee may seem irresistible, but we must *never* abandon her. When the feelings crash down on us and we want to give up, remember the intense anger and pain articulated by adult women who felt abandoned by their dads: "He's a jerk, an asshole; I hate him!" No short-term discomfort is worth dumping your daughter and leaving her with a long-term legacy like this.

Fleeing brings no freedom. Because if you abandon your daughter (physically or emotionally), you abandon yourself in very real ways. You abandon a relationship valuable to you now and in the past, while destroying the chances of enriching your future years— years when your daughter can be a vital part of your life.

Both overprotection and absence chip away at our daughters' well-being, cause great sorrow to them and us, cripple our relationships, and drive them toward the behaviors we dread most. Abandonment is a lousy way to end one of the most important relationships of our lives.

VARIATIONS ON THE THEME

Relationships can be particularly difficult if a girl feels sexually attracted toward another girl. Some of our daughters will grow up as lesbians, and that may test our fatherly obligation to help our daughters be true to themselves.

> *My first reaction was terrific guilt, like somehow I caused this, and sadness that I'd never walk her down the aisle or have grandchildren. But then I looked at the two lesbian couples I know. One couple has two kids, and both couples have been together a long time and their relationships seem to be as well adjusted as any marriages I know of. So while there may never be a traditional wedding, I think there probably will be grandkids. Besides, I love my daughter and I feel drawn to love the people she loves; her partner is like a daughter to me. Now, the bigger issue for me is the crap they get from other people for just being who they are.*
>
> *Ned*

It's fairly normal for a girl to feel sexual feelings toward another girl; that doesn't necessarily mean that she is homosexual. Some lesbian adults say they felt different starting at a very young age, others say they weren't aware of lesbian sexual feelings until later in adolescence. Homosexuality is not an illness, disorder, or moral failing. The American Psychological and Psychiatric Associations compare it to being left- or right-handed; it just is. There have always been lesbians and have always been those who are uncomfortable with them—just as there have always been people uncomfortable with sexuality itself.

A girl is likely to tell someone else (a friend, counselor, teacher, clergy, her diary) about any same-sex attraction before she tells her parents. If and when she does tell you, it may confirm feelings you already sensed about her, or it may be a complete shock. Either way, it's likely to be a tough time for all of you. Don't make it worse by rejecting her or pulling away.

> *I always thought homosexuals were immoral, so the best I could do when she told me was to keep my judgments to myself. But I know she wanted more from me and felt like I was condemning her, and that was painful for both of us. A friend convinced me to come with him to a local PFLAG (the Parents, Families and Friends of Lesbians and Gays support group) meeting. I was really skeptical for a long time, but these other parents seemed about as "normal" as me and, except for being gay, their kids seemed to be living lives like other young people. I think that hanging around these other parents got me over my judgmentalism and feeling like this wouldn't have happened if she lived with me instead of her mother. But my first response left a distance between my daughter and me and I'm still working on repairing that. This feels like the hardest thing I've ever been through, but she's my little girl. That's the bottom line.*
>
> *Gregor*

A girl discovering that she is a lesbian has a lot to deal with when it comes to the prejudice she's going to encounter in the world. So, listen to her respectfully and don't try to "talk her out of it" or dismiss her sexuality as just a phase. If you do, you're rejecting who she knows herself to be.

At the same time, watch for the problems she may face. Lesbian teens have higher rates of depression, drinking, and smoking, for example. Parental support is the best antidote for those problems.

Be honest with each other about the difficulties she's likely to face, but don't let them overwhelm your expressions of love and acceptance. As in every other aspect of life, we can't "protect" our daughters from being who they are or keep them locked up in a tower.

YOU, YOUR DAUGHTER, AND "THE TALK"

So how do we deal with the stew of emotions and thoughts that seems like the staple of every dad's journey through his girl's emerging sexuality? First, we need to recognize a simple truth: our fear about our daughters' emerging sexuality is not the same thing as their emerging sexuality. That means, to be effective fathers, we have to separate our apprehension from what may or may not actually be happening in our daughters' lives; otherwise we look through a cloud of fright, and miss a lot of what's really occurring. Our fear also prevents us from sharing important values and experiences with our daughters—the very things that can help them make good decisions.

My father was very concerned when I began dating, and I was quite a moral and prudish young girl! He was so hard on any young man who came to the door, and so suspicious of me doing something wrong, that I did go "underground." I got into more trouble with young men that way than I ever would have had my father been more trusting and open. Even my brothers said he treated me like a delinquent before I had the chance to act as one. I am sure it is hard for any father to watch his little girl go. But as long as you keep talking with her without judging or acting suspicious, she will talk to you. Daughters have a special place for their fathers; we need them to love us and trust us! As long as you do this, the chances of both of you surviving these years will be good.

Jamila

Talking with our daughters means listening to them and being honest with them—even when the conversation turns to sex.

Most folks (including us) think that conversations with a girl
about sex are for mothers only. But we fathers can't expect an honest and open relationship to flourish with our daughters if we never
communicate directly about sexuality, which, after all, is an essential part of her life.

Don't get me wrong—this communication isn't easy. The entrenched tradition that says "this is Mom's job" isn't our only disad-
vantage. Our ability to speak honestly and effectively with our
daughters about sex and sexuality is contingent on our possessing
accurate knowledge in the first place. Many of us still don't have a
lot of the basic facts of life readily at hand, or lined up straight. I'm
a good example. My father was a good guy, but when it came to the
facts of life, he was a flop. One summer during my mid-teens, Mom
announced that Dad would soon have "The Talk" with me. The
frequency with which he postponed "The Talk" told me that, without my mother's arm-twisting, he'd never do it at all.

Finally, the big Talk evening arrived. At the appointed time, I
joined my father at the picnic table that filled our back porch. For
quite a while, we talked about the Philadelphia Phillies' recent performance. Then, he took a deep breath (and a swig of beer) and
asked, "Do you know what your balls are?"

"Uh, yeah," I replied.

"Well," he said, "that's your scrotum."

"I know," I said. (I didn't know; my "balls" are my testicles, not
my scrotum. I didn't want to admit my ignorance to Dad, though.)

"Good," Dad answered. "So, do you think Richie Allen will hit
.300 this year?"

The stream of our version of "The Talk" flowed for the briefest
moment over the smallest stone of genital misinformation before
rapidly leaving for the less troubled waters of Cookie Rojas, Gene
Mauch, and the intrigues of the Phillies clubhouse. Ten years later,
chatting at the church fifteen minutes before my wedding, my fa-

ther asked me if there was anything I needed to know. I knew he meant well, but having already lived for more than a year with the woman I married moments later, I stifled a laugh before answering, "Thanks, I think I'm set."

This makes a great dinner party story, but it's a pretty sad legacy from both of my parents on one of life's most important elements—sexuality. My parents didn't even get past describing the plumbing accurately, much less talk about sexuality's potential to express love, values, spiritual intimacy, and the miracle of life itself.

Fathers *can* talk to daughters about these things. We often feel that these conversations are impossible because we invest too much foreboding in the idea of such Talks, with a capital T. But if we talk with a lowercase "t" all the time and grab the ongoing learning opportunities everyday life provides, it gets progressively easier.

> *Danni is very modest. Right now she's going through puberty and growing breasts, and she's very embarrassed about it. We've tried to open up the conversation in the household. "You know, you have to start thinking about wearing a bra." And it's not just her mom talking to her; I'm there also. So she doesn't feel like that's something Dad cannot talk about. Not that I feel real comfortable or anything, but I'm still talking with her about it.*
>
> *Steven*

Some of this discomfort stems from our lack of confidence in what we can offer or understand. We have to get over that doubt—we do have valuable information to offer our teenage daughters, even though we grew up as boys.

But, first things first. Before setting out to conceive children, a person should, at minimum, know the plumbing diagram. If we've never learned it, we need to start today. The basic biological setup is as easy to understand as household plumbing, and there are useful books, like *Changing Bodies, Changing Lives* (Times Books, 1998) and *The Teenage Body Book* (Perigee, 1999), that provide accurate answers to many questions daughters and sons might ask. However, we can't stop with explaining the location of the scrotum, clitoris, and other genitalia. That would be like installing plumbing in a bathroom and then never using it to brush your teeth or take a shower. We have to understand—and articulate—the value of sexuality and how people use (and misuse) it in the world. Otherwise, we neglect the most important lesson—why we even have our sexuality.

These conversations may be less complicated than we think. Writer and cultural critic Susannah Sheffer illustrates this point:

> *"What does intercourse really feel like?" Alison certainly got my attention when she asked me that question. When you assure young people that they can ask you anything, and, even more important, when you demonstrate through your responses that you are the sort of person who can be asked things, you have to recognize that this is the kind of question you might get. And you have to think fast, but think carefully, about how to answer.*
>
> *Speaking from a deep well of hope for Alison, I said to her, "It's like a hug." She stopped, almost dumbstruck. Then she looked at me and said slowly, "No one's ever said anything like that to me before."*
>
> *At fourteen, what Alison had heard about sex was overwhelmingly negative. Her sixteen-year-old sister had a bad time with a boyfriend the year before, and her friends talked mostly about what a letdown sexual encounters were. Her parents didn't mention sex at all.*
>
> *In answering Alison, I was trying to show her something she hadn't seen or even imagined. I was also, I acknowledge, putting a very positive spin on the subject. If I were aiming for strict honesty, I would say something like, "It can be like a hug," or "For some people, under some conditions, it can feel like a hug, although, of course, for others it can feel much more like a viola-*

tion." But I think I chose instinctively not to qualify the state-
ment right then. While I have no control over what Alison's sex-
ual experiences will be, and while I can't promise that she will
experience intercourse as a hug, I think I wanted, somehow, to
increase the odds of that happening with the words I offered her.

As much as we sometimes shudder to think of our little girl ever
having sex with someone, we must understand that she needs a
healthy sense of sexuality in order to be a healthy and happy
woman. It doesn't help to fall into the overprotection trap and lead
our daughters to see sexuality as inherently dangerous, dishonest, or
forbidden. We have to find ways to trust and respect our daughters
more than that. After all, if we ever hope to see grandchildren, our
daughters will, in most cases, have to have sex first.

In addition to their fathers' trust and respect, our daughters deserve accurate information about sexuality. We can prove our trust
and respect by providing that information. When we always give her
accurate information, we're showing that we're both trustworthy.

When my oldest started developing breasts, I knew it wouldn't be
long until she had her first period. I also knew that my ex-wife is
not comfortable talking about sex. Maybe it's because I grew up
on a farm that I felt I could do it, but I decided I had to start
talking to my daughters about it. So, I went and bought some
pads and next time they were over, I got out the pads and some
of their underwear. I explained to both girls what the pads were
for and what their periods were going to mean, then I taught
them how to attach the pads to a pair of underwear. Sure, their
faces were red, but they learned and they knew what to do when
they had their first period. Ever since then, they've come to me
with questions and talked with me about their boyfriend prob-
lems. I guess I proved myself to them.

Jeff

The more regularly you provide the facts, the easier it gets to do it. Plus, these everyday conversations deliver what she needs: accurate information about love, sexuality, abuse, safety, self-respect, menstruation, conception, desire, and what's happening with her body and emotions. That's a lot of territory to cover and, contrary to what most people think, there's plenty of acreage for fathers to cultivate.

Start by providing the facts about sexuality very early through everyday occasions that arise, whether or not they directly involve your daughter.

> *We have two cockatiels. And one day Alex came over and said, "Dad! The gray cockatiel is on top of the other one and he's killing him!" I looked and said, "Alex, they're not killing each other. They love each other and they're mating."*
>
> *"But, Dad! Look what he's doing!" So I dropped right next to her so we could both watch. After the birds were done and just flirting, we opened up the encyclopedia. And I read to her exactly what was going on: This is what is called mating. This is making offspring. And I explained, not the actual, physical act, but said that the same thing that happens with moms and dads happens to birds and every other animal that God makes. When Mommy and Daddy love each other, they love each other so much that you're here. And your brother is here. It's the same with the birds—in a couple of months, they're going to have little babies because they love each other that way.*
>
> *Frank*

Like Frank, we have to talk about sexuality and not just sex. Our responses to everyday events (mating cockatiels or impending menstruation) and the use of simple metaphors (intercourse is like a hug) will show our daughters how natural sexual behavior is, how sexuality can be an expression of and a path toward true intimacy, and how to make sense of their own sexuality and sexual feelings.

Open, positive conversations about sexuality also give our daughters a better foundation from which to deal with some of the world's ugly realities, like sexual assault and abuse. It's much easier to balance the positive and the negative when we consistently paint the whole picture, and don't focus *only* on the perilous scenerios. Still, if we're going to be honest, we can't leave our daughters unaware of sexual dangers; just like we must master the "plumbing" diagrams, we need to understand the nasty pitfalls girls face if we hope to help our daughters make sense of them and know how to respond. Some of these realities are tough to look at.

To take one example, a SmartGirl.org online poll indicates that many girls are forced or pressured into sexual activity. "Out of 339 teen girls surveyed, 28% said they had been pushed into having sex or performing sexual acts against their will. In many cases girls are NOT talking about these devastating incidents to parents and caregivers who can offer much-needed help.

"When asked whether they felt the forced sexual activity was their fault, 54% of the respondents who referred to an instance of forced sex said yes and another 10% said they didn't know. Additionally, because many of the incidents involved trusted boyfriends or acquaintances, girls were sometimes unclear about whether they had the right to say no. Twenty-one percent of this survey's respondents said that they had at times felt uncomfortable engaging in sexual activity, but gave in because they didn't know how to refuse. As one fourteen-year-old explained, 'I thought I had to because we were going out.' "

It may seem impossible to respond appropriately to these frightening realities. How can we talk about such awful things without scaring our daughters or reinforcing the impression that sexuality is dangerous and dishonest? The answer lies in simple, open conversation that trusts our daughters' brains, instincts, and savvy.

Sometimes this calls for courage we never imagined we had—and brings us unforeseen rewards, too.

> *My (white) daughter dated a Filipino hip-hop dancer who barely made it through high school but had talent. He traveled with bodyguards and the whole nine yards. The bodyguards were big, bad and mean except when they were in my house in the suburbs, and they came over a lot. It was hard to allow them in. There was an underlying fear. But it soon faded. Around here they were just good kids with kid thoughts and ideas. They relaxed and they told me that they felt comfortable at my house. It was a great lesson for me. It took me three years to find the real boy in there. I actually found myself caring for her boyfriend a lot and I believe I taught him a thing or two. He had no father to lean on. So here it is seven years later and their relationship is over. No kids from it, nothing but an empty spot. I miss him.*
>
> *Anthony*

The daughter in this story had her father's trust, even when it was hard for him to give. She responded by acting responsibly in the romantic relationship—for example, she didn't get pregnant. She saw her father embracing her friends (and her judgment in choosing them)—at first with difficulty, but then with enthusiasm and affection. In addition, the father gained a new friend, someone he now misses, because he took the risk of recognizing that there was a "real boy in there."

ONCE UPON A DAD

Even before boyfriends start coming around, it's smart to look back into our own adolescence and find the "real boy in there."

A few years ago, I had lunch in a Northern California Chinese restaurant with a construction worker who described himself as "your typical redneck." He told of his anger, hurt, and continuing bewilderment about the recent breakup of his marriage. He said that he and his ex were both struggling financially to support their daughter and their two homes. But Jim grew excited and animated when talking about his ten-year-old daughter's approaching adolescence.

There's a lot I can teach her and tell her. I was a boy, and I remember real clearly what I was looking for from girls when I was that age. Sure, some of it was physical, but most of it was really wanting to be close to a girl, discover what girls are like, have a friend. It was exciting. It was confusing and scary, but it was great! I want to share that with my daughter, the good and the bad, from the boy's perspective. And I can do it, too; she listens to me. I feel like that's a pretty big bit of information, a gift really, that I can give her and that nobody else can. I'll be able to tell her what boys her age are thinking.

Jim

Just as we didn't grow up as girls, our daughters are not growing up as boys. We can share with our daughter our knowledge and expertise about what it's like to be a boy. That's priceless to a girl trying to decode the mysterious minds of the "opposite sex."

The boy issue is a no-brainer. Some months ago, a poster of a new teen heartthrob appeared on her ceiling and I was getting the first favorable reports on Brian, a fifth-grade boy who treats girls with gentleness and respect. I made my daughter, Roxanne, who is almost eleven, a promise. "I'm not going to tease you about boys," I said. "That's because I want you to be able to talk to me about them. I used to be one, and I can tell you things about them you'd never guess." I know I'm seeking an unnatural, foredoomed alliance, but I'll see how far I can go with it.

Bob

The best way to pass along your expertise is to tell "I used to be a boy" stories on yourself. Telling stories about your adolescence fuels your daughter's trust in you, builds her savvy, and can actually make it easier for her to find and connect with trustworthy boys. Your life stories can demonstrate that not all boys are jerks or predators. This important lesson brings a wonderful side benefit: you feel more reassured that not every experience she has will be bad. If your son is listening in (or, if sis shares Dad's funny story with him later), you provide him a great role-model lesson. From an early age, we can grab the opportunities presented by our daughter's natural curiosity. Here's an example from Rick Epstein, author of *Rookie Dad: Meditations from the Backyard* (Hyperion, 1992):

> *"Dad, tell me about the first time you ever kissed a girl." I had stopped in to say good night when her request whisked me back to the moment when I risked a quick peck in Peggy Johnson's basement nearly thirty years ago. I lay down next to my daughter in the darkness and told her about my fifteenth summer, the happy season I spent haunting the Johnson residence under the vigilant eyes of Mrs. Johnson. The dad treated me with restraint—as if I was a protected species he'd like to take a shot at. I kissed Peggy on the cheek. She kissed me back. Bliss. Those were the days. My days, anyway. My daughter's days are impending.*
>
> *Rick*

My daughters liked the story of my "almost" first date. I met Debbie at a school dance my freshman year at an all-boys high school. She was a cute, blond freshman from our sister all-girls school. I also found out that she was bright and funny, so the following week, I screwed up my courage and asked her out for a date. Then, the night before the big event, Debbie called to say she'd have to postpone: "I bleached my hair tonight and it came out sort of green." As I recall, she was pretty calm about it and we shared a laugh over the absurdity of green hair while she reassured me by saying that she wasn't making up an excuse, and we could aim for the following weekend. Then we had one of those phone calls girls and boys have at fourteen, deep, exciting, giddy, profound and momentous. From thirty years away, the whole thing looks a little silly and absurd (like many adolescent things *are*), but I still remember the thrill of a phone call with "my girlfriend."

Back at school on Monday, the guys wanted to know how the date went, and I had to tell them it was postponed. Some of them razzed me, saying that she was just trying to brush me off. But others thought it was pretty cool that she'd called and told all. I thought it was cool, too; she liked (and apparently trusted) me enough to tell me a potentially embarrassing story straight away. I don't remember what we actually ended up doing on our first date a week later—except that my dad had to drive!

HEALTHY SEXUALITY: SAYING YES, SAYING NO

In our heart of hearts, we all want our daughters to enjoy healthy and mutual physical affection. Girls really can make good decisions, but we must trust them and talk to them about what good decisions look like in the realm of sexuality. We need to help them and ourselves distinguish between feeling sexual and sexual behavior; between sex and sexuality; between abstinence and repression. In short, we want our daughters to know themselves well enough to say "yes" when they mean "yes" and "no" when they mean "no."

As long as you raised her with love and attention and the old "right vs. wrong," she'll be fine. Now is the time to put those jealous feelings aside and ask her about her new beau. She may be a little nervous about talking to you about him (and rightly so if she feels your jealousy), but believe me she will talk. My daughter's first boyfriend was at twelve. She would write, "I love Seth" on her arms and legs. Then one day she said, "Dad, I dumped

Seth." To which I replied, "What happened?" She said, "He kept wanting to French kiss and I'm just not ready for that." Now I don't have to tell you that many girls would have given in to his advances if they felt they would lose him. My daughter had the strength and the discipline to dump the guy.

Ted

How many of us would have reacted differently? It's hard to rein in our gut reactions and not shoot (or scream) back with a rant about twelve-year-old girls French-kissing or being too young to have romances. It's hard to have faith in your daughter's judgment—or in how well you've instilled good sense and values up until now. But look at the result of this father's faith: his daughter was open with him about all the stages of her romance.

It's important to demonstrate trust in your children if you want to lay a strong foundation for their healthy sexuality. Sexuality expresses and builds the emotional and spiritual intimacy of a loving relationship. But that's not something we often think or talk about. For one thing, we get a distorted picture from our culture, which prefers the titillation of sex to the subtleties and complexities of love.

In addition, there's a harmful double standard at play in our culture. While we expect boys to act on their sexual desires ("boys will be boys" and "he's sowing his wild oats"), there is virtually no cultural permission for girls to act on their sexual feelings. An adolescent girl often feels abnormal or perverted if she *ever* desires sexual pleasure. Many of us think that's the way it ought to be—girls should not have or act on sexual desires. But that attitude trains our daughters to be passive and reactive in their sexual relationships— hardly a recipe for developing a nourishing sexuality that might keep them safe, healthy, and happy.

I want to help my kids escape the concern that other children will label them one thing or another—easy, frigid, whatever.

> *When I was in high school, the school's wealthy Italian Catholic*
> *"good girl" was, unbeknownst to everyone, being regularly raped*
> *by her cousin, my classmate. I only found out ten years later*
> *when we dated for a time. The labels are more than meaningless;*
> *they're dangerous, whether they hide abuse or give a child the un-*
> *deserved tag of slut, tramp, nerd, geek, or whatever. That's why I*
> *want my daughter to tactically guide her own self-image. If she*
> *decides to use her sexuality, let her do so with her eyes open. If she*
> *decides to preserve it, let her do so out of choice, not out of fear.*
>
> *Bob*

Most of us are so frightened of a girl's sexual desires—labeling them evil or dangerous—that we hardly know those desires exist. But sexual desire is a natural human quality. It's not doled out exclusively to the male gender. Denying desire to girls is denying an essential part of who our daughters are.

It's important to remember that acting sexually does *not* necessarily mean having sexual intercourse. Kissing is a sexual activity; so don't jump to the conclusion that in order for a girl to embrace her sexuality, she has to sleep around. We have to open our eyes to the range of safe and healthy ways our daughters can express their desire. That makes it easier for *them* to see the range of choices, understanding that there is plenty of middle ground between convent living and "going all the way." Within that continuum, our daughters can find the potential of their sexuality—for today and for the future. Hard as it may be to acknowledge with our own daughters, we must recognize that desire can't be detached from healthy sexuality. If we talk to our daughters only about abstinence, then we leave unaddressed the central issue of their desire.

The question boils down to: How do we help our daughters recognize their natural sexual desire and use it in a way that is true to themselves and their values and is a source of power rather than a source of manipulation, pain, or repression? A man who asks this question is *not* perceiving his daughter as a tart, encouraging her to be a slut, or becoming a candidate to abuse her. Indeed, I think fathers who think about these issues and discuss them openly with each other (and with their daughters) make great strides in empowering their daughters.

I want to be clear that none of these notions are incompatible with religious beliefs or spiritual traditions. I was raised in Roman Catholicism, often seen as one of the more repressed religious traditions on the subject of sexuality. But during my fourteen years in Catholic school, I learned that sexual feelings and actions were sacred and sacramental—concrete, living signs of God's love. Thus, the nuns' reasoning went, the most intimate sexual activity should be deferred until after the sacrament of marriage. Even the nuns understood that, as part of a sacrament, sexuality is also part of an individual's spirituality.

My limited adolescent sexual experiences confirmed this; I only had sexual contact (kissing, hugging, fondling) with girls with whom I was in love. There was an element of emotional and spiritual connection at work. We can argue about which came first—the desire or the love—but the point is that the two were connected. Until we fathers accept that our children can also have this spiritual connection, we'll just keep chasing ourselves in a circle, trying to control our daughters' sexuality—something over which we have less control with every day older she gets. If we spend all of our energies on saying no to our daughters' sexuality—and teaching them that they can only say no—none of us win. Until we can trust girls to safely say yes to their sexuality and desire, we have not fully enabled them to say no to sexual manipulation, abuse, and irresponsibility.

The point is simple: the confidence we have in our daughters' sexuality will reflect the confidence we have in every other aspect of her life. The confidence we have in other aspects of their lives will reflect our confidence in a healthy sexuality for them.

STANDING IN THE HALLWAY

Trust and respect grow best when planted and nurtured from the beginning. The way we father during our daughters' early years lays the groundwork for successfully negotiating their teen years and their sexuality. It is in the "each and every day" ways that we demonstrate our trust and respect for our daughters and build their trust and respect for themselves. It takes practice, but it builds confidence and serves both of us well as life rolls on.

> *I'm thirty-three and have two boys, eleven and five, and also a little princess just turned three. Raising boys seems to come much more naturally than raising this little girl. I'm going through the teenage fears already (ten years early) mostly because I work in law enforcement and see the less fortunate things that happen to our girls in today's society. The best thing I've come up with (it seems to work well) is to treat her as I want her boyfriend or husband to treat her. Most likely if she has a good relationship with me, she'll try to find the same thing in a companion. The teaching that will help her choose a loving, tender, sincere, caring, and kind companion starts now. Don't believe me? Go to a restaurant that waits on you hand and foot, always treats you fairly, kindly, and gives you consistent and courteous attention. Tell me you'll go somewhere else that offers anything less, even if it's closer or cheaper. Neither will she.*
>
> *Bradley*

Treating our daughters the way we want others to treat them means respecting their individuality and privacy. Thus, we have to recognize that their individuality and private space expands as they get older and become teenagers. That includes their physical space. Our adolescent daughters need both physical and emotional room to experiment and grow into the women they are becoming. Sometimes they create that room by pushing against us. We can actually show our respect by letting them push.

> *Clearly, she needs her space more now. So I'll knock before I enter her room. Oh, and it's part of my job to be shocked so that she has something to rebel against. When she gets dressed differently, or does her wild makeup, I'm not really bothered much by it. But I play it up, in a joking kind of way. If I don't, she has to go to greater extremes to find something to shock me. If I'm not shocked by excessive makeup or something like that, she has to go to tattoos.*
>
> *Larry*

Sometimes it's fun to play the role of "shocked father" about small decisions a daughter makes. If I was faster on my feet when Nia announced she was dyeing her hair, I might have donned the mock-shock "how could you?" pose. If we hit the right tone, and don't cross the line into teasing, these become good, safe opportunities for our daughters to reinforce their sense of self-respect.

The job can be particularly painful at times, because our daughters don't just rebel over music and makeup. Sometimes they push against us by shutting down the close contact we might have had when they were younger.

For most of Mavis's and Nia's early adolescence, they'd take their emotional upsets to Mom. On a purely intellectual level, this was no surprise to me. I figured the girls would gravitate toward Nancy because she had far more firsthand knowledge of being a thirteen-year-old girl than I did. Also, Nancy and I already had a parenting rhythm; the two of us seemed to alternate in skill and comfort at different stages of their childhood. For example, infancy was one of my strong times; I had a knack for picking up on the girls' nonverbal ways of communicating while Nancy (a very verbal person) waited impatiently for the day when they could communicate in words.

But when our daughters started turning "only" to Mom during early adolescence, I didn't react intellectually and logically; I was jealous. I felt hurt when one of the girls shut the emotional door on me. Sometimes there'd be such anger that she'd go upstairs and slam her bedroom door, too.

Fortunately, I had a great coach in Nancy. She reassured me often (and I needed it often) that "shutting the door" on Dad was a normal part of a girl's development. Indeed, Mom sometimes got the door slammed on her, too. Drawing on her own adolescence, Nancy said, "They need someone to push off from as they explore who they want to be; someone they love and respect. When I was a teenager, I also wanted to know for sure that my parents would still love me even if I changed and grew up. So, they're testing that with you—will you still care about them when they're not little girls any-more?"

I learned a painful lesson. Every time one of my daughters slammed the emotional door on me, my challenge was the same: hang in there. Have faith that my love matters more to both of us than the temporarily hurt feelings of a momentary explosion. That doesn't mean that those explosions didn't hurt—they did. But my task was far more important than wallowing in my hurt feelings or self-pity and deciding, "The hell with you! I'm not gonna get close to you ever again if you're gonna treat me like this!"

I had to trust that they needed—and wanted—me to be there when they emerged from their upset-du-jour. In a sense, my job was to not walk off when they "slammed the door." I might lick my wounds, but my biggest job was to stay in the hallway so that, when they "opened the door" again, they would see I was still there—still true to them and still loving them. I had to respect their journey through adolescence, even when it felt like I got run over.

Like trust, respect takes practice and courage. Respect for our daughters is a precious gift to them. It's hardest to provide when the bumps in the road are especially bad and our worst fears are real-ized. But those are the moments when its impact is most profound.

*I became pregnant—unexpectedly—at age eighteen. I was en-
rolled in an Ivy League college on a full academic scholarship.
First, I confided in my mother, who told my father, who was not
living with us at the time. I remember feeling so ashamed and
apprehensive over what his reaction would be. My world had
fallen apart in the weeks preceding the moment we first spoke on
the phone, like the ground was falling from beneath me. His first
words were, "Mom and I love you, and we will support you in
any way that we can."*

*My relief was overwhelming, but more than that, I felt the
physical sensation of being lifted upward, held up, and literally
supported by his words and the strength of conviction in his tone.
His reaction had been far more important to me than that of my
mother's, and I felt (and still feel) so grateful for the reaction that
he chose to offer me.*

*We corresponded through countless letters in the months that
followed, and visited in person a few times as well. However, it is
the letters that I remember most. It was the first time that I was
able to get a sense of what being a father was like for him; the
weight he felt and carried each and every day, and the magni-
tude of impact that these "each and every days" still had on him
long, long after these days had seen their sunsets. I have saved
these letters and treasure them as windows into the moments
he shares with himself and his relationship to himself as
"father."*

Denise

Even if we do well handling major crises and fears about outside influences, our daughters will continue to grow away from us. Their
independent dreams and judgment will diminish their reliance on
us—and thus diminish our status as all-knowing hero in their eyes.
It's tough to give this up, but it's all part of their growing into ma-
ture, confident young women.

When we take a positive approach to our daughters' emerging sexuality, we take a huge step in raising healthy, happy, bold, and savvy girls. But we also take a huge step toward keeping our relationships with our daughters relevant to them and us both. Although it may seem hard to imagine, that unconditional love we feel from our young daughters can survive adolescence and flourish in adulthood. We make that happen by remaining true to them, even as they develop into sexual beings.

When I struggled with the temptation to run away in terror from my daughters' adolescence, or to clamp down on them in fear, I turned to other fathers who'd been down that road before me. Dads who remained respectful as their daughters emerged sexually, emotionally, socially, and psychologically into womanhood assured me that the long-term dividends are excellent. When I thought long term, it was easier to respect my daughters' decisions and our relationship; and most of the time, they reciprocated. The payoff wasn't always immediate, but it was there. And it's still there.

Yesterday, my twenty-one-year-old daughter called me from school, confused about a conflict with two friends. For an hour, she alternately cried, worried, and asked me for advice. She didn't even ask for her mother.

Guess who had a big, proud grin on his face for the rest of the day?

TOOLS

TRUST-BUILDING TIPS

Trust and honesty are essential elements in every relationship. In a father-daughter relationship, they are especially important. Here are a few ways to foster an abiding connection with your daughter, your friend.

- PRAISE HONESTY FIRST

If you expect your daughter to be honest with you, don't punish her as soon as she says a truthful thing you might not want to hear. It is difficult enough for her to tell you something she knows you won't approve of, so praise her for being honest before you address the specific subject. Then you can evaluate what she has told you and decide what to do. Work through the situation with your daughter, proving that honesty is the best policy.

Say, for example, your daughter gets a speeding ticket for the second time. She delays telling you because she knows you will not take it well, but finally she admits her mistake. Try to understand her distress before you lash out; appreciate her honesty and then calmly and rationally talk to her about getting into trouble. Then move on to concrete suggestions, like taking a preventive/defensive driving course.

- LISTEN WITHOUT CRITICISM

You want her to talk to you openly, so try to avoid criticism even if that may be your first impulse. Your comments might seem natural, obvious, and not-so-harsh to you, but your daughter may interpret them differently. Be sensitive to her feelings. Remember, you're not speaking to one of your business partners or a golf buddy; it's your daughter. You want to encourage, not discourage, her. Keep your remarks gentle and tactful. Be constructively honest, not destructively blunt. Listen hard to what she has to say without interruption, and try to understand her point of view. Making that effort will have a huge impact on your ability to talk to each other.

- SAY YOU'RE SORRY

It's not always the easiest thing to do, but if either you or your daughter has betrayed the trust of the other, consider what you've done and how you've hurt the person you love. Then apologize without excuses or pulling your punches. Admitting your mistake and regret are the first steps toward repairing the damage.

SHARE A STORY

Sharing and respect are two-way streets. Tell plenty of stories about your own growing up so that your daughter gets a sense of who you are, your values, your interests. A wild adventure you had with a friend or an embarrassing moment in junior high will make your daughter realize that she is not alone and that you were young once, too. Once you confide a secret or two from your own past, your daughter will be a lot more inclined to let you in on her own thoughts and feelings.

Take a minute and think about the following questions—and jot down your answers:

What episodes from your adolescence do this chapter's stories bring to mind for you?

What things did you do in those episodes that you wish you hadn't done?

Were there any times when you felt like you couldn't be trusted? Why did you feel that way?

Did you ever feel that someone was only seeing you as a boy—and all that means—rather than seeing you for the individual you were?

Did that tick you off? What did you do or could you do about it?

Think about the most important "romance" you had as an adolescent. What were you longing for in striking up that romance? What did you want when you were in the romance?

Have you told any of these memories or stories to your kids?

MAKE A FRIENDSHIP BRACELET

Spend an afternoon with your daughter making friendship bracelets. The knot is a symbol of friendship, so when she wears the bracelet you've given her, you'll never be far from your daughter's thoughts. And in difficult situations, your bracelet on her wrist just might prompt your daughter to think, "What would my dad say about this?" Likewise, when you wear the bracelet she's made for you, your daughter will also be front and center in your mind, and you're more likely to think, "What would my daughter say about this?"

To make the bracelets, you will need:

Clipboard
Embroidery thread
Scissors
Yardstick

1. Choose two colors of embroidery thread.
2. Cut three twenty-seven-inch strands of each color.
3. Hold the ends of all six strands together and tie a knot about one inch from one end.
4. Secure the knotted end by clipping it onto a clipboard.
5. Separate the colors so you have three strands of one color on the right and three strands of the other color on the left.
6. Pick up the three strands on the left.
7. Wrap them over and under all three strands on the right, forming a loop.
8. Put the strands through the loop and pull tight, forming a single knot.
9. Pick up the three strands on the right.
10. Wrap them over and under the strands on the left, forming a loop.
11. Put the strands through the loop and pull tight, forming a knot.
12. Repeat steps six through eleven until your bracelet is the desired length.

13. Hold the ends of the strands together and tie a knot.

14. Trim the ends to about one inch.

Many girls already know how to make friendship bracelets, so your daughter may be able to teach you. A good thing about this scenario is the experience she gets from teaching you a skill and realizing that there's something she can do better than her hero!

SHARE YOUR VALUES

Setting clear expectations for your daughter and communicating openly and often with her about important matters—especially sex—is key to your relationship. Research shows that honest communication with your children about sex and your own family values can actually delay your teen's becoming sexually active!

- PROVIDE A MORAL FRAMEWORK

Your daughter needs you to set limits, but she needs to understand the values behind your family rules and moral standards. If you say, "Do this because I said so," you leave her little sense of power and responsibility. When you explain the reasoning behind your expectations, you help her refine her own moral judgments and conscience.

- TALK EARLY AND OFTEN ABOUT SEX, AND BE SPECIFIC

Initiate honest conversations about love and sex that respect her intelligence and opinions. Be candid about what you think and why you take your positions. Remember to involve her in the conversation too, so that it doesn't turn into a lecture. Ask her what she thinks and what she knows about sex, so you can clarify or correct any misinformation. Find out if anything about the subject bothers or worries her. Initiate these conversations early in her life and continue the dialogue through adolescence. Sometimes she may resist or seem uninterested in the subject, but hang in there. No matter what, she needs age-appropriate information and guidance on these issues.

- MONITOR AND SUPERVISE

Establish rules, curfews, and standards of expected behavior through an open process of family discussion and respectful communication. Make sure a responsible adult is supervising your daughter after school, and be aware of what she does in the hours after school and before you get home from work.

- KNOW HER FRIENDS AND THEIR FAMILIES

Get to know your daughter's friends and their parents. Invite her friends (including her boyfriends) into your home and talk freely with them. Encourage friendships with people who share your values.

5.

"WE'RE ALL SUSPECTS":
THE TOUCH TABOO
BETWEEN DADS
AND DAUGHTERS

The incidence of sexual abuse and the objectification of girls generates strong anger, revulsion, and fear in a responsible father. It is foolish and unproductive to ignore that fear and anger. However, we do great harm if, for example, we let the prevalence of sexual abuse make us afraid to touch our daughters, or afraid of how our healthy physical affection will be interpreted. If good touch is absent from our relationships with our daughters, then we cut off part of our humanity and our daughters' humanity. We are tactile beings who need physical expressions of affection, comfort, reassurance, and playfulness. Words are not enough to convey the depth and importance of our love for our daughters. Yet fear of being sexual—or being perceived as being sexual—can stop a father's hug in its tracks.

As a father, I am consistently affectionate, but *never* sexual, with my daughters. As a mentor and colleague, I found healthy ways to be in touch with more than forty girls and young women who worked on *New Moon* magazine. I take great comfort from hugs and enjoy physical play with little kids—a wonderful legacy taught by my father. Not every father relates to his or other children this way; my experience is neither universal nor unique. But no matter what our style of fathering, our kids need physical acknowledgment of our love for them. That's sometimes not simple or easy to do.

In this chapter, we'll look at the importance of father-daughter touch and how to differentiate good touch from bad touch.

What is good touch? Touch is good when it does the following for its recipient:

- Comforts her
- Affirms her as a person
- Supports her
- Respects and is sensitive to her person and her boundaries
- Is given with her permission
- Is given freely, with no quid pro quo
- Helps her feel strong, lovable, and able to delight in herself
- Is not sexual.

Good touch is not confined to fatherly hugs and kisses. Good touch can happen when, together with our daughters, we garden, play handball, do carpentry, take dance lessons, train the dog, wrestle, shoot baskets, go for a walk, or do any number of things. One great example of fathers' creative good touch comes from a Philadelphia ballet school. The most advanced class at the school was made up entirely of teen girls. By this age, the few boys who'd taken lessons had stopped and that left the advanced girls unable to learn an essential skill of advanced ballet—doing lifts and other moves with a partner. The solution? Several of the girls' fathers volunteered to come in and be lifters and partners in pirouettes. They were unskilled, but still useful to the daughters by literally providing physical support.

Still, it's not easy for fathers (or anyone else) to talk about good touch/bad touch issues. It feels awkward, odd, and even risky for me to write or say publicly that I am physically affectionate with my daughters. Part of me feels as if, by admitting that I touch my daughters, I'm confessing to some crime I didn't commit. Have you hesitated to touch your daughter or other girls you care about because of how they, or other people, might interpret that touch? Most fathers feel that the joy and comfort they get from hugging and kissing a daughter must remain hidden and unacknowledged lest others be suspicious or mortified.

We must cut through this thick cloud of suspicion if we want to begin having healthy, useful conversations about healthy and essential father-daughter touch. The true crime of abusive touch rightly sparks loathing because it is so deeply harmful. But we fathers need the courage to acknowledge that abuse exists and that its existence can get in the way of fathering a daughter in healthy, nonabusive ways. We need to talk with each other and with our parenting partners about how to provide our daughters with good fatherly touch.

BOUNDARIES AND CONNECTIONS

For much of my daughters' childhood, I had jobs with odd hours that allowed me to be home with them a good deal of the time, responsible for the mundane details of child rearing. I fed, bathed, dressed, tickled, held, and played—activities requiring a lot of physical contact. Even if I'd been around fewer hours every day, providing as much daily care as their mother provided helped create a foundation of nonsexual physical relationship. My daughters and I felt comfortable around each other and touching each other; we had each other's trust.

This physical contact started from my daughters' first day and enhanced one of nature's great miracles—a parent's ability to pick up signals for what their newborns need. The more I hugged, cuddled, and touched my premature infants, the better I got at recognizing those cues. This good touch also provided the most wonderful physical sensation of my life—having one of my infant daughters drop off to sleep on my shoulder, relaxing so completely that she seemed to melt into the indentation between my arm and chest.

As empathetic as I can be, I'll never fully know (as Nancy likes to remind me) what it is like to feel another life living inside me for many months, or to experience the pain and euphoria of giving birth. As close as I can come is this baby melting on my chest and into my heart.

As a daughter grows from infancy, there are fewer opportunities for her father and mother to comfort her with physical affection. That's because she is excitedly exploring new, independent territory, creating more distance from her parents. Well before adolescence, this distance starts to include a girl's body and the space around it. This is natural—it's healthy for girls to develop a sense of privacy and boundary about their bodies.

A key part of any child's development is her journey from total physical dependence to physical independence. This includes the development of body boundaries that help a child keep physically, emotionally, and psychologically healthy—while teaching the important lesson that she is a separate person from her parents. Our goal as parents is to help our daughters learn these lessons, despite knowing that they will inevitably start the move "away" from us.

Girls tend to have more complex body boundary issues than boys. Girls learn from culture and family that they have greater risk of physical violation. In response, girls feel the need to command their personal space. But they also place great importance on relationships. As girls develop, they don't always want to feel separate from others. They may go back and forth in an emotional and psychological tug of war with their desire for connection and space.

Pioneering research by the Harvard Project on the Psychology of Women and the Development of Girls revealed that girls' psychological development is facilitated by relationship and connection. That runs counter to the common idea (based primarily on boys' experience) that child development boils down to cutting the apron strings as the child casts off from his family. Rather than seeking separation, girls seek connection. Ironically, relationships are key for girls to reach self-sufficiency, healthy independence, and healthy interdependence. In a sense, the connection of a relationship is evidence that a girl is her own person—because it takes individuals to create a relationship.

Developing boundaries is an essential part of this process, but a girl's boundaries and their changing dimensions have more subtlety and motion than a father may have felt when defining his own boundaries as a youngster. Therefore, fathers have to be more tuned in and aware to pick up on the shape and status of our daughters' boundaries—and then make sure never to violate them.

While boundaries are essential for a girl, so is continued physical affection from her father. Her boundaries and Daddy's hugs are not mutually exclusive. Your daughter may still sometimes seek your lap or the "cuddle" spot beside you on the couch as a comforting and loving place. But at other times she will push you away. She might say "No" when you ask her for a hug, or dart her face away when you lean in for a kiss.

There is no sure way to predict when your growing daughter will welcome your affection and when she won't. This unpredictability may be most pronounced during adolescence, but is present well before then, too. You can be fairly sure of three things, however:

1. Your daughter is likely to accept physical affection from her mother more regularly than she will from you.
2. Because of number one, sometimes your feelings will be hurt and you'll feel unloved or underappreciated.

3. Despite numbers one and two, your daughter still needs your affectionate touch. It will help her thrive, feel safe, and know that the first man in her life loves her.

Even though I knew that my daughters' boundaries would expand as they grew up, it was a shock when they started to push away. My feelings were hurt when they began closing their bedroom door, or when they told Nancy not to tell me when they had their period, or when they turned away from my hugs.

Still, I respected the personal boundaries they imposed; I knew it was my parental duty during this natural developmental phase. I actually felt proud of the strong, firm way in which my daughters controlled their personal space. But I was confused and frustrated by my sudden inability to predict or "read" when they were and weren't open to my affection. I grieved over losing the touch we shared when they were younger. I felt as if I had failed them; that they didn't trust me anymore. I wondered whether their pulling away meant that they'd learned that it's not safe to trust males—and that that lesson trumped everything I'd done for them as a father.

By talking with Nancy and with more experienced fathers, I learned that I was misreading what my daughters were doing. I hadn't seen that their acceptance and rejection of my affection were *both* evidence of their trust in me—and evidence that the rejection would be temporary.

A daughter's approach-avoidance pattern with her dad is one important way she defines who she is and who she is becoming. As early as her toddler years and in varying ways, a girl pushes off against her parents in order to figure out where she starts and other people end. With Dad, she often does this by withholding her affection. When she first pushes me away, part of what she's doing is testing me to see if I can take it. Will I remain standing after she pushes, showing my love even though her shove almost knocks me over? Or will I turn and run, using my wounded feelings as an excuse to withhold my own affection and attention so that my feelings won't get hurt again?

If I stand in there, still showing her my affection, she learns that I am loyal to her and that she can trust me. Her next push away may be a sign that she feels safe enough to use me to explore and extend her boundaries. Her temporary rejection can mean she has faith that I won't reject her permanently. It's one more paradox of fathering, but my daughters demonstrated their trust in me by both accepting and turning away my expressions of affection.

My daughters and I are still close and, most of the time, we genuinely enjoy each other's company. They have the capacity to solve problems with or without me. Now that adolescence has ended, there are regular hugs again. I sometimes long to return to the melting, trusting, total touch we had when they were babies and I was new at fathering. But I know that time was meant to pass and I still draw immense comfort when one of my daughters sits on the kitchen counter to compensate for her height, arms around me, her thick hair snuggled against my beard.

DADDY TOUCH

If we're going to explore healthy touch between father and daughter, we have to acknowledge that the discussion will generate justified suspicion. The roots of that suspicion lie in the horrifying number of children abused by their fathers and by other men in positions of trust; in the sensationalized reporting of sexual abuse perpetrated by teachers and care providers; in the frightening sexualization of younger and younger girls in media and advertising. Its roots are in our society's entrenched denial of the fact that family members—usually a man—can perpetrate child sexual abuse.

In light of these facts, suspicions about any man touching a girl are well founded. I feel disheartened, sad, and angry about the warped sexual values so many of my male brothers act out. The childhood sexual abuse of people I love, including my wife and mother-in-law, also feeds my anger. As is common for partners of survivors, I have sometimes felt the brunt of the fury earned by another member of my gender; in this case, a long deceased relative of Nancy's. His violation scarred Nancy's life and the collateral damage obstructed our marriage many years after his physical violation "stopped."

When I see how my wife suffered from sexual abuse, I begin to mistrust other men. How can I tell which of you is abusive or unfaithful? I also begin to mistrust myself, because I know I have the potential to violate boundaries. I want to lash out against all abuse and all abusers. Yet, I also feel a deep need to do something more than grieve and rage.

I want a world where touch is healthy and nourishes, in the way that my infant daughter and I nourished each other as she melted into my shoulder and I melted into her heart. We fathers have an essential and difficult challenge in addressing the difference between nourishing touch and physical abuse. Fathers must recognize and help fulfill daughters' need for healthy touch. By being trustworthy, we earn the right to provide that physical affection—and the right to experience the joy of receiving our daughters' affection in return.

Nonetheless, there are times when, despite our individual trustworthiness, we are still considered suspect—seen as threats because we are men. That's why it's still often thought riskier to leave children in the care of men than in the care of women. Why? Because fathers through the generations (including you and me) haven't done enough to make trustworthiness a requirement of manhood. We've let a history of abuse distort our definition of masculinity.

TOUCHSTONES

It's time to reexamine our notion of masculinity. As we talk to each other and young people, let's start requiring and supporting the expectation that fathers are affectionate with daughters without being sexual with them. Let's stop tolerating in any way the male sexual abuse that scars kids and fuels suspicion of all men. Let's insist that this be a common goal for every father.

That will mean unlearning some lessons we absorbed about what it means to be a man and a father. When we have daughters, this challenge has special importance. Can we talk to each other as men about how we view girls and how we overcome the pornographic ways media conditions us to see them as sex objects?

> *I hate to admit it, but I enjoyed pornography before I had my daughters. But the thought of some total stranger trying to get himself off on, or some boy learning about sex from, a picture of a woman who could be my daughter . . . that's repulsive and scary to me. It's scary to think about my daughter being seen that way, and it's scary to think about boys learning sex that way— and that I learned it that way.*
>
> *George*

A father's old pornographic "education" can lead him to confuse his daughter's emerging sexuality with seeing her as a sexual object. That mix-up is dangerous for a girl. It also leaves a father without a healthy perspective should sexual energy ever arise between him and his daughter.

> *My daughter is a teenager and there are some times when I feel some sexual attraction toward her, and definitely times when it seems like she's flirting with me. Sometimes, there's just this sex-*

ual energy in the room. I've never done anything wrong; at least I don't think so. But you hear so much about how many pervert fathers there are and how much incest there is. How can I tell if how I'm feeling is wrong? I never talk to anyone about it because they'll think I'm sick and I could get locked up! Why do I feel like this and what do I do about it?

J.

Few fathers are brave enough to articulate these thoughts. That silence only adds to the confusion—confusion that leaves you terrified and nauseated with yourself. These thoughts can make you feel like the lowest form of pervert. They can also make you want to flee emotionally, if not physically—taking with you all the affection, attention, encouragement, and support your daughter used to get, and still needs, from you. She'll be hurt by your withdrawal, wonder why you disappeared, and think that she made it happen.

There has to be a better solution.

When our daughters were infants, Nancy and I went to "new parent" classes offered by the Minneapolis school district. One day, the teacher asked, "Have any of you new parents ever felt like hitting your baby?"

I was incensed. "How could you even talk about that?" I demanded, "No one should ever hit a baby!"

"You didn't hear my question," she replied. "I asked, 'Have you ever *felt* like hitting your baby?' not 'Have you ever hit your baby?' So tell me, haven't you ever gotten so frustrated by your babies' crying or not doing what you want that you felt like smacking them?"

I had to admit that—although I never had struck them—I had felt like it, especially during the worst colic episodes when it seemed like they'd never stop crying.

"That's my point," she said. "It's normal and OK to *feel* like hitting your kid; it's never OK to *actually* hit them. If you don't admit that you sometimes feel like hitting them, then it's much more likely that you actually *will* hit them. If you do admit the feeling to yourself, then it's much easier to find a healthy way to release your frustration so that it won't hurt your babies or you."

There's an analogy here with sexual feelings or energy that may arise between father and daughter. It's OK for those feelings to exist. It is *never* OK, under any circumstances, to act on those feelings. It is *never* OK for a father to share with his daughter (verbally or any other way) feelings of sexual attraction he may have toward her, because that is abusive, too.

But denying the existence of sexual energy that a father or daughter may feel only makes the environment riper for abuse. It's similar to feeling like smacking a baby; when a father acknowledges the feeling's existence to himself or another dad, then it's much easier to find healthy, appropriate ways to defuse it.

If these sexual feelings become obsessive or interfere with your relationships, then you need the help of professionals. In this case, chances are that underlying problems (perhaps even sexual abuse in your own past) are affecting every one of your relationships. Warning signs may include preoccupation with your daughter's sexuality, uneasiness around her and her girlfriends, or distancing yourself because you're afraid of what you might do. These feelings don't make you into a pervert, but they do signal the need to examine your upbringing, how you learned to be a man, your own sexual development, and so on.

But no past abuse, difficulty, or trauma *ever* justifies perpetrating more sexual abuse.

Doing anything sexual with a daughter is the surest way to guarantee that her life will be deeply damaged for a long time, if not forever. For example, many people in prison or in drug or alcohol treatment were sexually abused as children.

So, no matter how great our confusion or fear, there is never, ever any excuse for sexual abuse. None. There is also never, ever any excuse for tolerating sexual abuse. None. Ever. Period. (If we were having this conversation in person, at this point, my voice would be raised.)

If we want to end the scourge of sexual abuse, we fathers have to start addressing the taboos surrounding both sexual abuse and our responses to our daughters' sexuality. We have to model, encourage, and expect healthy affectionate non-sexual touch. We have to recognize the continuum of destructive behaviors and attitudes that contribute to (and create permission for) sexual abuse. We have to take an honest look at how often we engage in these very behaviors and attitudes ourselves.

For example, even if we never physically violate a child, our use of pornography can have an abusive effect on our children's lives.

Naturally, I assumed there would come a day when I would have to discuss the behavior of males with my daughters. But when at the tender age of six my oldest told us casually one evening that she had had sex with a friend's son, we were shocked.

We managed to remain calm as we got her to tell us what had happened. Apparently, when we were visiting some friends, she went into their son's bedroom to play. The boy had pulled down her panties, put his face near her vagina, and then told her that they had just had sex. This was the way, he informed her, that they did it in his dad's sex movies.

We explained to Lindsey that this type of behavior was not acceptable and what this boy did was wrong. "This is not what sex is," I told her. I instructed her that in the future if anyone tried this again, she was to just say "No." If that didn't work, she could yell for help.

Following this incident we stopped to talk to the boy's parents. We kept the discussion low-key, since we didn't want to start pointing fingers or making accusations. The parents' response was that they would talk to their son. On the way home Lindsey mentioned that the boy had approached her again about having "sex" with him.

"What did you do?" I asked.

"I told him no way," she responded, her voice proud and strong.

"Good for you," we told her. She now had the ability to stop the situation before it even happened. What troubled me was that we'd had to awaken that power in her at such a young age.

Bea

The little boy's father may never have laid an abusive hand on his son or his friends' daughter, but he sexually abused them both. The way this man used pornography may seem unremarkable, until you see the ripples and waves of harm that resulted. If I tell my daughter that she can be anything she wants to be and then turn around and start reading *Playboy*, I might as well have saved my breath. My actions speak far louder than my words and tell her that it's OK to see females as sex objects, rather than people with sexuality. My actions also reinforce the damaging stereotype that men and boys are only interested in titillation.

Couple men's widespread pornography use with the frequency of male-perpetrated sexual abuse and it is small wonder that men are viewed as threatening. We even view each other as suspect while we fear for our daughters' safety. Loving, nonabusive men feel unfairly singled out by the entrenched notion that it's not safe to leave children alone with a man—any man. But men are responsible for this notion—male perpetrators and the other men who do nothing to fight sexual abuse.

It's hard to know what to do when it seems impossible to even speak about the problem without being branded a pervert or accused of minimizing victims' hurt. However, retreating into silence or crying, "It's not fair!" does nothing about the problem. What can a father do?

If we openly and verbally support those among us who struggle to be good men and fathers, then there will be more fathers like us. If we also censure every fellow man who acts abusively—and explicitly make clear to our sons and daughters that we will not tolerate abusive behavior and attitudes—then that abuse loses the permission and acceptance it needs to survive.

If we educate ourselves about good touch and bad touch, the signs of abuse, and the incidence of rape in our community, then we'll have less tolerance for abuse and more ability to educate others. If we volunteer with local programs that promote healthy touch, work to prevent sexual assault, and help survivors recover—then we help those programs protect more girls while putting another chink in the notion that every man is suspect.

The culture of men will start to change when we begin to earn the trust we desire. That change lies in our work as responsive, supportive, effective, and loving fathers. Only then will we be able to live out that love—giving our daughters our full affection, confident that all of our children are safe.

TOOLS

GOOD TOUCH TIPS

There are plenty of activities you and your daughter can share to stay connected in a healthy physical way while respecting your daughter's need for physical boundaries as she grows up. Look at the following list for fun things to do together and then be inspired to find your own:

- Take dance lessons.
- Pillow fight.
- Gentle roughhousing.
- Hold hands while going for walks.
- Build something.
- Play in the pool.
- Lay in a hammock and look at the stars.
- Toboggan or sled.
- Give each other manicures.
- Groom the dog.

PROTECTING YOUR DAUGHTER FROM SEXUAL ABUSE

Review the following steps, based on the American Academy of Pediatrics recommendations, for safeguarding children against the threat of sexual abuse:

- Starting at an early age (three to five years), teach your daughter about private parts of the body and how to say no to sexual advances. Give straightforward answers about sex.
- Listen when your child tries to tell you something, especially when it seems hard for her to talk about it.
- Give your daughter enough of your time so that she will not seek attention from other adults.
- Know with whom your daughter is spending time. Plan to visit your child's caregiver without notice.
- Discuss safety away from home and the difference between good touch and bad touch. Encourage your daughter to talk about scary experiences.
- See if your daughter's school has an abuse prevention program for teachers and children. If it doesn't, get one started.
- Talk to your daughter about sexual abuse. A good time to do this is when her school is sponsoring a sexual abuse program.
- Once your daughter is twelve or thirteen, discuss rape, date rape, sexually transmitted diseases, and unintended pregnancy. Start to discuss rules of sexual conduct that are accepted by the family.
- Tell someone in authority if you suspect that your child or someone else's child is being abused.

(Adapted from *Child Sexual Abuse: What It Is and How to Prevent It,* copyright 1988 American Academy of Pediatrics.)

6.

"THAT WON'T HAPPEN TO MY DAUGHTER!": ALCOHOL, TOBACCO, AND OTHER DRUGS

*It terrifies me to think where I would be today if not for my dad.
There was a time when I really lashed out. I tried most of the
drugs. I was free-floating through life. But with the strong foundation I had from my dad, I was able to go out there, experience,
come back to the middle of the road, and maybe even come back
a little farther. I am the person I am today because of that unconditional love and support and caring and nurturing and him
being my best male friend.*

Elaine

Why do some girls have serious trouble and other girls don't? There
is no simple answer, and no simple way to prevent our daughters
from drinking, smoking, using other drugs, or having other difficulties. But we can be sure that our deep and consistent involvement in our daughters' lives will both lessen the odds of their

getting into trouble, and increase the odds that we will cope better with the troubles that do arise.

There are several good organizations and Web sites that help parents address smoking, alcohol use, drug use, mental health, and other crucial teen issues (see page 249 in the resource section). Rather than repeat in this chapter a lot of general information these resources provide, we'll concentrate more on difficulties and challenges specific to girls. Ironically, I've found only two books, *Taking Charge of My Mind and Body: A Girl's Guide to Outsmarting Alcohol, Drug, Smoking, and Eating Problems* (Free Spirit, 1997) and *Refuse to Use: A Girls Guide to Drugs and Alcohol* (Rosen Publishing Group, 1999) that focus directly on girls. That's a sign of how seldom these issues are addressed by gender.

Whether or not your daughter currently has a problem with drinking, smoking, drug use, depression, or other problems, I encourage you to tap the rich supply of general material already available. If your daughter does have a problem, it's essential to seek professional help. For example, no father can "cure" his daughter's alcohol or drug dependency. All of us need help at one time or another; it's a mistake and it's cowardly not to use the help that's available.

It's also essential that *you* participate in the parts of treatment that include family members. I've heard dozens of therapists say that the chances of recovery for their young female patients skyrocket when Dad is there for the family sessions—but, sadly, those same therapists say, fathers who do participate are the exception.

We also need to learn about the factors unique to girls' unhealthy behaviors, and what fathers can do about them.

HOW BAD IS IT?

It's still true after many generations: teens (and people of all ages) abuse alcohol and tobacco far more than any other drugs. By the end of the 1990s, the overall number of young people who drink and use drugs was down slightly. Still, almost one half of eighth graders and two thirds of tenth graders say they drank in the previous year. Studies by the federal government suggest that girls are closing the gap between their alcohol and tobacco use and the historically higher rate of use among boys.

For example, a 1997 survey showed that more than half of tenth grade girls drank within the previous year—a rate 40 percent higher than four years before. The rates of binge drinking and regular drunkenness are also growing faster among girls than boys; 20 percent of twelfth grade girls say they engaged in binge drinking recently.

Why the change? It's not clear. One factor may be that social attitudes have changed and we are less judgmental about female drinking than in the past. However, the underlying factors in an individual girl's decision to drink, smoke, or do drugs remain fairly constant.

For example, as we saw earlier, girls tend to silence their sense of self at the onset of adolescence and thus have a higher incidence of depression, which can trigger problem drinking. Adolescent girls who are heavy alcohol users are more likely than boys to drink as a way to cope with problems, frustration, or anger. When it comes to peer pressure, adolescent girls are more likely than boys to drink to fit in with their friends, especially older boyfriends who may have more access to booze.

Physiology plays a part, too; females get intoxicated on smaller amounts of alcohol than males. Girls have less water in their bodies to dilute alcohol, so will have higher blood alcohol levels than a boy after drinking the same amount. An enzyme important for metabolizing alcohol—alcohol dehydrogenase—is less active in females than males. Females have more frequent fluctuation in hormone levels, which also affects how they process alcohol.

Although we seldom think of it this way, tobacco is a very common "gateway" drug. In other words, girls who *smoke* are more likely to start drinking and experimenting with other drugs than those who don't. Why would a girl start smoking in the first place? Most teen girls say they start smoking to cope with worries about weight and stress. Dieting doesn't increase the likelihood of smoking among adolescent boys, but it does among girls. Here are facts about girls and cigarettes:

- Girls and women have more trouble quitting smoking than men.
- Girls with symptoms of depression are twice as likely to smoke as other girls.
- Twenty percent of U.S. eighth graders say they smoked at least once in the past month; by twelfth grade, almost 25 percent smoke *daily*.
- Regular smoking by tenth grade girls increased by nearly half during the 1990s.
- White girls have the highest rates of smoking and alcohol use while black girls report the lowest.
- Females are three times more likely to develop lung cancer than males who smoke the same amount. At least half of women who smoke will die of tobacco-related diseases.

If your daughter is a preteen, you may wonder what all this has to do with you. In the past three decades, the government reports, kids—and especially girls—are trying alcohol, tobacco, and other drugs at increasingly younger ages. The younger a girl starts using a drug, the greater the chance she'll become dependent or addicted later on. Adolescents who start drinking before they are fifteen are four times more likely to become alcoholics than those who start after twenty-one. A third of girls who try cigarettes keep smoking regularly into adulthood. If they reach twenty-one without smoking, there is very little chance they will ever start.

Drinking and other drug use make girls vulnerable to many high-risk behaviors. Girls who drink are less likely to insist on condom use and are thus more likely to get pregnant and develop sexually transmitted diseases (STDs). Most date rapes and unsafe sex involve alcohol and/or other drugs.

And despite these trends, the federal government itself admits that there has been little research done on female substance abuse causes, patterns, and effective treatment. In addition, many people continue to believe myths like "Alcohol isn't a drug." It is a drug—one that's legal for adults (not for kids) and thus more socially acceptable and much easier for kids to obtain than illegal drugs like marijuana.

It's not all bad news, though. Girls with strong relationships, a good sense of self, competent social skills, and involved, active parents are less likely to be substance abusers. Girls are less likely to drink or smoke if they're involved in community activities, academics, sports, creative arts, and other hobbies.

No matter how old our daughters are, we can and should inform ourselves and talk to them about substance abuse. Several recent studies found that fathers are less likely to talk to their children about drugs than are mothers—and are in more denial about how easy it is for their kids to obtain tobacco, alcohol, and other drugs. If we're silent, it's easy for our girls to see our silence as a signal that we have no objection to their using drugs. That means we have some work to do.

TAKE ME SERIOUSLY

One of the strongest desires girls have as they approach and enter adolescence is to be taken seriously—to be heard. As we saw in Chapter 1, what most girls encounter instead is the opposite: they're ignored, diminished, and objectified. When our daughters get into trouble as a reaction to these injustices, it's essential that fathers look beyond the immediacy of the "bad choice." There are many forces, both internal and external, encouraging girls to drink, smoke, do drugs, and engage in other destructive behavior. They want to rebel, fit in, be more sexual, experiment, act "adult," make sense of confusing gender expectations, get relief from the upheaval of adolescence and discord at home—it's a long list.

Meanwhile marketers and media flood our daughters with images and messages that insist drinking and smoking make people sexy and happy and bring them cool friends. After years of consuming this advertising, it's easy to see why girls perceive alcohol and drugs as a solution: a way to ease pain and engage in a satisfying fantasy. After all, beer and cigarette ads never say cigarettes bring you cancer and booze can make you drunk and more likely to be raped.

Tobacco companies, brewers, distilleries, and drug dealers have a big incentive to market in ways that attract children's attention. There's little chance that a nonsmoking twenty-one-year-old will ever start smoking; so cigarette manufacturers need to get girls started before then if they want lifelong customers. Problem drinkers make close to half of all alcohol purchases. The earlier a child starts drinking, the greater the chance that she becomes an alcoholic, so again the market is motivated to target youngsters. The same marketing principle applies to sales of illegal drugs, which is why dealers often give free samples to new "customers."

Marketers also sell our daughters (usually with great success) the idea that substance use is a path of rebellion and independence. This is the most irresponsible and disingenuous advertising of all. Rebellion and independence are, of course, significant, healthy emotional reactions for adolescents. Alcohol, nicotine, and other drugs are addictive substances. As Dr. Jean Kilbourne says, "rebellion" that feeds corporate profits isn't much rebellion and "independence" that feeds addiction isn't freedom. The marketers of addictive substances do not take our daughters or their well-being seriously.

We've seen how marketing, media, cultural attitudes, and trends in teen behavior combine to create an environment where it's easier than ever for girls to choose substance abuse. You are no doubt already familiar with alcohol and tobacco as "substances" with the potential for abuse, but you may not be up on today's drug scene. What follows is a brief refresher course.

The "Other" Drugs

Some aspects of the drug world are the same today as when we were teens. After alcohol and tobacco, adolescents use marijuana the most. The government reports that use of heroin has declined, but use of inhalants, methamphetamines, and "club" drugs has risen. There is not much research broken down along gender lines, but surveys that have been done indicate that girls are catching up with boys in the use of many illicit drugs.

Marijuana isn't healthy. Its active ingredient, THC, damages brain cells. It is worse for one's lungs than cigarettes (it has more tar). It affects one's sense of time and one's coordination (a skill central to risky activities, like driving). It can be laced with more serious drugs like crack cocaine, and other bizarre substances like embalming fluid. Finally, a person can become chemically dependent on marijuana and require treatment to break the dependency.

It can be hard to tell if a teen is smoking marijuana, because the side effects sometimes mimic normal adolescent behavior: acting silly, seeming distracted, or losing interest in activities, family, and school. Other symptoms are clearer clues: dizziness, bloodshot eyes, loss of short-term memory, or difficulty walking.

So-called club drugs is a catchall phrase for a wide range of chemicals often used at clubs, concerts, and "raves"—all-night dance parties. Club drugs include Ecstasy, GHB, and Rohypnol. Ecstasy makes one's heart and breathing race and can lead to major organ failure. GHB and Rohypnol are depressants also known as "date rape" drugs because they can be slipped undetected into drinks (they have no taste or odor), immobilize a victim, and make an assault easier. Rohypnol can also bring on a type of amnesia that leaves a girl uncertain of how she was assaulted. Symptoms of club drug use may include problems remembering recent events, loss of coordination, dizziness, fainting, depression, confusion, sleep problems, chills or sweating, and slurred speech.

Fortunately, more than 90 percent of teens say they've never tried Ecstasy, the most common club drug. Unfortunately, many of those who ingest GHB and Rohypnol do so without foreknowledge and against their will.

Hallucinogens like LSD and PCP are still in circulation. As the name suggests, these drugs bring on hallucinations and can induce severe paranoia. They affect heart rate, blood pressure, and breathing—and may interfere with hormones needed for physical growth. Signs of use include dilated pupils, dizziness, nausea, depression, anxiety, paranoiac behavior, and lack of muscle coordination.

Methamphetamines, cocaine, and crack cocaine induce wild mood swings and delusions, and can produce permanent psychological damage. Symptoms of methamphetamines may include any of the following: inability to sleep, increased sensitivity to noise, nervous physical activity, like scratching, irritability, dizziness, or confusion, extreme anorexia, tremors or even convulsions, and increased heart rate. Cocaine users may suffer from red, bloodshot eyes, a runny nose or frequent sniffing, a change in eating or sleeping patterns, acting withdrawn, depressed, tired, or careless about personal appearance; losing interest in school, family, or activities. These drugs are very addictive, hard to kick, and foul up one's physiology to the point that a young person may suffer strokes, heart attacks, and failure of the kidneys, lungs, and liver.

The cheap, easy-to-obtain groups of drugs known as inhalants tend to attract young people at an early age. Paint thinner, glue, and similar substances induce a quick, but very dangerous and short-lived "high." They immediately affect brain and heart function and can kill on the very first use. Death by inhalant is ugly—suffocation, choking on vomit, or heart attack. Signs of use include slurred speech; drunk, dizzy, or dazed appearance; unusual breath odor;

chemical smell on clothing; paint stains on body or face; red eyes or runny nose.

Each drug (including alcohol) has accoutrements and paraphernalia that can point to a problem, just as changes in behavior or mood can. Trust your instincts and don't turn a blind eye if you notice a personality change—or a roach clip, razor and mirror, straws or pipes, glue tubes, or empty liquor bottles lying around.

The U.S. Department of Health and Human Services, the Partnership for a Drug Free America, and many other organizations have extensive information about drug use and the effects of each substance. Tap into these resources for your own knowledge so that you're armed with information and perspective when father-daughter conversation turns to chemical use—hers or her peers'.

Peer Pressure

> *Probably my greatest fear is that she'll meet a group of kids and get involved in drugs or get with the wrong group of people. There has been no hint or inkling of that kind of problem with her yet. The kids that she hangs around with now are perfectly nice kids. But I'm afraid that someday drugs will make an appearance. I think that's a difficult subject, and I'm not sure I want to handle it.*
>
> Stan

None of us want to confront our children with the issue of substance abuse; parental life would be so much easier without it. But we do have to deal with it, even when it means addressing topics our daughters want us to keep out of—like relationships with their peers.

Your daughter is going to be influenced by her peers. In most cases, and for the majority of her adolescence, that's a good thing.

Peers influence each other to perform at a higher level, be interested in other people, develop new interests, gain more perspectives, and explore their own values. For example, a good grade doesn't carry near as much satisfaction if you can't compare it with how your peers scored. So, first, a dad has to remember that not every peer is a threat and not all peer pressure is evil.

At the same time, we have to be realistic about the school and peer culture our daughters inhabit. For example, it is virtually impossible to send your daughter to a school where she would have no access to alcohol, drugs, or cigarettes. The threat of a particular school's drug culture will always be a relative thing, so you can't rely on a school to keep your daughter away from drugs.

In many communities, most teen social life revolves around parties where there is alcohol available. This is one teen phenomenon that hasn't changed since we were kids. Too often, keg parties are even endorsed—and the booze supplied—by parents. It's not uncommon for other drugs to be available, too. That means, for both parents and kids, there's usually an ongoing tension between having a social life and drinking, smoking, or using drugs.

> *I nag because I'm more fearful than I thought I was about the world. For my daughter, I worry a lot. She likes herself. She's pretty responsible and her friends seem to be, too. When she goes out with friends, she tells us everything. But at the same time, I'm always saying, "Don't do this, you have to be back by this time, wherever you're at." Because I think the world's not necessarily going in the direction I want it to go in. I worry about her future and if she's going to be safe.*
>
> *Hank*

Of course, a responsible father wants his children to have a social life; that's where teens learn the most valuable lessons adolescence has to offer. But a responsible father also doesn't want his kids to be drunk or stoned, either.

Our daughters feel intense pressure and tension about these choices on a daily basis. They spend much of their day at school or "hanging out" with peers whose social life also revolves around the limited opportunities available. Even girls who are adamant about not using chemicals are left frustrated because there seem to be few venues for socializing outside a keg party.

In some cities, the so-called club scene has become a prominent part of the youth social life—especially for girls. Many dance and "rave" clubs serve liquor and, of course, are not supposed to admit people under twenty-one. However, it's usually easier for a girl than a boy to appear older than her age. Teen girls who combine high heels, makeup, clothing, and attitude can "pass" for an adult and gain entry to the club scene—and the dangers of club drugs.

If so much of teen peer culture intertwines with alcohol, tobacco, and drug use, then that presents us fathers with a challenge. What can we do to help our community provide realistic alternatives? One thing we can do is work with other adults and kids to create places that will be simultaneously safe for young people and attractive enough to ensure that young people utilize them. Communities across the country are struggling to make this happen, and we owe it to our daughters to be part of that effort and part of the solutions.

We also need to be a visible and vocal part of the solution at home. We must talk openly and rationally with our daughters about alcohol, tobacco, and other drugs. We have to acknowledge their frustration when they feel like they're being forced to choose between drinking and not spending time with their friends. We have to open our homes as safe and substance-free gathering places. This shows our daughters how seriously we take their concern for friendship and health, while also providing a practical, healthy alternative for other kids, too.

As fathers, we have a responsibility to tell our daughters: "The safety and sanctity of your life comes first for me, no matter what anyone else says and no matter what you do. Here are the things I value in you, no matter what some of your friends may value you for." It's difficult to overemphasize the importance of telling our daughters this. If you are silent, how can she know what's important to you?

Despite the troubling trends described by all the survey data, studies of adolescents continue to show that they give more weight to their parents' values and opinions than they do to their peers'. That's a powerful advantage to have. We have to get over our tendency to be intimidated by our daughters' peers, thinking, "My daughter will never listen to me, so why bother saying anything." We have to speak up, ask questions, and share what we know and what we believe is the right thing to do.

Of course, you have to back up what you say with action; speaking up brings obligations. If you tell your daughter that her safety comes first, you have to respond to her requests for safety whenever and wherever you're asked, no matter how inconvenient. When it comes to drinking, this principle is well expressed in the contract that Students Against Driving Drunk/Students Against Destructive Decisions (an example of positive teen peer pressure) encourages parents and children to sign. Here's part of what the parent agrees to: "I agree to provide for your safe, sober transportation home if you are ever in a situation that threatens your safety and to defer discussion about that situation until a time when we can both discuss the issues in a calm and caring manner."

The SADD contract seems like a big stretch for many fathers, but such arrangements often bring better-than-anticipated results. Say your daughter gets drunk one night. If you're willing to promise your daughter that she has a safe way to get home in return for waiting a few hours before firing off questions, then she gets a real feeling of how much you value her. And, those few hours give both of you some time to cool off and reflect on what happened and why. The "time-out" may even provide her with the gift of a hangover, which might carry more wisdom about alcohol abuse than any lecture you can provide. With cooler heads, both of you are in better positions to talk about the good and bad choices that were available the night before, as well as the good and bad options the future will hold.

> *I like SADD, although I have to admit, I'm not crazy about the "no questions asked" part. But it seems like a decent enough trade off. So far, I only had to do it once. She was sixteen, it was a Friday about eleven, and she was at a party at a friend's house. A bunch of them were going off to someone else's house, but they'd all been drinking. Turns out my daughter had been drinking, too, but . . . Anyway, she called, I got her, the ride home was pretty tense, and she went right to bed. The next day we talked about it. I was calmer than the night before, though I was still really pissed at the parents of the other kid who didn't seem to sweat the fact that these kids were getting drunk at their house. I ended up thanking my daughter for calling me and promised I'd do it again the same way if she ever needed me to. It really surprised me that I said that. And she eventually told me that she was scared. That was something. So far, she hasn't put herself in that position again. And I really meant it when I thanked her.*
>
> *Dick*

It's much harder to have a good morning-after conversation about drinking, smoking, or other drug use if that conversation is the first time we've ever brought the subject up with our daughters. The communication has to start early, because a typical adolescent takes her first drink at age thirteen (and that means many start younger). As with sexuality, everyday talks get our ideas across better than a crisis-triggered Big Talk.

The Role of Desire

The desire we discussed in Chapter 4 plays a big part in how girls relate to alcohol and other drugs. Adolescence is a time of yearning; a big element of that yearning is sexual. Girls pine for a secret kiss with their "crush." They desire the excitement of sexual activity and want to understand their emerging sexuality.

As boys and young men, we had more permission to express and act on sexual desires. In my high school, a guy with a reputation for sleeping around was a stud. A girl with a reputation for sleeping around was a slut. That double standard continues today, and girls know it. Meanwhile, the media sell sex as the way to rebel and be cool, while cultural mores and many parents continue to treat girls' sexuality and sexual desire as bad. This creates a confusing, contradictory environment where it's easy for girls to feel confusion, anger, self-doubt, and like they're getting unfair treatment.

One way girls may try to escape from that frustration is with alcohol or drugs.

> *Alcohol made it so I didn't hear the voice in my head that says, "You're a bad girl if you have sex. Only loose, immoral sluts do that." It relaxed me some and quieted down that little voice so I could do the sexual things I wondered about. But because I was drinking, I didn't really get to experience what I wanted anyway.*
> *Louise*

Girls may use alcohol as a tool (albeit an unhealthy one) to explore their sexuality—and to ignore the double standard that restricts their desires and denies their legitimate adolescent yearnings. They may also use drugs and alcohol to drown out guilt about their sexual desires and sexual behaviors.

Very often, fathers are the firmest enforcers of the idea that girls *should* feel anxious about sexual activity and avoid it in every circumstance. That can contribute to sexual anxiety and guilt, for which alcohol and drugs seem to offer quick relief.

It's a fair bet that you want your daughter to be valued for reasons *other than* her sexuality, especially by the boys and men with whom she has significant relationships. But she learns how to properly value her sexuality when you also want your daughter to be valued for reasons *in addition* to her sexuality. In other words, value her without denying her sexuality. She is likely to feel more in control of her sexuality, less vulnerable to abuse, and more able to fulfill her desires in healthy ways. A daughter living with expectations like this has much less motivation to turn to alcohol or drugs.

Sexual desires are not the only yearnings our daughters have. Girls yearn to be themselves, seek justice, be creative, make the world better, and have a host of other longings. As Nancy Gruver writes, "When we try to squeeze and stamp out girls' sexual desires, it is very difficult for girls to trust and pursue their other desires. How well can they learn to reach for their dreams when we work so hard to deny them one of the most central human desires? Then, to make matters even worse, when girls can't seem to fulfill their nonsexual desires and find their goals, we ask, 'Why don't you know what you want? Why can't you figure out what you need?' "

I'm not suggesting that the nonsensical messages we send girls about sexual desire are the only reasons a girl develops alcohol or drug problems. But clearly it is a common factor. It's painful to try and stay true to yourself when so much of what you encounter diminishes and dismisses your inner self. Alcohol and other drugs can be ways for girls to "forget themselves"; forget who they are. Sadly, chemicals also block out the healthy, creative search for ways to grow during adolescence.

The combination of peer pressure and sexual pressures deeply entwined with chemical use is a significant threat to our daughters. That combination is a powerful reason to start early in encouraging your daughter to be true to herself and believe in herself.

Our Own Behavior

Throughout this book, I've repeatedly emphasized the importance of listening to and communicating with your daughter. Drug, alcohol, and tobacco use is one case where what you *do* is exponentially more important than what you say or hear.

How we use tobacco, alcohol, and other drugs tends to act as the norm for our children throughout their lives. For example, statistics show that adult alcoholics are most likely to have grown up in a family where a parent drank to excess. A teetotaling family— where alcohol was forbidden—is the next most likely environment to generate an alcoholic. An adult alcoholic is least likely to have grown up in a family where parents drank moderately.

Many children growing up in alcoholic and teetotaling families do *not* become problem drinkers, just as some children growing up around moderate drinkers *do* become problem drinkers. In other words, our behavior will not predetermine our daughters' fates— but it will influence them. If our daughters see a healthy example (as opposed to a bad example or no example at all), they are more likely to follow that healthy example.

I happen to be an alcoholic and, thankfully, I got sober before my daughters were born. As of today, they've never seen me drink. I used to think that, because I didn't drink, I hadn't modeled for my kids an example of responsible alcohol use. I felt I hadn't said enough to my daughters about alcohol; that maybe I should have a big "T" Talk on the subject. I never had that Talk, but I never hid the fact that I have a drinking problem and that's why I regularly spend evenings meeting with other alcoholics. Nancy and I also didn't hide the fact that some other relatives have similar addictions, nor did we ban alcohol from our home. When Nancy and dinner guests occasionally have some wine, it's no big production.

Still, I was uneasy when the girls went off to college; would they go overboard now that they were away from home? Would they have any internal compass for moderation and safety? Turns out, the answer is yes. That's something I didn't quite grasp, especially when remembering how drunken my young college years were. I recently asked one of my daughters to explain.

*Well, I know you're an alcoholic; I saw you go to your meetings
every week. I know other relatives have a problem with alcohol
and drugs, and not all of them have gotten sober. And I know
that there's probably genetics involved. Maybe I'm being too con-
trolling, but I figure I can't become an alcoholic if I don't drink.
So I don't.*

Nia

While folks might want to argue the merits of her strategy, its effect
is practical and positive. She's content living without using a drug to
alter her mood. What I learned from her answer is the influence of
my everyday conversation and behavior; my words and actions were
healthy, consistent, and part of life from her earliest memory. I had
communicated clearly enough, without resorting to a Big Talk.

Indeed, our Big Talks carry much less weight than our Big
Behavior. I find the question of *what* you use alcohol or drugs for
more illuminating than the question of *how much* alcohol or drugs
you consume. For example, do you use alcohol as a self-prescribed
medication in order to get through anxiety or anger? When you
come home from work, does your daughter see that one of the first
things you do is to fix yourself a drink, get out a cigarette, or light
a joint? Do you drink or smoke when you are feeling stressed or
upset?

Does your daughter see you drink only on occasions when
friends are present or during a special holiday? Does she see family
members use alcohol as part of traditional rituals, but not in a way
that the alcohol is the center of the ritual?

In other words, we have to look in the mirror before we can
hope to reasonably and effectively deal with our daughters about alcohol, smoking, and other drugs. A father probably has a problem
with drinking if he uses booze to get through the day, manage difficult people, or to cope with feeling. Until he addresses that problem, he can't expect his daughter to give much (if any) weight to

what he says on the subject. Even more important, his own life and well-being will be handicapped.

If I use illegal drugs, I am sending a clear message that breaking the law is acceptable, no matter what I say to my daughter. Instead of learning healthier (not to mention legal) ways of celebrating or coping with difficulty, she learns how to use the drug to escape. As with alcohol, she may also suffer the loss of her father through incarceration, accident, or emotional and psychological withdrawal.

If I don't want my daughter to take up smoking (a practice nearly guaranteed to shorten her life through ugly and painful diseases like emphysema and cancer), then I shouldn't smoke—or I should stop today. It's common sense that kids whose parents don't smoke are less likely to start themselves. They are also less likely to develop asthma and other respiratory problems aggravated by secondhand smoke.

It is not easy to break an addiction or chemical dependency. But that temporary discomfort and long-term effort is worth it to increase the quality and quantity of time we'll have with our daughters (since we'll probably live longer), and to increase the chances of our daughters being healthy now and in the future. Plus, it makes our lives more meaningful, useful, and acceptable to ourselves.

It's simple: in the case of chemicals, your daughter will respond a lot more to what you do than to what you say. If you have a problem with alcohol, tobacco, and/or other drugs, get help for yourself now.

COMFORT OR PROTECT? RESPONDING WHEN TROUBLE ARISES

It's frightening to reflect on all the difficulties and dangers our daughters may encounter as they grow up. Whether or not these dangers materialize, we may feel drawn further into the overprotection trap, as if shoving our daughters into the storm cellar while we wave our shotguns wildly at the tornado. Especially as our daughters get older, our role is to be by their side with support and comfort, rather than sitting on the cellar door to keep them from entering the turbulent world. We need to go beyond reflexive overprotection and into the more demanding practice of supporting and comforting. As the writer Susannah Sheffer puts it: "If protection says 'I will try to keep you from this,' comfort says, 'I am with you, and I will help you learn to get through this as best you can.'"

One of my daughters struggles with depression, so I've worried that she'll follow me into the quagmire of alcoholism. I'm afraid that she'll never fully appreciate and give herself credit for her wonderful qualities and accomplishments. Of course, if she chooses to, she can find resources to address these problems if and when they arise. That is no guarantee that everything will work out OK for her, however. As hard as that is to accept, it's a basic truth of parenting.

My daughter was in chemical dependency treatment last year and the hardest thing was to fight my urge to go in there and rescue her. Everyone told me that the best thing for her was to have her face the consequences of what she was doing. I knew that in my head, but it was really hard to do. I really needed support from other parents, especially one or two other dads, but, boy, that was really hard to ask for, too.

She's getting better, but still struggling—I mean, she's only a kid. But I'm starting to see that sometimes the pain's a real tool. It helps her see how serious this is and gets her moving to do what she needs to do to get better. That's really hard to watch because she's my little girl and Daddy's supposed to be her protector. I know in my head that protecting her from the hurt or from the consequences, in a way, protects her from getting better. But, damn, that's hard to let her hurt. It's harder than going through all the chaos she put us through when she was drinking.

Chet

What Chet describes is probably the hardest road for any father to walk when his daughter becomes dependent on or addicted to drugs or alcohol. The chaos and pain can be so great that we will go to great lengths to deny their existence or severity. We will be tempted to try all manner of "solutions" before seeking effective help from others. We'll turn to shouting, pleading, lecturing, punishing, and dozens of other strategies before admitting that we can't solve this problem for them.

Fortunately, there are many, many people and organizations that can help a father find the support he needs and help him create an environment to increase the chances of his daughter's recovery from addiction. The most effective chemical dependency programs for adolescents involve family members in the treatment process; and the more the family participates, the better the chances for success. Usually, a father is the family member least likely to participate. That's unfortunate for two reasons: a father's nonparticipation leaves him out of a crucial experience of his daughter's life, and when fathers do participate, recovery rates for their daughters increase markedly. Participation isn't ever easy or convenient. It will disrupt work and stir up difficult feelings. But a daughter's life is worth that.

Al-Anon Family Groups are one resource readily available all across the country. Al-Anon members are relatives and friends of alcoholics who gather together to help one another. The only requirement for membership is that there be a problem of alcoholism in a relative or friend. Al-Anon suggests that relatives live by the well-known Twelve Steps, principles shared with Alcoholics Anonymous. There are no dues or fees for Al-Anon membership, and the focus is on helping each other live a better life—not on trying to "fix" the person using drugs.

The notion that we cannot fix or cure a chemically dependent child is often the most difficult for us to accept. But it is a reality. Your daughter is the only one who can truly decide whether she will pick up a drink or take a snort today. You can't do it for her. What you can do, however, is love her enough to let her face the consequences of her substance abuse—and love her enough to not let her choices determine how you choose to live your life. Just as only she can decide whether to drink or use today, only you can decide whether to base your mood, your self-worth, and your usefulness to others on whether or not she drinks or uses today.

Paradoxically, when you let go of having your life revolve around her behavior, your daughter will often feel a greater incentive to admit to her own powerlessness over the chemicals she uses. To quote from the book *One Day at a Time in Al-Anon*, "There is no need for me to accept blame for another person's irrational actions. I will deal honestly with my own shortcomings. If I do this honestly, the change in me will be reflected in every person whose life touches mine."

It's hard for a man to ask for help or admit that his children are having problems. But it is impossible to deal with a child's substance abuse without the support of others. Your sanity and the prospects for your chemically dependent daughter's recovery may very well depend on the amount and quality of the help you get for yourself.

Chemical dependency in your daughter is a hard and painful way to learn a lesson every dad must learn: the older she gets, the less control I have over my daughter's fate.

When our daughters are very young, we really can protect them from most danger and fright. As they get older, we're usually able to convince them that we'll take care of troubles that come up, even if we can't always solve them. But when they hit adolescence, their knowledge and powers of observation begin to prove that Daddy doesn't have all the answers—indeed, he's got insecurities and fears of his own. Two things can happen when that time comes.

We can remain silent and try to push stubbornly forward in our traditional protector role. The flaws in that role and our own imperfections remain visible to our daughters, however. Disillusionment can set in as our daughters see that, with our human weaknesses, we don't measure up to the role we're attempting to play.

Or, we can talk openly about the ways in which uncertainty, grief, fear, or pain are as much a part of our lives as are passion, euphoria, beauty, and love. In fact, we can tell them, "The best part of life is knowing that someone cares about us, not in knowing that someone will always be there to fix what's wrong or hoping that nothing ever goes wrong." Instead of disillusionment, our daughters learn that no human (not even Dad) is omnipotent, that comfort and love are even more valuable than solutions to our problems.

Late one night a few months ago, my daughter Mavis called home, deeply frustrated over problems she was having at school. When I answered, Mavis immediately burst into tears and spent the next half hour pouring out her anger and frustrations. Perhaps because I was tired, or perhaps because I'm finally getting wiser, I just listened. I didn't offer fixes or suggestions. I heard her out and told her I understood. I longed to be there and give her a hug, but sensed that my attentive ear was the affection she needed right then. By the end of the call, she was calmer and said, "Thanks, Dad; you were a real comfort to me." Those words made me feel loved, loving, proud, and satisfied.

Our daughters need us to respond fully and responsibly to whatever difficulties they may encounter or bad choices they may make. They're watching for it and, no matter how hard things get, we can deliver. Sometimes our love, comfort, and support comes in small, symbolic rituals like the nightly bedtime kiss; other times it comes in large acts of heroism, like letting our daughters face the necessary tough consequences.

By consistently coming through for them, we teach our daughters how valuable they are and how to embrace the challenges that the rest of their lives will surely bring.

TOOLS

HER FUTURE'S SO BRIGHT

If your daughter's future appears bright to her, that significantly increases the likelihood that she will *avoid* bringing harm upon herself by way of unsafe sex or drugs. So, help her make plans for the future, talk to her about what it takes to realize her aspirations, and help her reach her goals. Encourage her to volunteer for community service as a way for her to learn job skills, meet good adult role models, and get involved in worthy projects. Support her involvement in and exposure to extracurricular activities and organized sports.

"I'LL ALWAYS . . ." AGREEMENT

Draft an agreement in which you and your daughter each commit yourselves to take care of yourself. For example, you might vow to quit smoking and she vows to not start. You could promise to get a yearly physical and your daughter might promise to avoid parties where alcohol will be consumed. Plus, the agreement can include steps that each can take to help look out for the other. Your daughter could encourage you while you quit smoking, and you can promise to always come get her if she finds herself at a party where people are drinking or doing drugs.

A contract encourages communication about specific situations involving alcohol, drugs, peer pressure, and being healthy. Continuous and open father-daughter communication is critical in helping your daughter make healthy decisions.

SADD: CONTRACT FOR LIFE

*The nonprofit organization Students Against Driving
Drunk/Students Against Destructive Decisions designed this
straightforward contract to keep kids safe—and to facilitate
communication between young people and adults about smart
decisions related to alcohol, drugs, peer pressure, and behavior.
After you both sign it, keep this agreement posted on the family
message board or refrigerator, so that, every day, everyone
remembers that they can count on each other.*

Young Person

*I recognize that there are many potentially destructive decisions I
face every day and commit to you that I will do everything in my
power to avoid making decisions that will jeopardize my health,
my safety and overall well being, or your trust in me. I understand
the dangers associated with the use of alcohol and drugs and the
destructive behaviors often associated with impairment.*

*By signing below, I pledge my best effort to remain alcohol
and drug free, I agree that I will never drive under the influence of
either, or accept a ride from someone who is impaired, and I will
always wear a seatbelt.*

*Finally, I agree to call you if I am ever in a situation that
threatens my safety and to communicate with you regularly about
issues of importance to us both.*

Young Person: ⸺⸺⸺⸺⸺⸺⸺⸺⸺⸺⸺⸺

Parent (or Caring Adult)

*I am committed to you, and to your health and safety. By signing
below, I pledge to do everything in my power to understand and*

communicate with you about the many difficult and potentially
destructive decisions you face.

   Further I agree to provide for you safe, sober transportation
home if you are ever in a situation that threatens your safety and
to defer discussion about that situation until a time when we can
both discuss the issues in a calm and caring manner. I also pledge
to you that I will not drive under the influence of alcohol or drugs,
I will always seek safe, sober transportation home, and I will
always remember to wear a seatbelt.

Parent (or Caring Adult): _____

"WHAT WOULD I DO IF . . ."

Rehearse difficult situations with your daughter, and give her words
to say when confronted by peer pressure. I know, it might feel a little dorky at first—for both of you. But it works.

   Pretend you are a friend, acquaintance, or even a stranger who
approaches your daughter with an offer of drugs. You might say
something like, "*Hey there, cutie. How would you like to try this*
stuff out? It will make you feel better than you've ever felt." She
plays out her appropriate reaction. Be provocative, tempting, and as
realistic as you can be in your manner and approach. Say things
like, "*Oh, it's really harmless. Everybody does it.*" Try to catch her
off guard. Be creative with your words and actions and try to anticipate everything that might really happen. She should, of course, be
strong in her response to you, but avoid putting herself in harm's
way. Let her know she can always use you as an excuse. "*My dad*
would absolutely kill me, and I just can't afford to get in trouble
with him right now." Although it might be difficult for your daughter to picture herself in such a scenario when acting out with her

dad, this role-playing exercise will better prepare her to say no when she is confronted with a similar situation.

Remember, just like doing a theatrical play, this exercise is much more successful when you do multiple rehearsals. After finishing a role-play, talk to each other about what each of you said, how each of you felt. Then, brainstorm even more effective responses—and practice again.

BE IN-THE-KNOW

Monitoring your daughter's whereabouts and activities isn't easy. But knowing her comings and goings is a very good way to help her avoid drugs and alcohol, especially as she gets older. It works like this: if you talk to your daughter regularly and she speaks to you freely about what's going on in her life, where she's going, and with whom, then monitoring her activities for safety purposes occurs naturally.

The trust and ease grow when "I'm going to be at . . ." communication goes both ways. Have a reliable system to leave messages for each other, either by phone or on a message board at home. Know where she is at all times. Do the same thing for her by letting her know where you are at all times. Whether it's a grocery store run or a tennis match, she has a right to know where you are as well.

- Know her friends (and their parents) and interact with them whenever you have an opportunity.
- Steer her away from kids who use drugs or from families whose values about drugs and alcohol are not your own.
- Know her plans for the next day.
- Know what she's doing after school, and curb the amount of

time she spends without adult supervision. Have a responsible adult in your home during this critical time, or enroll your daughter in after-school programs or activities.

- Know what she's watching on television or listening to on the radio.
- Limit her time on the Internet (running around in the backyard and park still remains fun and interactive, despite the onset of technology!). Know where she goes when she's online.
- Know how she's getting along with peers in school, and be on top of her academic performance.
- Have a curfew and enforce it.

7.

"DADDY, WHEN I GROW UP,
I WANT TO . . .":
SCHOOL, WORK, MONEY, POWER,
AND THE FUTURE

Growing up, I thought fathers were supposed to relate to the boys, and the girls were supposed to relate to the moms and pick up those roles, especially about work. I try to let my daughters know that they don't have to follow a typical woman's role, and I don't have to be the typical father.

Fred

SLEEPING BEAUTY'S WAKE-UP CALL

The world of work and money is a profound part of our heritage as men. We were raised expecting that we'd be the breadwinners in the family. We were taught that men at work are proud, take risks, have discipline, and think ahead. As men, we've also learned that work can bring benefits in addition to money alone. There's challenge, creativity, accomplishment, and a sense of self-worth. These are all huge assets for our kids—especially our daughters. Here's why.

Our daughters grow up with Disney heroines on the one hand (a Cinderella or an Ariel whose life decisions seem to end once they get a man) and real heroines on the other hand (accomplished pioneers like astronauts Sally Ride and Mae Jemison). For a real-life heroine like Mae Jemison, life gets interesting once she discovers her passion for space travel and her willingness to make an enormous effort. Yet real women like Jemison and Ride still have less visibility and influence than Disney's swooning, get-me-a-man motivated cartoon characters. Maybe that's why surveys of girls continue to show that, while most expect to work for pay when they are women, they *also* anticipate that a man will take care of them financially. This astounding attitude is evidence of how powerful the unrealistic Disney-like myths remain in our daughters' impressions. That's why sharing our work heritage—including our work ethic, obligations, and experience—is so valuable for our daughters' futures.

> *I've told her from the get-go, if she thinks some guy is gonna take care of her every need and comfort, then she's living in la-la land. She sees her mom and me working and most of the time liking it. Her husband could get hit by a bus or she could get divorced. There will be times when she has to bail herself out—ain't nobody else gonna do it for her.*
>
> *James*

It's now true that nearly every one of our daughters will hold a paid job during her adult life, just like nearly every one of us has. And while no dad hopes his daughter's adult relationships will fail, there's also a decent chance that she will divorce sometime during her adult years. She'll have to learn how to live independently.

When we share our work heritage and career experience—with both sons and daughters—we give them a firmer grip on their future than any fairy tales can. If we encourage our daughters' talents and dreams, we guarantee that they won't sleep through life waiting for a charming stranger's wake-up call.

In reality, your daughter will have years—maybe all of her adult life—during which she and/or her family depend on her income; a job won't be optional. Because women marry and have children later than ever, and on average spend additional "single" years after divorce or a spouse's death, our daughters will have to support themselves even when their families don't rely on their income.

It all boils down to this: my daughter isn't Sleeping Beauty, there is no rich Prince Charming waiting for her, and life isn't a fairy tale. We both need to realize this if she's going to be successful.

SCHOOL BELLES

School is nearly always the first step a girl takes outside the family toward the "real" world. We can help our daughters immeasurably by looking closely at the opportunities girls have and the obstacles they face in school.

In theory, schools play a fundamental role in motivating girls, fostering their interests, and preparing them for work and career. Schools should nurture and challenge girls, helping them to bloom and thrive. Girls especially need schools that help them feel comfortable in their own skin, free from restrictive gender expectations, confident in their special talents, and pushed to discover new abilities.

Schools can hold the potential to let girls explore a wide range of interests in a safe setting, without having a livelihood or a job at stake. Say your daughter is passionate about writing, and by junior year becomes editor for the school newspaper. Also in junior year, she has a great chemistry teacher who is tuned in to her learning style and knows how to focus her natural curiosity on the fascinating atomic puzzles of science. Think about it: when your daughter is thirty-seven, it's markedly more difficult to switch from being a newspaper editor to being a chemist—or to attempt to be both at once. What's great about a good school is that it provides room and encouragement for your daughter to pursue many paths—and even discover new ones—with relatively little risk.

A good school is like a social incubator for girls. They are forced to get along in diverse groups of peers and adults. Girls begin to learn from someone they wouldn't choose as a best friend, understanding that people who are different still can offer intellectual, emotional, social, and spiritual stimulation. If her French teacher doesn't have the best people skills, your daughter still may be able to relate to the teacher's love of the language. The best sprinter on your daughter's relay team may drive her nuts, but a good school environment will help her to work with her teammate nevertheless. In other words, a good school aims to help kids sort out problems and find what they need—even in trying circumstances.

I dreaded sending my daughters to seventh grade, often the crucible where girls feel the most heat to silence their voices, and the time when many girls really start to struggle emotionally and academically. But they were fortunate in the environment created by the four teachers who team-teach seventh grade at that school. Ms. Durant, Mrs. Armstrong, Mr. Weber, and Mrs. Ball were (and still are) each quirky in his or her own way. What I found most valuable was that these teachers were open and unapologetic about their eccentricities. They celebrated and reveled in them.

This teacher attitude helped create an atmosphere that encouraged the seventh grade kids to relish their own (and each other's) unique qualities, at a time when kids feel so much pressure to conform and when kids are so quick to cruelly label one another as odd or different. Thanks to Mr. Weber, my kids can now easily identify marsh marigolds and dozens of other boreal fauna. But far more important, my daughters learned how to recognize and respect the dozens of different characteristics in themselves and in their classmates. That was a nearly ideal school experience.

But our world is seldom ideal, and the same goes for our schools. Schools today have a burgeoning number of issues to address, and they rarely have all the resources they need. Among the most persistent problems is gender inequity.

Years of research consistently indicate that classroom teachers (female and male) tend to call on girls less often than boys, give girls less sustained and intensive help, and direct the highest percentage of their attention to boys who engage in problem behavior. (You can learn about the research from numerous American Association of University Women publications and books such as *Schoolgirls* and *Failing at Fairness.* See page 248 for information.) Girls tend to be rewarded more for the appearance of their schoolwork than they are for its substance, and they are praised for being quiet and self-effacing, like school belles. In early grades, girls and boys have similar math scores. But girls' scores steadily drop with age as they are subtly steered, and steer themselves, away from "boy" subjects, like math and science. By the time our daughters reach college and graduate school, embarrassingly low percentages of them major in hard sciences or math. This came as a shock to one schoolteacher who became a father.

> *No one had ever told me I couldn't do anything because of who I was. But now I recognize the cold truth that my wonderful, inquisitive, blossoming daughter Kate would probably be told over and over again as she was growing up that there are some things girls really shouldn't do. She may not hear this directly. In fact, the people who give the message may not even hear themselves doing it. But the fact is that girls are shortchanged in the opportunities they are offered. One of the greatest offenders in the challenge of equity for all children is the education system, and I, as a teacher, was smack in the center of it. Was I doing anything in my class to discriminate against girls? Was I doing anything as a father to limit Kate's self-expectation?*
>
> *I'll be damned if anybody is gonna tell my kid or any of my*

students they can't do something just because they're a girl, or Latina, African-American, hearing-impaired, non-English speaker—whatever. As a classroom teacher, I began to read more about the issue. I took more workshops that focused on equity as an important issue in school reform. I worked on ways to reorganize my class and my teaching.

As a father I reexamined my interactions with my daughter, from the kinds of games we played and the books we read to the more subtle subjects and phrases I used to communicate ideas and beliefs. I keep trying.

Bob

Let me emphasize Bob's observation that "the people who give the message may not even hear themselves doing it." Few schools or parents malevolently plot against girls' well-being. Nevertheless, teachers and fathers can reinforce arbitrary gender stereotypes even when they have the best intentions and when they want girls to have the same chance at success as boys do.

When we look at gender-equity problems in schools, it's also important to look at how we fathers teach our daughters at home. Our attitudes about what skills our daughters should have, and our attitudes about their competencies, will color what they look for and expect to find in school. It's a problem if we're teaching skills at home in a way that reinforces the very things we're trying to get our schools to change.

I was with a neighbor outside working on something and he sent his little son and daughter to get a Phillips screwdriver. The boy said, "I don't know what a Phillips screwdriver is." The dad said, "Bring a bunch out and I'll show you." The dad started showing the difference between the Phillips and the regular, but he was only talking to the boy. So I grabbed one of the Phillips and asked the girl, "Have you ever seen a screwdriver with the four things shaped like a cross that's different than a regular flathead screwdriver?" Meanwhile, the father kept on explaining it to the son and not saying a thing to his daughter. I think it was totally unintentional and unconscious—but it made me think hard about what I expose my daughter to versus what her brother is being exposed to. This guy's a good father; I'm sure if I asked him, he'd want the girl to know how to use a Phillips head. But he just wasn't showing her.

George

The accumulation of all these subtle, unconscious, and unintentional messages whittle down a girl's perception of herself as capable with tools, mechanical things, numbers, physical problem-solving, technology, and science.

We may not believe that *we* would ever reinforce those ideas. That's a belief that education researchers Dr. Myra Sadker and Dr. David Sadker encountered regularly over more than twenty years observing teachers in classrooms. They and their colleagues observed teachers from elementary school through college. Over and over, teachers were stunned by the dozens of subtle—and sometimes quite overt—ways they reinforced gender stereotypes and operated on gender assumptions that limited girls and boys.

The data (some of the observations included videotaping) show nearly all of the teachers' most constructive feedback is directed toward boys, while girls get the less detailed or more critical feedback. This behavior varies little whether the teacher is female or male. Boys are chosen to answer questions more frequently, even when more girls than boys have their hands raised. Boys are more likely to call out answers without being called on. When girls call out, they are often instructed to "raise your hand first." As one teacher who is also a father wrote:

It's hard to admit, as a seasoned professional, that you're producing outcomes that you don't want, even realizing you're doing it. That's true whether you're a teacher, a father, or both. And that's

*why it's so important to pay close attention to how gender issues
affect our kids.*

Marty

Many years ago, the late Dr. Myra Sadker told me a story about her youngest daughter, Jackie, who did very well in an all-girls' high school before beginning at a coed college. Early in her freshman year, Jackie called home to say that one professor—a woman she respected—was not calling on her.

"We said, 'Why don't you call out?' " Myra recalled. " 'Don't wait for your raised hand to be recognized—call out the answer.' And Jackie said, 'I did call out, and the teacher told me to raise my hand.' " Myra said she and David, her husband, were flabbergasted because this college professor's behavior was right out of their research—even after twenty years of drawing attention to such classroom inequities.

"We had to laugh, it was so typical," Myra said. "But Jackie knew what was going on. Most girls don't. It doesn't even reach a conscious level with them; they just stop trying."

It's not hard to imagine why many girls stop trying when they get less recognition for their academic accomplishments and abilities. When life in the classroom teaches our daughters that society pays much more attention to males, it's also easier to understand the drop in self-esteem our daughters suffer during adolescence.

Gender-equity efforts help schools and their staff overcome teaching patterns and institutional barriers that interfere with how both girls and boys learn. The good news is that most gender-equity solutions require an infusion of awareness and action more than they require an infusion of cash. That means many of the problems can be addressed with support and advocacy from parents and individual educators.

Many educators are responding with simple and effective strategies to the challenges of gender inequity in their classrooms. They observe one another's classroom techniques and feed back precise information about teacher-student interaction along gender lines. Parents can participate in the process, too, by encouraging classroom observation or volunteering to help do it. In some schools, students themselves have participated—gaining experience in the methods of social science field research while providing concrete information that the "observed" teachers use to constructively break down gender inequities.

Teacher behavior is not the only area to examine if we want to fully address gender inequities in schools. The educational materials that teachers and students use often tell a story we really don't want our daughters or our sons to hear.

Here's a simple exercise you can try next time you're at your daughter's school. Peek into a classroom. Take a close look at the posters, pictures, and articles you see on the walls. Borrow your daughter's social studies or history textbook and flip through the illustrations, chapter headings, and featured historical figures.

How many female names and images do you come across?

Do this exercise and you'll encounter a damaging attitude so prevalent that parents, kids, and educators just accept it as normal. That attitude says that half of the human race has accomplished virtually nothing worthy of a student's study in school. This is simply not true, and it's not the function of schools to teach untruths to boys or girls, even if they do it unconsciously.

A Hunger for Knowledge

Now that we have defined the problems, we can begin talking about the many ways a father can help his daughter make the most of her schooling. We can leverage our "first male" role in helping girls break out of traditional gender notions about education and career.

When she was ten or twelve, we had this father-daughter conversation where I told Julie that she could do anything she wanted to do, with one exception. I said you have my encouragement to

*participate in any kind of activity, but I don't want you to cheer
for boys' teams, I want you to be involved. She tested the limits of
that theory by being on a girls' dance line and they went to a
state tournament. She also went on a one-month Outward
Bound survival program absolutely on her own, not even with a
friend. She went to France to study economics, in French, at a
time when France was a socialist country. She is a really strong
and independent person. Her husband and I laugh and kid each
other because she is so strong. And I love it—I just love it.*

Bob

A father has a direct impact when he is vocal about his daughter's
academic and extracurricular activities. Even when our involvement
is as simple as asking our daughters about their schoolwork, they're
better off. Imagine the effect on the world if even a few more fathers got more engaged in their daughter's lives and schooling.

*I love doing her science projects with her, and encouraging her to
think about doing things on the computer. We've been doing a
project on how and why siphoning works. She had to come up
with a hypothesis, even though she didn't quite understand what
a hypothesis was. So we talked about it. "It's a guess, it's an educated guess. What do you think will happen, and why does it
work? 'The air pushes the water.' 'Okay, let's go prove it, or dis-
prove it. And then you revise it.' " We have fun doing those kinds
of projects. I absolutely enjoy science, and that's a lot of fun, par-
tially because I get to show off a little bit, too.*

Jerry

It feels good to show off what we know to our kids. When our
daughters see us excited and proud about our knowledge and skills
(no matter what they are), their own pride in learning is affirmed.
Whether fathers share knowledge they gained from work or hobbies, they seem to have a special ability to spark interest in daugh-

ters. This helps girls learn that they can handle the knowledge and skills needed to be an adult with responsibilities, careers, and hobbies.

> *I think my father has always given me a hunger for knowledge. He's taught me that no matter how far you go, you can always go a step farther in learning. He's taught me to look below the sur-face of people and situations and not just take a first glance and make a judgment. And I think that's helped me a lot as I've been traveling a lot around the world and meeting new people.*
>
> *Cynthia*

There are all kinds of ways to encourage this hunger for learning and new challenges. When his daughter Eve was a preteen, novelist Scott Turow wrote a mystery story with her that appeared in the book *Great Writers and Kids Write Mystery Stories* (Random House, 1996). The project sparked great excitement in Eve. A story she'd already begun while visiting her grandmother served as their mu-tual starting point. They ended up with what Eve called a half mys-tery, half magical tale. Scott and Eve battled over differences in writing style, age, and outlook, but worked through them to finish with an intense shared experience.

Our family often had wandering and wondering dinner conver-sations where, fueled by our daughters' natural curiosity, we'd end up unable to answer a question or two. I usually responded by look-ing the answers up in the encyclopedia. As a result, I am known around home as *the* encyclopedia guy. More nights than not, I'd jump up from the table and grab a volume to search out the fact in question, like "Which president had the most children?" (John Tyler had fifteen, eight with his first wife, Letitia Christian, who died in the second year of his presidency; and seven with Julia Gardiner, whom he married during his term's last year—the first president married while in office!) My daughters and I actually get excited about learning facts like this, and next thing we know, we're discussing ways to measure time, the size of Texas, the impact of television, and other topics beginning with the letter T.

This is fun and good for our relationship. It also reinforces a curiosity so strong that my daughters now get the encyclopedia out themselves at dinner. They're proud of this simple family tradition of learning, a tradition that challenges and stretches how they think about the present and the future. I believe that this simple encyclopedic activity helped lay a foundation for their current interest in history, social anthropology, journalism—and their desire to be eclectic, lifelong learners. They love studying a variety of things in college.

We have to be eclectic ourselves as we approach our daughters' learning. For example, you have to watch out for the way your own expectations may affect her desire to learn during her teen years. If you stay within "traditional" ideas about girls, you may expect that your daughter's adolescent school experience is mostly about boys, with little room for learning and achieving. In her study, "Smart Girls, Gifted Women," researcher Barbara Kerr quotes a woman describing how radically her father changed his tune when she entered adolescence.

> *Until I was in junior high, my dad was my best friend. We read together and played chess together. He was proud of my intelligence and he showed it. Then when I entered junior high, he began to show ambivalence toward my achievements. He still said "Great" when I got good grades, but he began asking me about boyfriends and praising me for looking pretty. Somehow this made me feel bad, but I never could express it. I was just frustrated with him and felt betrayed. He just wanted me to be like the other girls.* (Cited in Sadker and Sadker, *Failing at Fairness,* Scribners, 1994.)

Our daughters' social lives are important issues for fathers, as we've already seen. But be careful not to concentrate solely on one aspect of your daughters' lives, and thus limit your contribution to her academic growth.

When you focus on your daughter's intellectual or avocational achievements, she feels support and encouragement for her talents, while you can begin seeing a more balanced view of her entire life. At home, ask straightforward questions about school and extracurricular activities to start things rolling. Granted, you have to set aside time for these conversations, and your daughter may not always be in the most forthcoming mood. Just keep trying at every opportunity, whether it's during a quick trip to the store or over Sunday brunch.

I never did well in science classes, so I wasn't sure how to talk with my daughter Nia about a chemistry class she was taking a couple of years ago. But I tried with basic questions like, "What are you working on now?" Some days the answer was short: "Next Tuesday's test." One particular day, however, her answer ran more than an hour, as she started describing the atomic concepts she was learning. She even attempted to get me to understand. Although I haven't retained any of the information, I kept the memory of how her face glowed with eagerness as she demonstrated her mastery of the subject matter—and her pride that she knew something I didn't know.

Conversations like this stimulate your daughter's love of learning. When you start asking questions when she's young, you feed her natural curiosity. Paying attention to what sparks her imagination can draw out even more interests and confidence that she can achieve. Ask some successful women you know about fatherly influence. It's fascinating how many give a lot of credit for their accomplishments (in career and hobby) to the interest and encouragement they got from their fathers.

You convey that crucial interest and encouragement by participating in her academics and showing up for her other activities. That means helping with homework struggles and attending parent-teacher conferences. It means attending her concerts, games, exhibits, meets, demonstrations, performances, and all the milestones that mark the progress she's making in mastering skills. Sometimes, these events may not be your first choice of how to spend an evening or afternoon; I despised ballet when my daughters started taking it. I'm still not a huge fan, but I attended every recital for almost ten years, even though I did occasionally grumble about it under my breath. Your daughter needs you to make those relatively small sacrifices so that she learns how highly you value her interests and accomplishments. She gets the message that these things are important for *her*, as your questions and presence demonstrate that her academics and other activities are a priority for *you*.

Taking Initiative

Education is a key piece of her future strength, and an arena where we have plenty of influence. One father found that direct involvement in his daughter's education changed the whole course of her life.

When Robin Sadker was young, she loved to play with puzzles and numbers and did very well in grade school math. Before entering junior high, each child in her large suburban school system took standardized tests to help determine what "track" they'd be assigned to in junior high subject areas. When the results put Robin on a mid-level math track, her father David and her mother Myra didn't understand. They asked for an explanation, but were told that the tests determined the learning track, and in such a huge school district, administrators simply couldn't open the door to making exceptions. David and Myra asked for a meeting with school officials and, David says, "Even though we both had doctorates in education, I felt intimidated. They brought more doctorates to the conference than Myra and I had." The officials listened sympathetically, but reiterated their position. Then, David asked to see Robin's answer sheet from the test. Out came her file and, lo and behold, attached to the answer sheet was a note from the school nurse: "Robin wasn't feeling well and I took her to my office halfway through the test." Robin never made up the test and so she was graded for only half her answers—the answers she left blank were scored as incorrect and relegated her to a mid-level math track.

There was no malevolence at work here; in the best school systems, some details fall through the cracks. But David knew enough about his daughter's enthusiasm for math to know that something was wrong when a test scored her low on math skills. "If we hadn't gone in there and kept asking questions," David says, "she would have been bumped off the advanced math track in seventh grade and denied the chance to follow her passion for math and sciences." She also might not have found her way to her current career as a physician, which she sees as her life vocation. She is a doctor thanks, in a substantial degree, to her parents' sixth grade advocacy.

Fathers influence what happens at school in hundreds of other ways, too. Simple acts like reading to a daughter's class helps her and her classmates know how much they matter. Plus, it's fun.

I've made an effort to go on field trips with my daughter's class. And often times I'm one of only one or two dads. But I've always had a really good time doing that, because I get to see her in her element, and observe her, and mix with her friends. I get along with her friends pretty well. I think I always will because I have this joking way about doing things. I think I come across a little different than the average dad because I'll do physical goofy stuff. I'll make a jerk out of myself in front of them. And kids like that. "Oh, your Dad, he's so stupid!" That's the kind of stuff I like to hear!

Brian

The junior high school my daughters attended had never done a school play before. Since I love theater and used to do a lot of it, I signed on to direct a show—we even convinced a couple of teachers to perform, too. Mavis played a role in the play, Nia ran props, I got to work with many of their peers, and they got to see me respect, be creative, and have fun with their friends.

The National Coalition of Girls' Schools actively encourages fathers to take advantage of the impact they have in and around a school setting. Their material tells stories about dads like the engineer who tells his coworkers he's late for a dentist appointment, excuses himself from a client meeting, and rushes out to work with eighth grade girl scientists determined to build their own remote-controlled car for a regional technology contest.

Fathers matter to our daughters' education from its first days. At Hockaday Girls School kindergarten in Dallas, Texas, fathers in the "Dictation Dads" program write down stories that the girls tell. In a training session, dads learn to take dictation and encourage girls to express their thoughts without leading them. The girls can't write yet, but their fathers make them authors anyway—and many of the stories appear in the school's literary magazine.

These are a tiny sampling of the hundreds of ways you could get involved directly in your daughter's school. There are common threads in these examples—a father's participation and initiative in his daughter's school builds up her personal confidence. These fathers become good role models for every kid in the school. When men talk about their work, or share expertise gained in their field, they introduce girls to a wider range of career choices. When they share all this with girls, the girls get the message that these careers and talents are as possible for women as they are for men.

CHOOSING HER PATH

Even today, kids tend to divide up careers by gender stereotype. When I ask a classroom of young children to shout out the names of "jobs for boys" and "jobs for girls," the results are very predictable. Under the boys column go careers like pilot, President, pro-athlete, firefighter, police officer, doctor, engineer, and other jobs that have been traditionally male for generations. Particularly troubling is how seldom the boys' job list includes the word *father*. Under the girls column, the list will be shorter, and include the traditionally female jobs of nurse, mother, teacher, librarian, maid, and the like.

How can these career stereotypes still be prevalent in this more enlightened age? In part, because children's books, TV, and classrooms still regularly portray males in active, complicated, and high public responsibility jobs, while females are shown as passive or as caretakers. Family and cultural attitudes reinforce these out-of-date stereotypes, too. Little wonder if girls feel unsure about investing the drive or ambition to go for their dreams.

As the first male in our daughters' lives, we can step in and debunk these arbitrary limitations right from the start. Just like our willingness to take dictation can transform our little girls' imagination into published stories, so can the range of our work skills or hobbies become wonderful tools for our daughters. When that skill or hobby is a "nontraditional" one (for either girls or dads)—car repair, chess, cooking, cards, gardening, fishing, bicycling, archery, carpentry—our involvement carries the extra weight of conveying the message, "I don't care what 'convention' says about this, I'm your dad and I say we can do it!"

Our daughters need to feel our high level of interest and support as they begin to make big life decisions. This isn't easy during those adolescent times when they appear to tune us out or shut us down.

> *She's a teenager now, so I can't just go up to her anymore and say, "Let's talk about school," or "Let's talk about what you want to do next year." We need to block out some time when we can get into a conversation. She's good at a lot of things, so I ask about that: "How's the music going? Do you like Jazz Band? Do you want to continue that?" But she's not willing to share her feelings*

as openly as when she was younger. And frankly, I'm having a
little bit of trouble pulling it out. Because she can do pretty much
anything and be successful at it, I'm trying to understand what it
is that she really wants to do, so I can encourage her.

Willy

It can be hard for a dad to keep up with all of his daughter's interests. It can be hard for him to help his daughter juggle the growing list of extracurricular opportunities now open to girls—sports teams, sports camps, music groups, music camps, study abroad. But his bigger task is to encourage and support the interests that she does have.

Encouraging her interests and introducing her to new ones is a long-term investment that can pay unpredictable dividends. My daughter Nia describes it better than I can:

We always went to plays together, worked on tech stuff for plays,
and generally enjoyed all things theatrical. I'm studying costume
design in college, and when I worked on a play called Arcadia, *I*
called you and told you how wonderful it was, and how you
must read it and direct it if you ever get the chance. So you went
the very next day to find it at the library, and when you couldn't
find it, you read a synopsis and requested a copy through interli-
brary loan. All because I was excited and wanted to talk to you
about it.

Nia

You must believe and help your daughter (and son) believe that there are no activities and academic subjects that are just for boys, or just for girls. Encourage her to experiment and explore different activities—without regard for whether other people put those activities in the girls column or the boys column. Try to point out every example you can find of girls or women engaged in spheres dominated by males. Rather than making a big deal out of it, it's better if you cite your examples matter-of-factly. That sends your daughter the message that such a role model is entirely acceptable and welcomed—at least by you.

For example, I recently saw a news story about two girls playing varsity high school football in small towns near Duluth. One is a placekicker and the other plays offensive guard. The girls acknowledged that their choice was unusual, but they played anyway because they love football. The male coaches praised their talent and toughness. The girls projected confidence about themselves, and the coaches expressed confidence in the girls. It seemed clear that this confidence carried over into other aspects of their lives.

I've also seen this kind of physical and psychological confidence in my daughters and the other girls who took ballet with them. Ballet certainly goes in the "girls" column of activities. Ballet also demands specialized physical strength and skill along with great physical and emotional stamina—just like football does.

My point is this: a girl doesn't have to do traditionally "boy" stuff to develop confidence in her physicality, stamina, teamwork, artistry, and other skills. However, whatever her passion, she needs you to encourage and support it. When you drive her to practice, games, or recitals, you demonstrate an investment in her interests. When you call or e-mail to see how her afternoon game went, she has the opportunity to share her excitement or work out her disappointment with you. And, with the concrete evidence that dad is backing her up, she can step confidently out into the world of her future.

Eventually, our daughters start making choices among their various interests, and those choices can affect major life decisions, like whether or where to go to college. When Nia decided to go away to school, she knew exactly which college she wanted, and so only applied to that one. She didn't need a lot of guidance from me.

Mavis, on the other hand, considered several prospective schools and potential majors. Somehow or other, I became the help-pick-a-college parent. I cheered her on, reminding her about application deadlines and brainstorming admission essays. She decided on five campuses she wanted to visit, so I took two weeks off, and we hit the road to see them all.

The morning of her first visit and interview, Mavis was as tense as I'd seen her in years. After some gentle prodding as we drove toward the school, the dam of emotions broke. She was terrified of what the admission counselor would ask her and what people would think of her. She was sure that her experience, education, and qualifications wouldn't measure up. I kept driving as she let every doubt and fear gush forth.

I listened sympathetically, but also felt her words tap some fears of my own. I'll admit to selfish motives: I wanted Mavis to be a sought-after student so the light of her many accomplishments would reflect well on me. So, I had a little voice in my head also worrying what would happen if Mavis's colleges of choice turned her down. But as Mavis released her worries, I tried to set my smaller (and less important) ones aside.

I let her vent until it seemed she was done. Then, I began some gentle cheerleading. "I don't think it's very likely that they'll reject you. They were eager to adjust their schedule so you could visit this week." She seemed to agree with that, so I switched into a more joshing tone of voice: "On the other hand, what school would want a kid who has traveled overseas, helped start a national magazine, written chapters in a couple of books, and earned a bunch of tae kwon do belts?" Mavis delivered one of her patented over-the-top-of-her-glasses looks of annoyance, and then started laughing.

We didn't completely dissipate her nerves, but by the time we arrived on campus, her perspective was somewhat restored. While waiting for Mavis's admissions counselor to emerge, another admissions counselor came into the visiting area and chattered enthusiastically. "You're Mavis Gruver, aren't you? I know all about *New Moon* and I think it's great. I was so excited when I heard you were coming and I was hoping that I'd get to meet you in person. This is so cool!" Mavis was a little embarrassed by all the woman's gushing, but also looked proud—and no longer worried about whether this school was going to take her in (they did).

As I saw it, my job was to help Mavis keep her bearings, and keep her confidence afloat until she took over again and propelled herself to her destination.

Our fatherly support and attention foster confidence in—and can help other people in the family have confidence in—our daughters.

> *My stepfather Mark was talking to me about his father being disappointed in some decisions he made at my age. I'm making college decisions, and this is the first time when I'm going to go out on my own. I feel like I'm getting an immense amount of support from Mark, because he's making it clear that he trusts my judgment and won't have any reason to be disappointed. My mom and I are fighting here and there; Mom wants me to go to college, and I don't want to go right away. But I know that whenever I make my decision, everybody's going to support me— my mom, my real dad, and Mark. I don't feel like I'm going to get this feeling of secret disappointment from my parents because Mark knows what it felt like to get it from his dad.*
>
> Serena

Giving your support requires sharing your own experience and trusting your daughter's sense of self. That's really hard to do sometimes, especially when you can't clearly see where the path she chooses will lead. After all, even the best father cannot predict the future.

> *I want my daughters to be able to think about things and still be their own person, do what they want to do without always worrying about what parents want them to do. But we always let them know that choices come with responsibilities. And we've*

told them that if you're going to climb up the scale, you have to perform to a certain level of expectation, especially with school. The scary part is that I don't think they can really decide how to do their own thing until they've been away from home for a while. I think it takes them a few years to finally discover what they want to do and what makes them feel good. So I always try to influence them until that point. Sometimes I may get a little heavy-handed, but then I go back and think, "Well, I screwed up on this one," and I'll tell them when I feel like I've screwed up, so they can learn from it, too.

Jerry

It's important to keep the conversations going, even when you screw up or when your daughter isn't terribly communicative.

Your pride in your daughter's accomplishments acts as a powerful motivator for her. But try to share your accomplishments with her as well. When you do that, you open a new window for her. She sees how you use your interests, talents, and goals to enjoy your work and to overcome its rough spots. She feels you sharing something that's a big part of your life, and that can be a solid confidence booster. You might be surprised at the impression you make on her with your work ethic and parts of your job that seem quite ordinary—and how that impression can influence the way she approaches her adult careers.

TAKE OUR DAUGHTERS TO WORK

When I was a preteen, my father worked at a now-defunct Philadelphia department store called Lit Brothers. Dad was a buyer and had an office in among the stock shelves just off the sales floor. Once or twice a year, my older sisters and I would each get a day alone at work with him. He'd take me to lunch at Lit Brother's dining room; at age 9, linen napkins with my grilled cheese sandwich seemed like the height of elegance. I'd see the bright lights of the sales floor and the finely dressed saleswomen, then wander around the dim warren of shelving and desks in the windowless stockroom, feeling as though I was backstage at an elaborate theatrical production.

I doubt my father thought his job had any resemblance to Broadway, but it did in my childhood eyes. Those memories are vivid because, when he took me to work with him, my father gave me a glimpse into what he did all day and where he spent so much of his energy and creativity—something I couldn't see otherwise.

I tried to carry that tradition on as a father. My daughters still remember their visits to the radio station where I worked when they were young. They loved seeing all the gear and gizmos that made it possible for them to hear their father's voice come out of the radio in the morning while they ate their cereal.

Our daughters always had glimpses of our work, some more intense than others. At Nancy's old job, the girls volunteered every year at a Senior Citizens' Expo. They were deeply involved in creating *New Moon* magazine, a family-run business. Anyone who has been in or around a family business knows how consuming it is and what passion it requires. As girls, our daughters consistently saw the effort, energy, and excitement needed for—and generated by—our jobs. We didn't hide it.

Now that my daughters are young women, I see a similar passion in their commitment to college and campus volunteering. Because they got to see how their parents work, they accept passionate commitment as normal adult behavior and recognize its rewards—and some of its liabilities.

Several researchers have found that successful career women had a strong girlhood interest in their father's work. The key wasn't what kind of work the fathers did, but that they talked about that work with their daughters. Since a father is so important in a daughter's life, any insight he shares about what's important to him carries special power.

Psychologist and researcher Lise Motherwell interviewed women whose fathers were creative and committed scientists, artists, or writers.

There was something important about knowing that their fathers could feel so strongly about something. They wanted [more of that energy] directed at them, but they also wanted to know how they could feel that way in their own lives. The idea that they could feel passionate about work, and not just about people, was very powerful. It opens up new possibilities for girls.

In addition to sharing our work with our daughters, we need to pay attention to our daughters' work, even in the days before they're old enough to be paid for their efforts. For example, if our daughters help out with younger cousins or neighborhood kids at a family reunion, they will beam when we thank them for the help, ask them about how it went, and help them figure out how to make things even more fun next time. When fathers provide encouragement for their daughters' paper routes, baby-sitting, and other kid jobs, it reinforces the power and excitement of their own "work."

Once we're aware of how vital work is going to be for the rest of our daughters' lives, we'll start seeing learning opportunities pop up everywhere.

Anna was having a birthday party with some of her girl friends. It was getting close to fishing season, and I had been looking for night crawlers in the backyard. The sun was going down and the girls were still here, and I said, "It's raining. That's a good time for night crawlers to be out." So I took the girls in the backyard. It wasn't really dark yet, but because it was raining, the crawlers had already started to come out. And I showed them how they needed to sneak up and grab, and really needed to hold on. They experimented, and they got better and better. And pretty soon they were all excited, and they just started collecting night crawlers left and right. Then we stuck them in the refrigerator, much to their mother's dismay. The next morning was opening day of the fishing season. They loaded up all these night crawlers in Styrofoam containers, put them in the little red wagon, headed down to the main drag, and set up their stand, yelling, "Night crawlers!"

Russ

It's great when those opportunities break through stereotypes about "what a girl is supposed to do." A girl who collects night crawlers (and has a father who doesn't discourage her just because worms are squishy) stands a better chance of meeting other challenges.

Of course, no one can make a career out of selling worms on the street corner. Life will be more complicated than that, and a woman with a career faces substantial challenges along the road.

I do know that since having a daughter, I have a lot more respect for what jobs women perform in our society. When I was younger, I didn't pay much attention to that. I'm also very aware that women make less money, have less respect in the corporate world today. I think that's probably where the big change in my awareness is.

Jeff

That awareness provides a special perspective for us both at work and at home. When we imagine our daughter employed at our workplace, we have a lot less tolerance for the difficulties women encounter on the job.

Women often view the workplace as a place with significant potential for danger and injustice—for good reason. Women are targets of sexual harassment and workplace violence more often than men. Women continue to be systematically paid less than men for equal work. Women continue to be scarce in higher echelons of management—at the current rate of "progress," it will take centuries before the number of female Fortune 500 CEOs even approaches the number of males. There are still very few employers who recognize the psychological, familial, and social benefits of parents and stepparents being involved with their families. Putting our daughters' faces in these scenarios can motivate us to make our workplaces more respectful and supportive for women.

COMPOUNDING OUR INTEREST

When our daughters have careers (and even before then), they will earn money. Money doesn't have a gender, but it does come with the responsibility to manage it. No woman should be dependent on a husband, boyfriend, or anyone else to deal with money—the very same money she will help earn and which will help keep her and her family functioning.

The importance of girls managing money gains urgency in light of some important facts. The age at which people marry has steadily risen over the last few decades, increasing the odds that young women spend their early adulthood living independently. Many marriages end in divorce, and single mothers with children are the population most likely to slip into poverty. Even if they remain married, women are substantially more likely to outlive their spouses. Nearly all adult women in the United States are employed in paying jobs for substantial periods of their lives. These are all concrete reasons for us to start talking money with our daughters.

My husband and I got married the summer after high school and we were able to buy a small house in the country the next year. Once we got into the process with the bank, I got kind of angry. Nobody had ever told me what a mortgage was or what compound interest is. I'm the assistant manager of a hardware store; I'm not stupid. Why didn't my father ever talk to me about stuff like this? Why didn't our high school take a couple of hours and explain it to us before graduating us out into jobs? I mean, how hard is that to teach?

Mary

It's not very hard to teach. A few simple financial concepts can go a long way: *Don't spend more than you earn. Don't pay 18 percent interest on a credit card if you can pay off the balance every month instead.* But what I find interesting is this young woman's question, "Why didn't *my father* ever talk to me about stuff like this?" I think children look to their fathers for knowledge about money and career because cultural stereotypes say those topics are within the man's realm. There's a good side to this gender stereotype—the world of work and money is a big part of our cultural heritage as men, so we're in an excellent position to share what we know with our daughters. For better or worse, we're the first ones they're likely to ask.

Money is a loaded topic for many of us. Still, we have to turn away from any fear and emotion money may generate, and not leave girls in the dark. When our daughters were ten, we decided they were old enough to start learning simple lessons about managing money. Neither Nancy nor I had a very good handle on that skill until we were adults, so we figured if the girls started young, they'd be ahead of the game. We started with what we saw as the basics; I took them to our local bank to open their own checking accounts. I had no idea how strange some people thought this idea was—including the woman at the bank.

"Of course," she told me, "children under eighteen can't have a checking account unless a parent's name is also on the account."

"Yes," I replied, "I was planning to be the joint account holder."

"OK, but I still don't know; they're only ten. We've never had someone that young with a checking account."

"Is there some rule against a ten-year-old having one?"

"No, but I still don't know if we can do it."

We went round and round some more (and I got more feisty) until the banker finally went along, but not without many more doubtful looks.

I was surprised by other people's resistance to something as simple as opening a checking account for a ten-year-old girl. But basic money management is a skill too important to be derailed by someone else's preconception that little girls shouldn't worry their pretty little heads about money. Plus, most girls are able to handle the responsibility well if we're there to answer questions and explain the process.

From age ten on, my daughters handled their own income and expenses. Allowance, baby-sitting earnings, gift money, wages, quarters found on the sidewalk—it all went into the checking account. Nancy and I no longer paid for amusements or gifts for friends and family. We gave them a clothing allowance by age twelve, and put them in charge (making visits to Target more attractive than pricier stores). Even though they were young, the girls quickly adapted to the arrangement and we seldom heard them complain about it. They didn't spend much on themselves. They preferred, for example, to wait for birthdays to get clothes from grandparents and other relatives—a smart strategy, I always thought. Their only complaint was over the weird looks salesclerks gave when a twelve-year-old pulled out her checkbook. But because my daughters' money added up in the till just the same as an adult's, the clerks always found a way to take the check in the end. If a cashier needed a driver's license number on the check, Nancy or I would provide ours.

Now, as young adults, our daughters are still fairly frugal. They're using some of the money they saved during childhood to help pay for college. They are much less intimidated by and much more responsible about money than I was in my twenties. Given the careers they're currently considering (journalism and costume design), they will probably spend at least part of their adult lives with relatively low incomes. They don't seem too concerned about that and, to be honest, neither am I. I share their confidence in their ability to manage money because they've spent more than half their lives doing it for themselves.

Many other simple opportunities to teach girls about money come along to fathers every day.

> *I heard somebody talking about explaining the utility bill to his kid, and that gave me the idea of having her sit with me while I pay the bills on Saturday. I talk to her about what the bills are, and we get into conversations about how the city figures out how much water we're using and what a cubic foot is and things like that. I had to laugh because when she asked me how they measure a cubic foot of water when the water pipe is round, I didn't know! But I just talk about it with her and sometimes I've let her fill out the checks. I tell her why I pay some bills right away and hold off on others. It's just time we spend together and I think she's learning something. I think it makes money seem like it's less scary, not the big monster everyone makes it out to be.*
>
> *Chet*

Money doesn't have to be a monster. It's a tool. Just like a power saw or a pipe wrench, it's a tool we need to teach both our daughters and sons how to use safely.

There are many good ways to do this. The girls who created the book *New Moon: Money* (Crown, 2000) came up with dozens of examples, like a simple budget sheet for a proposed girl-run cupcake-decorating operation. A list adding up one-time and ongoing costs (which includes the important step of assigning a value to the girl's time) helps determine the volume of cupcakes and unit price needed to generate a profit. This one-page exercise teaches essential business concepts in a way anyone can understand.

Money management helps make it possible for our daughters to succeed in life. Money can help them fulfill dreams. It can keep them and their families sheltered and fed. It can help them live their values through philanthropy, political contributions, and donations to other causes and organizations.

In other words, money can give our daughters power, something every good dad wants for his girl. But having a career and earning money are not the only ways that our daughters can turn their education, work, and values into power and influence.

GIRL POWER

We want our daughters to have a good education, fulfilling careers, and well-managed checking accounts. But both of us have to remember that these are only tools, vehicles through which our daughters can apply their incredible power and creativity.

A couple of years ago, we found that my elderly mother could no longer live alone. My sister and brother-in-law began adding a handicap-accessible room onto their house for Mom, but it would be months before it was done. So my daughter Mavis announced, "I want to go live with Grandma until Uncle David finishes the addition. All of you grown-ups have full-time jobs, and I have more flexibility to do this."

I wasn't sure it was a wise idea. We'd always encouraged Mavis's volunteer spirit, but I didn't want her to sacrifice her own goals just because someone else was in need—something I feel women already do too often. But she went and spent the summer sleeping on the floor of Grandma's small apartment, cooking, taking her shopping, for walks, and to the doctor. Sure, Mavis was sometimes frustrated and emotionally stifled sharing a small space with a seventy-three-year-old, in a town where she knew no one her own age. But she was not denying herself. Clearly, she'd made the choice with her eyes wide open and from the best parts of who she is.

Mavis was putting her independence, strength, and values into powerful, effective action. Notice that money isn't on the list of tools she used. If money is power, then it's only one kind of power.

Girls of every age have force, ideas, and passion to share. They have Girl Power. Girl Power doesn't revolve around the money girls may have and their influence as consumers. It doesn't require status or stellar grades. Girl Power springs from a strong voice, concern for others, and love of fairness.

Using Girl Power, girls push to make things better for less fortunate people, protect the environment, and build community among their peers and in their neighborhoods. Girl Power propels girls forward to find new talents to use and new causes to fight. Girl Power refuses to let our culture silence girls or put girls—or boys— in suffocating gender straitjackets.

Make no mistake, it's risky for girls to fully use the power they hold within. The world may respond with threats or ridicule. It's also often uncomfortable to live with Girl Power's uncompromising commitment to doing the right thing. Fathers may be challenged on the compromises we've made in our lives. But Girl Power also reveals vibrant courage and imagination shining through our daughters' lives.

As fathers, we shape our daughters and their attitude toward life. So, when we help our daughters take risks, dream large, and overcome barriers, we help them tap into their Girl Power. In the end, Girl Power is the antidote to the troubles girls face today. So, we know we've fathered successful daughters when they celebrate their Girl Power and strive to be what Girls, Incorporated, calls "strong, smart and bold."

And, reflected in the light Girl Power shines on the world, we fathers can find proof that we have those same qualities of courage, strength, and imagination within ourselves.

TOOLS

SCHOOL INVOLVEMENT

School opens up a whole new area of dialogue for the two of you. Be willing to discuss, intervene if appropriate, or assist if she is having difficulty at school, either academically or socially. Here are just a few of the many ways you can get involved:

- Lead nature walks for science class.
- Referee on field day.
- Chaperone trips to the zoo or museum.
- Read aloud to the class on story day.
- Be an after-school tutor.
- Offer to teach skills from your field of work or interests.
- Start an after-school book club or community service club.
- Meet your daughter's teachers.
- Volunteer to be an in-class assistant.
- Sign up to be a student mentor.
- Help with homework.
- Host a safe prom night party.
- Keep a file of her schoolwork at home.
- Inform teachers about any concerns or specific goals you have before an upcoming school year.
- Host a field trip at your workplace.
- Plant flowers in the school yard with your daughter's class.
- Help out in the school library.

HOMEWORK HELPER

Homework is part of your daughter's life. If you make it a part of your life, too, it can pay dividends for both of you. She gets support with problem areas and the chance to exchange ideas and questions with a good listener. You get the chance to spend valuable, productive, high-quality time with your daughter, watch her learning—and brush up on Shakespeare, too!

Here are few ways to help your daughter's homework:

- Set aside a homework time, making sure it is the same each day so she gets into a routine and gets her work done.
- Let your daughter study in whatever ways work best for her, even if it means she listens to music while working. Different study techniques are good for different people. Obviously, if the work doesn't get done when the music's on or she's curled up in a mound of pillows rather than at her desk, then talk about these habits with her.
- *Don't* do the homework yourself! Just offer your assistance and a sympathetic ear. If you cover for your daughter, then you, she, and the teachers miss opportunities to help her learn how to solve the problems.
- Be patient. Pay attention to what she says, and try to understand how her mind works. Show her respect when sitting down to help her with a school assignment or project, especially if she's having trouble with it.
- Initiate conversations about what your daughter is learning in school or something in the news that relates to her studies. Listen to her views, her opinions; get to know her values, her ideologies, her personality. You will both be stimulated by these conversations. They will also help your daughter to think about important issues, and build the confidence she needs to form and voice her own opinions.

CAREER FANTASY

If, at age ten, your daughter loudly announces, "I'm going to be a teacher when I grow up," don't be surprised if she ends up a fire-fighter or a lawyer. The specific careers she wants to pursue as a kid are less important than the fact that she imagines and pre-tends about having a career.

So, if your daughter wonders early on about her interests and talents, don't get stuck "holding her to" the ideas she generates. Imagining careers is her "practice" for the time when she starts to make real-life decisions—her own decisions—about where she wants to go in life. Talk about the importance of choosing an occu-pation that makes her happy and fulfilled, and that maximizes her potential. Ask your daughter to make a list, just for fun, of possible careers: those she could actually see herself pursuing, those in which she has interest, or those to which she thinks she might be well suited. Ask her to be creative and to think outside the box. The two of you might even take a personality or interest inventory test (you can find them online or in a bookstore) to see what it has to say about your respective personality types and career matches. Here are some occupational ideas to brainstorm, just for starters:

Actor	Doctor
Architect	EMS technician
Artist	Engineer
Banker	Entrepreneur
Biologist	Environmentalist
Chef	Farmer
Chemist	Firefighter
Computer programmer	Geologist
Dancer	Government official
Director	Interior designer

International relations

Inventor

Investment broker

Law enforcement

Lawyer

Military officer

Nonprofit organizer

Nurse

Outdoor instructor

Photographer

Pilot

Playwright

Politician

Psychologist/Psychiatrist

Public Relations

Publisher

Retailer

Scientist, Researcher

Ship captain

Singer

Social worker

Special education

Teacher

Tour guide, Traveler

Travel agent

Web Page Designer

Writer, Journalist

8.

"HOW OLD ARE YOUR DAUGHTERS?": IN THE COMPANY OF FATHERS

She's my connection to eternity. It's like being born twice.

Luther

LEARNING FROM DADS

Nearly every father I spoke to for this book went on at length about how important his daughter is to him; how much he has learned; how much he's been changed; and how much he worries whether he's getting this fathering thing right.

However, most of the fathers I interviewed also said that their conversation with me (a stranger) was the first time they'd ever talked directly to anyone about being a dad. This tended to be true even for active and involved dads.

> *Rarely do I talk to other fathers, period. I mean, unless I'm talking about business, like community projects. All of my community projects are actually for kids; I'm motivated by how much my own kids matter to me. But even those business and community project conversations are pretty distant.*
>
> *Jim*

Of those dads who said they do talk to someone else about being a dad, most cite only one person: the mother of their children. Very few talk to other fathers—even their own fathers.

Given how little practice these dads seemed to have, many incredible things gushed out when they let loose and started talking to me: insight, humor, affection, understanding, and deep commitment to their children—even in the toughest circumstances. Very few fathers held back when this opportunity to speak (in the form of an itinerant interviewer) came along. What they had to say could easily fill a twenty-six-volume encyclopedia. We really have wisdom to share with each other about real issues facing fathers.

If fathering is so essential to all of these dads, why do only a handful of them share their experience and worries with another father? Why do we keep something this important so hidden and silent? It's not as though the other dads we know have nothing to offer. Even the newest rookie dad has knowledge and inspiration to share.

> *I had no sense of how exhausting it could be, between the sleepless nights and my work. I could not believe what you would do to be able to sleep! I also had no idea how wonderfully fun and rewarding it was. I could sit, from the time she was a baby, and play with her for hours, just watch her and talk to her, and stare at her. I still think that's the most amazing thing I've ever encountered in my life. As a reporter, I've interviewed presidents, and been on network TV. But still, the most amazing thing was watching her head come out. And the second most amazing was*

watching her sister be born. I was just struck by how all-encompassing fatherhood was for me, and continues to be.

Larry

Every one of us can tell a story—or ten—like this. Get two or three fathers together, and you've got an encyclopedia of fathering information. We've got a World Book of fathers all around us every day. But how do we open that volume? Each one of us has many experiences, doubts, feelings, joys, questions, and perspectives that are valuable for other dads. Even if we don't have an ironclad solution to a problem for our neighbor, daughter's stepfather, brother-in-law, coworker, or friend, we can provide assurance that, as a father, he's not alone.

Father-to-father conversations can give us a sounding board, advice, alternative viewpoints, a sense of belonging, and other benefits. Still, not many of us engage. Those dads who do indulge recognize how much it helps to have another father's perspective or, at the very least, to know that someone else has gone down this road before.

Jim is an interesting guy—he looks for as much information from me as possible. I give him what I can; some raw data to analyze, a second opinion, a different point of view. I think sometimes men have tunnel vision—they see it their way and that is the way it is. Sometimes you get a second man with a little different perspective on things and that is good.

Tony

So how do we introduce conversations about fathering?

Men's Groups

One of the best rituals that I've got is this group of guys I jog with. I know them, and I know their kids, and they know my kids. And so in the course of an hour's run on Sunday mornings, we will go through whatever is happening. Somebody will say, "Here's what my kids are doing," and ask for feedback. It was not hard at all to start talking. After so many miles, we found each other willing to talk about issues that are personal to us.

Jamal

For a lot of us, we have to be doing something else before we feel ready to start talking about our kids. A jog, card game, yard project, round of golf, or any number of other "guy" activities can serve as safe places for us to jump in. For others, a more formal, organized setting dedicated specifically to talking about raising daughters works.

I go to a men's group once a week. It's not a drumming, running naked through the woods group. We work on breaking through to emotional honesty in a safe and supportive environment. That's been real good. I've been going for five years now. I find that it's really helpful for figuring out how I want to be a father.

Mike

Whenever I mention men's groups, there's at least one guy who rolls his eyes or makes a wisecrack. Men's groups have a bad reputation with many men; they're considered weird, bizarre, creepy, or just ridiculous. There are probably men's groups that are all of those things. But that doesn't mean every men's group is. It doesn't mean that it's against the law for you and me to start up groups with our own rules; and it's also no excuse for staying silent about our fathering.

A big part of the problem is that there simply aren't enough men's groups or fathering groups out there. The smaller the number of groups, the smaller the variety, and the fewer chances for a dad to find a group where he'll feel comfortable talking and listening. Somebody must be responsible for this shortage. That somebody is me and you. It looks like we've been too afraid to take the risk and do the work to get what we need from one another.

Dr. Steve Bergman, psychiatrist at Harvard Medical School and Wellesley College's Stone Center Gender Relations Project, is a father who has tried to follow the example of the Women's Movement, which began with small support, or "consciousness-raising" groups. Those groups generated innovative thinking about women's roles in our culture. Bergman (among others) thought, Why couldn't men do the same?

When his daughter was five, Steve noticed several other fifty-year-old fathers at her preschool, and invited them to start up what he called an "Old Farts Group" to talk about being an older father of young kids. Things started with promise, but then Steve hosted a meeting where all the guys had an excuse for not coming. The one fellow who hadn't left town said he couldn't get a sitter, so Steve invited him to bring his daughter over and they'd share child care. He said OK, but never showed up.

It's hard to sustain a group of men who gather for something other than camping, skydiving, and the like. Our unwillingness to share our fatherhood in groups is a huge problem for fathers and all men. Steve and many other people studying manhood in America think it will take a kind of cultural movement to loosen the male gender straitjacket and undo fathers' status as second-class parents. "The solution in any historical movement is small groups that then merge and produce writers, speakers, etc.," Steve says. "We have to be honest: so far, we can't sustain the groups."

I think we haven't formed or sustained groups because we are afraid. It takes courage to admit we don't know everything and to ask other fathers for help. It takes leadership to keep the conversation going even when other fathers are too "busy" to participate.

For the last couple of years, I've belonged to a book group made up of a half dozen men whom I don't know all that well. An acquaintance invited me at the start and, for my part, I invited the father of a young woman I'd worked with—an interesting guy I wanted to get to know better. There's a business consultant, a naturalist/teacher, a psychiatrist, a city planner, and a man who manages the office of his chiropractor wife. We try to meet once a month, and each man has the chance to pick a book twice a year. Not everyone makes every meeting—I'm one of the worst offenders. About half the time, the meeting date that works for everyone else falls on a day that I'm traveling for work. But the group keeps going.

We've discussed novels, a collection of environmental essays, a memoir about sailing to Greenland, and even a volume of poetry. These are all pretty safe topics and, while no one has revealed any deep, dark secrets, we really enjoy each other's company. Recently, I tried to push the envelope a bit by picking Will Glennon's *The Collected Wisdom of Fathers: Creating Loving Bonds That Last a Lifetime* (Conari Press, 2002) as our book of the month. I figured even the one group member without kids could relate, because he does have a father.

The night we got together to discuss *Fathering*, I thought the conversation got off to a slow start. It seemed like there was more off-the-topic small talk than usual, and a couple of the guys didn't seem as enthusiastic about the book as I was. The guy with no kids didn't show up, and the rest of us talked about our own kids. But it seemed to me as if we only talked about them a little bit, and only after prodding each other with plenty of questions.

When the group broke up for the evening, I felt slightly disappointed. I had hoped that, since we'd grown comfortable with each other over the previous year, we might be ready to use our fathering experience to jump into a deeper level of conversation. I didn't feel as though that hope was fulfilled as much as I wanted.

The next day, however, I got a phone call and two e-mails from three of the guys thanking me for the topic and saying it was the best book group meeting we'd had yet. They were excited and stimulated by a conversation that I saw as halting and uncertain. They've mentioned several times since how much they enjoyed the discussion, even though they weren't ga-ga over the book. I learned something important here.

I have to set aside some of my expectations when sitting down to talk fathering with another dad. What I think is irrelevant might be central for him; a conversation I find stumbling and disjointed might be the first time he's ever spoken to another father about being a dad—and those words might amount to great eloquence for him. It turns out that our book group's halting discussion on fathering had laid a foundation for more interesting and personal talk down the road. It's slow going, but it's progress.

It matters less what form a fathering "group" takes than that we start talking to someone beside ourselves about being a father. Two dads willing to talk and listen to each other amounts to a group—and it's a good start. We have a thing or two to learn from the fathers who are already doing the most talking: divorced dads and stepfathers.

LIVE-AWAY DADS

Lots of us are divorced or otherwise separated from our children. But live-away dads* who stay involved with their kids may be the best mentors any father can find. Live-away dads are pioneers in how to be an intentional father.

My biggest surprise about divorce is the way I spend time with my daughter now; it's incredible and completely unexpected. When I was married, I worked a lot, and I didn't spend very much time at home. Being divorced, I now have these regular

---

*"Live-Away Dads" is the term used by William Klatte in his book of the same name (Penguin, 1999), the best resource available for a man whose family is breaking up. It's more positive than noncustodial father (which implies that kids are property) and covers men who are divorced, men never legally married, and men in a host of other situations where they live in a different home than their kids, but still remain a big part of their kids' lives.

days in the week to be with my daughter. I have lots more time with her now than I did when we were living together, which isn't at all what I expected, and it really made me realize how stupid it was not to spend more time with her when I was living there. Like my work was more important than my daughter? It's ridiculous. I know there are times it bugs my ex to see me more committed to our daughter now than I was then, and I can see why she'd feel that way. But now, I schedule time with her and I'm concentrating just on her. It's like I have to really be a father on purpose now.

Paul

This dad's story struck a strong chord for me. It made me realize how often I took it for granted that my daughters would be around when I got home from work or a trip. I took it for granted that I could go do something special with one of my daughters whenever I wanted—even though I seldom went and did something special as often as I could have.

Divorce is a terrible fire to pass through in order to understand the rewards of concentrating on our kids. But every father can learn from live-away dads who stay actively and constructively involved with their kids.

There was so much that was so hard about this divorce, it's hard to pick one thing. You have a "Brady Bunch" mentality whether you want to or not, and to lose that notion of family was very difficult for me. What helped me through it was how I dealt with my children. I remember the anxieties I had, and realize how good my relationship is with my daughters, how good friends we've become, and how much we share about life, our goals, and hurdles. I realized that if I just spend time, good time, with my daughters, and I'm a responsible role model, that it all comes back in spades.

Billy

Whether living with or away from our kids, the building blocks for a strong father-daughter relationship are the same: making time, paying attention, thoughtfully living out our intentions, being a father on purpose. But live-away dads and stepdads often understand this more clearly than other fathers. In order to keep the relationship alive, they *have* to make time and pay closer attention to their daughters.

The activity that live-away dads tend to do more often than live-with dads is perhaps the most important and revealing—talking honestly with their daughters. The following conversation between a California live-away dad and his twelve-year-old daughter was one of the most moving I heard during the interviews I did for this book.

> *FATHER: The most painful thing that's ever happened to me in our relationship happens once every week—Sunday night when you leave to go back to your mom's. I mean, I just cry; I'm really grieving.*
>
> *DAUGHTER: You cry?*
>
> *FATHER: Yes.*
>
> *DAUGHTER: I never knew that. I try not to show it, but I'm really, really sad when I leave Mom's to come here, and when I leave here to go home to Mom. It's very hard. I'm just sad to leave either one of you. I guess I grieve, too, but it happens to me twice a week.*
>
> *FATHER: You do? I didn't know that! Yeah, it makes sense that you would feel that going both ways. Boy, it's so obvious, but I never really realized it before. I'm sorry. I'm so glad we're talking about this.*

This short exchange brought tears to both father and daughter; they reached out and hugged each other tightly. Clearly, sharing this "secret" about their sadness strengthened the bond between them.

There was little doubt that this new awareness would positively influence their understanding of each other, especially during those weekly transitions between Mom's house and Dad's house.

The breakup of an intimate relationship, like a marriage, is often caused by a breakdown in communication. Paradoxically, the more we pay attention to our kids and make specific time to talk to them (as live-away dads must do), the more our kids will communicate with us, feel close to us, and feel they can trust us. Another paradox is that the best divorces are the ones where both *parents* communicate about what's best for their kids.

> *I am a divorced father who shares all the responsibilities for raising my two daughters with my ex-wife. The relationship between LEW (lovely ex wife) and me is much better now that we are divorced. We could not live together. It is much healthier for both my daughters as well.*
>
> *Sam*

When I hear a live-away dad talk about building relationships with his ex and his children, I'm always struck by how relevant his words are for me, a man who lived with his children in an "intact" family. Maybe that's because so many of the issues are the same for both of us. What are the most important things to do for our daughters when we don't live with them anymore?

- Support her close relationship with all of her parents and stepparents.
- Don't play her off against her mother (or stepparents).
- Communicate with her mother (and stepparents).
- The more you stay involved in child rearing, the better off every family member is.
- Give her loving support, clear limits, and regular routine.
- Remember, girls learn how to relate to men through their fathers. That means you.

I'm not divorced, but all of these concepts are crucial for me, too, as a live-*with* father.

It may be that live-away dads and stepfathers are our best teachers because these are the men most likely to *say something*. It's awfully hard to learn from or listen to dads if no one is speaking. Stepdads and live-away dads are much more likely to talk with one another about their situations. It's as if we fathers have to go through great crisis and difficulty before we'll let go of our "pride" and unlock our tongue to talk to another dad about being a dad.

> *Being a stepfather has been important work for me. One of the hard lessons is that I'm not nearly as together as I thought I was. I think having a stepdaughter allows one to see—you can't hide. You see all aspects of yourself. Not just the good things, but the things that you wish weren't the way they were. My stepdaughter keeps giving me invitations to work on things and to become a better person. It's been good, but it's also hard. It's intense. I have to work to stay present. Most of the men I know have lots of places to hide, whether it's reading or watching TV. They just take themselves out, even if they're standing right next to you. My stepdaughter is pretty good at calling me on that.*
>
> *Mark*

It's good to have supportive daughters who call us on hiding out or being dishonest. But we shouldn't rely exclusively on our kids to teach us important lessons about fatherhood—we also need to learn from other fathers.

The commitment, bond, and communication among involved live-away dads and stepdads is a fabulous example for every one of us. Our challenge is: don't wait for the family roof to cave in before examining our priorities, fathering on purpose, and talking with other dads. Nearly every one of us wants to learn about being a better dad. That means that we have to start talking to each other and building the kinds of common bonds on which stepdads and live-away dads come to rely.

UNCHARTED TERRITORY: EMOTIONS

What keeps so many of us from forming that bond? We're afraid. We don't want to open our mouths and say something stupid, or something that makes us look stupid. We don't want to expose our uncertainties and ourselves—we want to act like we know it all. We're afraid of venturing into emotional territory.

Fathering is emotional territory. There's no getting around it. There's also no getting around the near certainty that—because few men grow up feeling at home in emotional territory—we're likely to stumble along our way. We'll get lost or at least feel lost. The directions and our destination won't always be clear. Having daughters can help us learn about and identify our emotions. Communicating this to other fathers can deepen, cement, and affirm the process. We may get more emotional than we want to be, and start to choke up in front of our friends and then be embarrassed about what they'll think of us.

If our friends are honest men concerned about being good fathers, they'll probably think we are brave to bare our softer sides. They may be initially taken aback, but probably not for long.

I was at a conference in Milwaukee a couple of summers ago when I met a guy from the East Coast who has three kids. One evening was dinner on your own and I suggested to Steve that the two of us get our meal at the soon-to-be-demolished Milwaukee County Stadium. As usual, with the perennially hapless Brewers, there were many good seats. We got our bratwurst and settled in. Before the first inning was over, Steve and I were talking about our kids. I talked about how hard it was to "let go" of my daughters now that they were moving away from home, and especially letting go of my role as the daddy that my girls depended on for everything. Steve talked about the excitement and trials of raising his two sons through adolescence and the awe he had for his preteen daughter's openness, insight, and eagerness to express her opinions.

For the rest of the game, only a slick fielding play or a home run interrupted the conversation. That was one of the most enjoyable and memorable nights of my fatherhood because I'd found another guy eager and open to talk about his life as a dad.

Find a father you trust and stick your toe into the conversational waters. Try it at the ballpark, basketball court, watercooler, bowling alley, or swimming pool. You can always pull your toe back out quickly if you want. Sure, it's unfamiliar water, but you won't drown. With practice, those conversations will grow a bit wider and deeper. Over time, you may develop a friend or two whom you can turn to when fathering seems particularly hard and uncertain. You can share the excitement and fun of fathering, too. It takes time to build that kind of father-friendship, so be patiently persistent. It's worth it.

HER GIFT TO YOU

Having daughters provides countless opportunities to widen our notion of what it means to be a successful man. Our daughters bring out what many dads call their "feminine side." That's the "side" where life with a daughter stirs up a father's intense and unaccustomed feelings of longing, love, fear, incompetence, affection, and other emotions usually considered "unmanly." Often, we get disturbed and confused by all this turmoil. We feel weak or stupid or like failures. After all, children furnish daily reminders of our fallibility.

> *One time I had a piece of sheet metal in the back of my Suburban. When I turned my back, the thing rolled and cut her leg open. It wasn't bad, but the bleeding on a shin is tremendous.*

And it was the worst feeling in my life. I felt like I was a complete and utter failure. I felt so dumb to let her get hurt like that; it was a low point in my life. "You're worthless, you're horrible, you're stupid," it just avalanched on top of me. We handled it, and she was fine, even though there was this "it shouldn't have happened" component to it. But I think that's okay. It's okay to feel bad about it. That stuff happens.

Randy

Stuff does happen to us when we raise daughters; much of it is unfamiliar. When the unfamiliar happens, many of us hunker down, silently removing ourselves a safe and remote distance from the situation or feelings. Others of us lash out in a rage because we feel outnumbered, and don't know what's going on or how to explain it. These are patterns we learned as boys about how "real men" respond to difficulty and danger.

Raising a daughter is unmapped territory for a father. But it's territory where there's no use for running away or stomping angrily around in circles. In daughter territory, we learn that we lose none of our true masculinity when our daughters draw out our "feminine side." When my daughter Nia, after eleven years of training, danced a lead part in a ballet, I sat in the darkened auditorium feeling chills, my eyes filling with tears. I was choked up with love, pride, and awe at her amazing passion, emotion, and determination. My own emotions welled up within me, catching me by surprise. After all, I'd proudly observed other displays of Nia's talents and I knew I was going to feel proud watching her that night.

But the intensity and suddenness of my tears was, at first, disturbing. As a man, I'm used to having greater control over my emotions. But as the power of the moment continued, I realized that these new feelings were exactly what I wanted to feel as Nia's father. She drew those emotions out of me, and that brought me closer to her. Being a father means being a man, and being a father means tapping deep and sometimes unfamiliar springs of feeling and experience.

That's very hard for some fathers to admit. Emotional expression can be threatening to many men, much to the chagrin of researchers like Steve Bergman:

People tell me, "You're just talking about the feminization of men! You just want men to become like women." We're not talking about the feminization of men, but about the "relationalization" of both genders. If, in this culture, that is taken as feminization, then we are in big trouble. That's what we're up against.

In our research, we ask thousands of eighth grade boys, "What do you want girls to know about you?"

It rips your heart out to hear what they say: "I'm not really like this. I'm a nice guy underneath. I act like a pervert, but I really care. Don't believe my behavior and my actions."

Does acting like a jerk really do our sons any good? As grown men, we know better; we know that the strategies for attachment and intimacy with a life partner do not include conquest and the masquerade that men's activist Jackson Katz calls our "Tough Guise." I enjoy being a man and doing "guy stuff" like going to a ball game and hanging out with male friends. I've never found that to be incompatible with nurturing my daughters, being openly affectionate and caring, resolving problems head on without violence, and admitting my mistakes. To me, "real men" are the guys who see this kind of ongoing, intimate involvement in fathering as a badge of honor.

Having these kids laid a foundation for me to be at peace inside and with the world around us. It's a foundation for being able to give, and for being able to forgive. I've fought that stigma of

being a big tough black guy. There's been some of that all my life.
I used to have a quick temper. But through my kids, I was able
to see the whole of life, and not just that narrow vision from
stereotypes. I don't want to lose that. It's helped me to separate the
negative from the positive and to see people as people.

Gerald

We need real boys and men in our world more than we need men and boys strutting around trying to prove they are "tough." Jackson Katz argues convincingly that when we continually masquerade behind a "tough guise," we lose track of our ability to connect with the brotherhood of living, breathing men. That's a connection too vital to miss.

I have a friend who grew up on a Midwest farm. As a young boy, he and his father were visiting their neighbor's farm, and my friend wandered by himself into the barn. He accidentally knocked over an unlit kerosene lamp. When the neighbor found the broken lamp, the boy said he didn't know how it happened. The neighbor believed him—because the boy's father had such a strong reputation for honesty. On their way home, the boy's father asked, "Did you break the lantern?" and the son said yes. So they made a U-turn and went back to the neighbor's place.

I still get teary eyed about this—we drove up as our neighbor,
John, was just going into the house. There was no way I was
going to get out of the car. My dad said, "My son wants to tell
you something." I said, "I'm sorry, John. I broke your lantern."
To this day, what I remember about this experience is John lean-
ing down, looking through the open car door at me. I'm looking
down and crying. And he said, "Well, by God, it takes a real
man to admit that he lied." He didn't say another word. My dad
got back in the car. My dad didn't say another word. We drove
home. We went and slopped the hogs and milked the cows. "By
God, it takes a real man to admit that he lied," and somehow I

*felt like I was, that I was a good person. That I was willing to
admit that I had screwed up. It was like this coming of age
thing. Like being accepted into manhood. Accepted into the company of these honest men.*

Gene

We, our sons, and every boy need to be welcomed into the company of men with integrity and respect. That need becomes more
vivid when we have children of our own and imagine our sons
(or our daughters) battling with our culture's male gender straitjacket and its narrow ideas about manhood. We need to be their
example—men courageously sharing our integrity and respect.
Ironically, our daughters can help us learn how.

*I think that if girls can have that kind of emotional, honest, soft
kind of relationship with their fathers, it could go a long way to
changing things for the better for men and boys.*

Bob

Daughters bring so many of us a wider range of experience than we
felt able to have as eighth grade boys. That daughter-driven experience enhances our true masculinity. We need courage to resist the
pressure to conform to a harmfully narrow definition of manhood.
We need courage to venture farther into the unfamiliar territory of
emotional, "soft" relationships. Our very own daughters can be
valuable teachers, giving us courage and sharing the wonderful gift
of emotional awareness.

Nearly every time I ask a father of a daughter if he's learned anything from having a daughter, the answer is "Yes!"

*What's striking about having a daughter is her very candid,
heartfelt comments. With your spouse, there's always a kind of
sense of caution or carefulness. You have to avoid treading on the
other person's psychology too much; you've got to live with them.*

There's kind of an implicit contract there. But, without too much exaggeration, having a daughter is kind of like having, for a short period of time, a Greek oracle in your life. She'll go away eventually. But meanwhile she sits there and tells you things that you need to know—that your wife won't tell you. You have an advantage in life because you have that candor coming out.

David

The more I listen to my daughter, the more I understand about myself. All the mistakes I've made (and, no doubt, the mistakes yet to come) provide my daughters with ample opportunity to practice forgiveness, acceptance, and seeing the good in people. But, through my relationship with my daughters, I also learn one of a man's most important lessons—that I don't have to be perfect for someone to love me deeply.

LETTING GO WITHOUT SAYING GOOD-BYE

As a father, you hear the name "Dad" and "Daddy" quite a bit. One day I was driving home with Erika, when she would've just turned twelve. It was quiet in the car, which is really rare, because we usually listen to music or talk. All of a sudden out of nowhere, she started to ask me something and when she said "Daddy?" it struck me. In that little moment, I felt how amazing it is that I'm her father.

Rik

The most powerful name anyone will ever call us is Daddy. If you take nothing else from this book, take the courage to absorb all of what the name "Dad" means. Listen to your daughter and talk with another concerned father. What you hear will drive home how much you matter to your daughter, how much she matters to you, and how much fathers matter to each other. Yes, we'll stumble and blunder no matter how hard we try to listen to girls and talk with dads. But that's all part of the profession. And, for a man, there's no better career move in the world than earning the title of Father.

This Christmas my twelve-year-old daughter presented me with a typed letter and montage of framed and matted pictures of us since she ws an infant. The letter is a culmination of almost nine years (since my divorce) of great tenderness and closeness we've shared as single dad and daughter. I framed and display it proudly in my home. Here it is, word for word: "Dad, over this past year I've been thinking about how lucky I am to have a father who cares about me like no one else. Sure there are a lot of others who care about me just as much, but, Dad, you make me feel like I am talking to someone my age. Like a best friend. Someone I can call in any type of situation, someone who can act like a teen, and a parent at the same time. Someone who can make me feel comfortable talking about anything*! Dad, I love you more than anyone could ever love you, and I mean anyone! Sure, Grandma, Grandpa, Aunt Cindy, and Uncle Jeff could argue, but they don't have the kind of relationship that you and I cherish together.*

"Now that I am older, I look back at the old times, and I don't see you and Mom separating as being a bad thing. I see it as something that God knew was the right thing. And now God's not the only one who knows it was the right thing, I do. Because I wouldn't have had nearly as much love surrounding me as I do now.

"Well, Dad, I am ending this letter letting you know that you always have and you always will have a huge part, not only in my life, but also in my heart. I love you, Dad."

Phil

Stories like this confirm that each one of us has a tremendous influence on our daughters, and they on us. This reciprocal father-daughter influence will last the rest of a father's life, even when he is no longer the most important man in his daughter's life.

Our daughters' dreams will take them places we can't imagine. If we fear those great unknowns, then we're much more likely to hold our daughters back through overprotection or other futile tactics. If we remember the imagination of our own youth, and learn to see our daughters' unknown journeys as great adventures, then we're much more likely to nurture their strengths and get excited about their future, passions and dreams.

If we do a decent job of this, we can be pretty confident that they'll be OK as they grow into womanhood. And if we do a decent job of this, we feel so close to them that it's impossible to imagine letting them go—letting them grow into women and move away from us physically and emotionally. The ultimate paradox of fathering a daughter—the toughest thing a father of a daughter ever does—is letting her go.

When my daughters finished their high school years, Mavis went right off to a college eight hundred miles away. Nia elected to stay home, work, go part time to the local community college, and travel a bit. I saw this as a real bonus; I'd get to delay saying goodbye to my "last remaining daughter."

Indeed, it was a bonus. While we had our friction, we got along well. She probably said, "Dad! Duh; I'm grown up. You don't have to tell me" less often than she had every right to (very considerate of her, I thought). But much of the time, it felt like we were living as housemates and friends, having adult conversations and enjoying time together. Still, at her age, she can take only so much of living at home. After a year and a half, Nia also went away to an even more distant college.

So there I was, losing my last remaining daughter. I helped her set up the dorm room, antenna attuned to any sign of nerves or uncertainty on her part. I hovered—the behavior Nia likes least from me. But, hey, it was for her own good! I wanted to be sure the other kids liked her and that she wouldn't feel lonely or overwhelmed when we left. It was lost on me that my fears were more suited to dropping a ten-year-old off at camp than a twenty-year-old at college.

Nia was (for the first few hours of registration red tape and furniture moving) patient and tolerant. Once the room was set up, while sneaking in some more hugs, Nancy and I did a couple of final not-really-necessary checks on everything (acting as if there were no Wal-Marts or Targets in that part of the country). Finally, Nia herded us downstairs to the lobby of her dorm. Reluctant to actually get in the car and drive away, I reached out for one final hug. In a firm, loving (and only slightly annoyed) voice, Nia held up her hand and said, "Yes, I love you. Now go away."

A little part of my feelings hurt when she said that, but I also felt very proud and ready to lovingly let her go. All in all, it's hard for me to imagine a better phrase to cap off the most important phase of being a father—the time when my daughter is a child. With "Yes, I love you. Now go away," my daughter told me how important I still am to her, and that she is ready to be on her own.

I believe that's the best and most valuable thing I can ask from being a father: my daughter loves me and she feels strong enough to live her life on her own terms.

TOOLS

TEN TIPS FOR DADS WITH DAUGHTERS

1. **Listen to girls.** Focus on what is really important—what my daughter thinks, believes, feels, dreams, and does—rather than how she looks. I have a profound influence on how my daughter views herself. When I value my daughter for her true self, I give her confidence to use her talents in the world.

2. **Encourage her strength and celebrate her savvy.** Help my daughter learn to recognize, resist, and overcome barriers. Help her develop her strengths to achieve her goals, help other people, and help herself. Help her be what Girls Incorporated calls **Strong, Smart and Bold!**

3. **Respect her uniqueness.** Urge her to love her body and discourage dieting. Make sure my daughter knows that I love her for who she is and see her as a whole person, capable of anything. My daughter is likely to choose a life partner who acts like me and has my values. So, treat her and those she loves with respect. Remember (a) growing girls need to eat often and healthy; (b) dieting doesn't work; and she has her body for what it can do, not how it looks. Advertisers spend billions to convince my daughter she doesn't look "right." **I won't buy into it.**

4. **Get physically active with her.** Play catch, tag, jump rope, basketball, Frisbee, hockey, soccer, or just take walks . . . you name it. Physically active girls are less likely to get pregnant, drop out of school, or put up with an abusive partner. Studies show that the most physically active girls have *fathers* who are active with them. Being physically active with her is a great investment.

5. **Get involved in my daughter's school.** Volunteer, chaperone, read to her class. Ask tough questions, like: Does the school have

and use media literacy and body-image awareness programs? Does it tolerate sexual harassment of boys or girls? Do more boys take advanced math and science classes and if so, why? (California teacher Doug Kirkpatrick's girl students weren't interested in science, so he changed his methods and their participation soared!) Are at least half of the student leaders girls?

6. **Get involved in my daughter's activities.** Volunteer to drive, coach, direct a play, teach a class—anything! Demand equality. Texas mortgage officer and volunteer basketball coach Dave Chapman was so appalled by the gym his nine-year-old daughter's team had to use, he fought to open the modern "boy's" gym to the girls' team. He succeeded. Dads make a difference!

7. **Help make the world better for girls.** This world holds dangers for our daughters. But my overprotection doesn't work, and it tells my daughter that I don't trust her! Instead, work with other parents to demand an end to violence against females, media sexualization of girls, pornography, advertisers making billions feeding on our daughters' insecurities, and all "boys are more important than girls" attitudes.

8. **Take my daughter to work with me.** Participate in every April's Take Our Daughters and Sons to Work (sm) Day and make sure my business participates. Show her how I pay bills and manage my money. My daughter will have a job and pay rent someday, so I need to introduce her to the world of work and finances!

9. **Support positive alternative media for girls.** Join with the family to watch programs that portray smart, savvy girls. Subscribe to healthy girl-edited magazines like *New Moon* and visit online girl-run " 'zines" and Web sites. It's not enough to condemn what's bad, I must support and use media that support my daughter!

10. **Talk to other fathers.** Together, we fathers have reams of experience, expertise, and encouragement to share. There's a lot

we can learn from each other. And we can have a lot of influence—for example, Dads and Daughters protests stop negative ads. We can make things better for girls when we work together!

TEN TIPS FOR LIVE-AWAY DADS

(Dads who live away from their children due to divorce, separation, or conflict with the child's mother.)

1. **Hang in there for the long haul**. My involvement in my daughter's life may be different than my dreams for the two of us when she was little, but it is no less important. I remain a tremendous influence in her life and need to stay involved in a calm, loving, and committed way forever.
2. **Develop healthy social and emotional supports for myself**. Some live-away dads struggle to handle anger and loneliness with maturity. These feelings are normal, but I must be careful not to become emotionally dependent on my daughter. Instead, I need to spend time with healthy adults and have my emotional and social needs met through them.
3. **Remember that my daughter lives in two homes**. I need to be patient if my daughter doesn't do chores or follow rules the way I want. She has different rules in her mother's house. She may sometimes be upset or moody when she leaves my home or her mother's home. I need to remember that my relationship with her is much more important than getting her to do things the way I think she should.
4. **Father the best I can when she is with me**. I cannot change how her mother raises her or make up for what her mother does or doesn't do. I can't correct excessive leniency by her mother with

excessive strictness on my part. Instead, I need to father her calmly. Give her choices. Be a patient and loving father, not a demanding and critical perfectionist. Be the dad she can always talk to and trust to support her—even when she makes mistakes.

5. **Keep my daughter out of the middle—even if her mother doesn't.** Speak well about my daughter's mother even when I'm angry at her—and even if she talks poorly about me. Negative talk about my daughter's mother is a little wound to my daughter, and causes her to think less of herself, her mom, and me. I'll resolve adult conflicts away from my daughter and allow her to be the child.

6. **My daughter and her mother are different people.** I'll not misdirect anger at my daughter's mother toward my daughter. When my daughter does not listen to me, does less than her best in school, or makes other mistakes (normal behaviors for most kids), I'll be careful not to confuse my daughter's mistakes with her mother's actions, and instead, I'll see what I can do to make things better.

7. **Give my daughter consistent time and attention.** My daughter needs my healthy attention in person, on the phone, over the Internet, through the mail, or any other way. I can't try to buy her love with things—even if her mother does. My daughter needs my presence, not my presents.

8. **Listen to my daughter.** Lecturing and arguing get me nowhere. It does not help if I minimize my daughter's feelings or falsely tell her everything will be okay when I can't guarantee that it will. Instead, I need to listen and be there for her. Accept my daughter for who she is; not who I *want* her to be, think she *should* be, or think she *would* be if she were raised only by me. I'll take the lead in communicating—even when I feel unappreciated. I may not agree with everything she says or does, but when I listen, I build the emotional connection that will help her listen to me when it really counts.

9. **Focus on my daughter's positives**. Many men were raised by fathers pointing out what we did wrong, so we could fix it. That may work on the job, but intimate personal relationships are not like a job. Focusing on negatives undermines her strength and confidence—already stretched by living in two homes.

10. **Be her father, not her mother**. I am a powerful and encouraging role model, and I'll tell her that she has a special place in my heart. My masculine actions and loving words can help her realize that she too can be adventurous, playful, and successful—and should expect respect from affectionate, honorable men.

ACKNOWLEDGMENTS

This book will never know how much its many mothers and fathers gave, but it does know their names.

The candor of the fathers and daughters I met in one-on-one interviews, at the First Unitarian Church of Oklahoma City, the Rochester, Minnesota, Community Education program, and on the DadTalk Internet group is an honor to witness.

My good friends Joan Drury, Don Chapin, Gary Spoerle, and Maureen Michelson provided space and time to begin this project. Joan's huge gift of two quiet months on Lake Superior's North Shore helped me sift through reams of interview transcripts. Joan and Maureen also formed a cross-country cabal with my wife and agent to prod me to start the book.

The extraordinary Amber Winonah Rysdam Miller transcribed nearly every interview tape, and added her insight as a daughter completing adolescence. Special thanks to Mark King for providing transcripts of his interviews with me.

Dozens of *New Moon* magazine fans responded when I first sought fathers to interview. The following families even put me up in their homes (though some had never met me before): Dabney, Peterson-Fox, Airhart, Muller, Freedman, Fellner, Mitchell, Peacock-Broyles, Lerner-Sadker, Llewellyn, Naclerio, Nemeth, Georgeiff, Richard, Melly, Karr, Kelly, and Gruver. I learned a ton from the editors of *New Moon* magazine—dynamic proof of the constructive power girls generate when adults let them work. I was also blessed with learning, challenge, and support from my former adult *New Moon* colleagues: Barbara Stretchberry, Tya Ward, Mary Jeronimus, Angie Miller, Linda Estel, Deb Mylin, Andrea McKinnon, Sherry Boyce, Barb Sheedy, Bridget Grosser, Amanda Norenberg, Beth Cooper Benjamin, Dyann Logwood, Ophira Edut, Shelly Johnson, Crys Lundberg, Mary Streufert, Rain Newcomb, Autumn Libal, Karen Ostovich, and Lynette Lamb.

Support and inspiration also came from a network of amazing colleagues and friends: David Sadker, Drummond Pike, Will Glennon, Joe Jennings, Phyllis Lerner, Don Streufert, Michael Kimmel, Margo Maine, Michael Levine, Rosalie Maggio, Steve Emmett, Sarah Stinson, William Klein, Bill Klatte, Frank Barnes, Robert Vokes and Linda Vokes, Steven Botkin, Jim Pipher, Hollie Ainbinder, Holly Hoff, Leroy Fykes, Jean Kilbourne, Kathy Kater, David Pate, Mike Hayes, Mary Pipher, Annie Rogers, Karen Zittleman, Euan Kerr, Susannah Sheffer, Sean Taylor, Jenna Cornick, Jessica Flipp, and Dusty "Daddy" Johnson.

I learned how to father from two good men: my dad, Joe Kelly, and my grandfather, Frank "Bepa" Barnes. Far from perfect, they freely showered their attention, affection, and passion for justice on my sisters and me.

My first editor, Suzanne Oaks, and her colleague, Claire Johnson, graced us with very sharp analysis and sound guidance that made this book make more sense—and a lot easier to read. Trish Medved, and her colleague, James Benson, continued the support I felt from everyone at Broadway Books, and shared great stories about Trish's daughter. Publicists Erin Curtin and Betsy Areddy put up with my many questions and worries. Their enthusiasm never flagged.

Everyone should be so lucky as to work with Robin Dellabough. She is funny, honest, businesslike, determined, brave, and everything else you want in a good friend. She's also a literary agent with a magical knack for getting an author's voice from his mouth to the reader's eye. Robin finally convinced me that this would be fun, and she was right.

The day that Robin and I finished the proposal for this book, Dads and Daughters' Deputy Director Heather Henderson died. A teacher, partner, catalyst, communicator, organizer, writer, Web-maven and friend, Heather's death painfully clarifies the need for this book and the DADs organization; her heart still pulses through both.

Michael Kieschnick is first of all a good father to his son and daughter. He also created Dads and Daughters. A visionary who connects the personal and the cultural, Michael had the insight to recognize the unique influence of one dad on his daughter—and the ability of mobilized fathers to make the world better for all daughters (and, therefore, better for sons). He also had the courage to make his vision a reality and the faith to keep it alive.

I embarked on this project to explore the ways I've been changed by two remarkable women, Mavis Barnes Gruver and Antonia Brenckman Kelly. They influenced me so much that I changed careers to work with them. They've grown and moved away now. Still, nothing tops being their dad.

My longest-serving colleague and fellow student of daughters is Nancy Gruver. I still scratch my head at how this beautiful tornado of affection, brains, passion, creativity, and persistence decided to marry me. While taking on a huge load of new projects, including her own forthcoming book, Nancy was also this author's memory jogger, concept challenger, idea stimulator, and most fervent believer. Every single night there's a good reason to put Nancy on my gratitude list.

RESOURCES

RECOMMENDED READING FOR DADS

On General Fathering

Beyond Dolls and Guns: 101 Ways to Help Children Avoid Gender Bias by Susan Hoy Crawford (Heinemann, 1996).

The Courage to Raise Good Men by Dr. Olga Silverstein and Beth Rashbaum (Viking, 1994). Raising full-blooded boys who have strength, compassion, fear, love—in other words, the full experience of being human.

Covering Home: Lessons on the Art of Fathering from the Game of Baseball by Jack Petrash (Robins Lane Press, 2001). In fathering and baseball, you have to practice the fundamentals, develop good habits, avoid errors, work on your control, and always remember that you can't win them all.

The Expectant Father by Armin Brott (Abbeville Press, 2001). Lays a good foundation for starting out as an involved dad, and staying that way.

The Collected Wisdom of Fathers: Creating Loving Bonds That Last a Lifetime by William Glennon (Conari Press, 2002). A fathering bible. Not simply a "how-to" book, but a deeply enriching "why-to" book. I highly recommend it.

Fathering Daughters: Reflections by Men edited by DeWitt Henry and James McPherson (Beacon Press, 1999). Compelling essays by dads about the magical relationship between father and daughter.

Fatherneed: Why Father Care Is as Essential as Mother Care for Your Child by Dr.

Kyle D. Pruett (Free Press, 2000). Practical ideas for dads and stepdads in all situations, and ways that absent-dad families can find what they need.

Parenting Our Daughters: For Parents and Other Caring Adults by Judy Gordon (Girls Count, 1999). A resource that helps adults help girls develop into resilient and successful women.

Reviving Ophelia: Saving the Selves of Adolescent Girls by Mary Pipher (Ballantine, 1995). The classic *New York Times* best-seller that describes the serious issues girls face, and what we can do about them.

The Shelter of Each Other: Rebuilding Our Families by Mary Pipher (Ballantine Books, 1996). Compelling evidence to assign family problems as much to culture as to parents, while inspiring us to create community—probably our biggest family challenge today.

200 Ways to Raise a Girl's Self-Esteem by Will Glennon (Conari Press, 2000). Practical tips and wonderful ideas to draw on every day.

The War Against Parents: What We Can Do for America's Beleaguered Moms and Dads by Sylvia Ann Hewlett and Cornel West (Houghton Mifflin, 1998). Two prominent social critics present a passionate challenge to how little support society gives parents.

What Parents Need to Know About Dating Violence by Barrie Levy and Patricia Occhiuzzo Giggans (Seal Press, 1995). Straightforward advice on topics ranging from how to recognize warning signs to how to encourage healthy teen relationships.

Working Fathers: New Strategies for Balancing Work and Family by James A. Levine and Todd L. Pittinsky (Harcourt Brace, 1997). A provocative, sorely needed, and easy-to-grasp look at our culture's assumptions about a father's family role—and what we can do to change them.

200 Ways to Raise a Boy's Emotional Intelligence by Will Glennon (Conari Press, 2000).

On Body Image and Eating Disorders

The Body Project by Joan Jacobs Brumberg (Vintage, 1998). A fascinating comparison of adolescent girls' diaries, showing how today's girls make their bodies (instead of their lives) into "projects."

Body Wars, Making Peace with Women's Bodies by Margo Maine, Ph.D. (Gurze Designs & Books, 1999). Guide for parents, educators, therapists, patients, or anyone who wants to fight against the forces that prevent women from being comfortable in their own bodies.

Fasting Girls: The History of Anorexia Nervosa by Joan Jacobs Brumberg (Vintage, 2000). Dispels the myth that anorexia nervosa is a new disease and tells why it's become such an epidemic in today's culture.

Father Hunger: Fathers, Daughters and Food by Margo Maine, Ph.D. (Gurze Designs & Books, 1991). The classic study of how fathers influence girls' relationships to their bodies, self-image, and food. An essential book for dads concerned about eating disorders.

Healthy Body Image: Teaching Kids to Eat and Love Their Bodies, Too! by Kathy Kater (National Eating Disorders Association, 1998).

On Divorce

How to Survive Your Parents' Divorce: Kids' Advice to Kids by Gayle Kimball (Equality=Press, 1994). More than 250 kids talk frankly about what they've been through, what they need, what works, and what doesn't. This short book is essential reading for any parent or child living in divorce.

Live-Away Dads: Staying a Part of Your Children's Lives When They Aren't a Part of Your Home by William C. Klatte (Penguin, 1999). Simply the best book available for a dad who, for any reason, lives away from his kids. Effective, loving ways to build connection by using your most effective tool (and the only tool you can really control): yourself.

On Education

Beyond the "Gender Wars": *A Conversation about Girls, Boys and Education* by AAUW Educational Foundation (American Association of University Women, 2001). This short report demolishes the useless boy vs. girl debate in education and recasts the issues in ways that provide progress and hope for all.

Failing at Fairness: How America's Schools Cheat Girls by Dr. Myra Sadker and Dr. David Sadker (Scribners, 1994). This easy-to-read classic provides powerful evidence of how schools reinforce harmful gender straitjackets for girls and boys; plus, there are effective strategies to combat the problem.

Gender Play: Girls and Boys in School by Barrie Thorne (Rutgers University Press, 1993). Refreshing insights on gender self-segregation on elementary school playgrounds, and how this shapes kids' ideas of their gender roles.

Schoolgirls by Peggy Orenstein (Doubleday, 1994). An intimate and provocative glimpse into the lives of adolescent schoolgirls at two West Coast middle schools by journalist Orenstein (formerly managing editor of *Mother Jones*).

On the Media

The Beauty Myth by Naomi Wolf (William Morrow, 1991). A must-read classic on how cultural and media images of "beauty" are used against girls and women.

Can't Buy My Love: How Advertising Changes the Way We Think and Feel by Dr. Jean Kilbourne (Touchstone Books, 2000). Kilbourne paints a gripping portrait of how the barrage of advertising affects kids, especially girls, with false promises of rebellion, connection, and control.

Dr. Dave's Cyberhood: Making Media Choices That Create a Healthy Electronic Environment for Your Kids by Dr. David Walsh (Fireside, 2001). A fun and very practical guide to keeping children safe and savvy in the media neighborhood they visit every day.

Selling out America's Children: How America Puts Profits Before Values and What Parents Can Do by Dr. David Walsh (Fairview Press, 1995). In a good short book, Walsh, head of The Center for Media and the Family, tells how kids and adults can counteract excessive marketing to kids.

On Sexuality

All About Sex: A Family Resource on Sex and Sexuality by Planned Parenthood Federation of America (Three Rivers Press, 1997). Planned Parenthood gets a lot of flack from many quarters, but this book proves that no one is better at providing realistic, understandable information about sexuality—which is what we and our kids need to make healthy decisions.

Changing Bodies, Changing Lives by Ruth Bell Alexander (Times Books, 1998). A classic, comprehensive, and honest guide for daughter or dad; the physical, emotional, sexual, and social changes girls and boys face.

Homosexuality: The Secret a Child Dare Not Tell by Mary Ann Cantwell (Rafael Press, 1996). A parent's look at myths and lessons we teach our kids, and new ways to parent and mentor lesbian and gay young people.

The Teenage Body Book by Kathy McCoy (Perigee, 1999).

Ten Talks Parents Must Have with Their Children About Sex and Character by Pepper Schwartz, Ph.D., and Dominic Cappello (Hyperion, 2000). Advice on exactly how to begin and what to say not just about sex, but safety, character, peer pressure, ethics, meeting people on the Internet, and mixed messages from TV.

On Sports

The Frailty Myth: Women Approaching Physical Equality by Colette Dowling (Random House, 2000). This book includes a lot about male perspectives on girls in sports, and how dads can help get girls out of thinking they can't "measure up" when it comes to physicality.

The Stronger Women Get, the More Men Love Football: Sexism and the American Culture of Sports by Mariah Burton Nelson (Avon, 1994). A leading writer on women and sports, Burton Nelson exposes the cost to men and women of the uneven playing field. This is a classic book.

Organizations, Web Sites, and Other Resources

About Face. The Web site of a group of young female activists who skewer media appearance obsessions. Very funny and educational. Web site: www.about-face.org.

At-Home Dad. National newsletter for at-home dads. Phone: (508) 685-7931, www.athomedad.com.

BodyImageHealth. Designed to promote healthy body image attitudes and prevent eating and weight concerns before they start. Web site: www.BodyImageHealth.org.

The Center on Fathers, Families, and Public Policy (CFFPP). The center provides policy research, technical assistance, training, and public education on the barriers faced by never-married, low-income fathers and their families. Web site: www.cffpp.org.

The Center for Media Education. A leader in creating a quality electronic media culture for children and youth, their families, and the community. Web site: www.cme.org.

Center for Media Literacy. Excellent resources to make our kids and us more media savvy. Phone: (800) 226-9494. Web site: www.medialit.org.

Daughters: For Parents of Girls. The award-winning national newsletter with practical information on raising healthy, confident girls. Phone: (888) 849-8476. Web site: www.daughters.com.

U.S. Department of Health and Human Services Fatherhood Initiative. Good statistical information and outlines of budgets and government definitions of fathers and their roles as parents. Web site: www.fatherhood.hhs.gov.

Eating Disorders Coalition for Research, Policy, and Action is a national nonprofit working for federal investment in the healthy development of children. Dads and Daughters sits on EDC's Board of Directors. Web site: www.eatingdisorderscoalition.org.

The Family Violence Prevention Fund (FVPF). This organization works to end domestic violence and helps women and children whose lives are devastated by abuse. Site includes information on how to take a stand against domestic violence. Web site: www.fvpf.org.

The Fatherhood Project at Families & Work Institute. Check out their links page for great ideas. Web site: www.fatherhoodproject.org.

Gender and Diversities Institute. The institute is committed to achieving gender equality, sustainable development, and human rights for everyone. Web site: www.edc.org/GDI.

Girl Power—Fathers Are Powerful. Offers research and statistics, activities for dads and daughters, resources. Web site: www.girlpower.gov/AdultsWhoCare/fathers/index.htm.

Girls Incorporated. Provides resources for adults to help girls become strong, smart, and bold. Web site: www.girls-inc.org.

Girl Scouts of the USA. Helps create strong girls, and has close to 100 years experience at it! Plus, there are opportunities for fathers to volunteer. Web site: www.girlscouts.org.

Gurze Designs & Books. Publishes and distributes books on body image and eating disorders. Phone: (800) 756-7553. Web site: www.gurze.com.

Harvard Center for Eating Disorders. Good, solid research and information. Phone: (617) 236-7766. Web site: www.hedc.org.

Making Your Voice Heard: A Media Toolkit for Youth. Filled with activities and projects to help teens challenge negative portrayals; from the Canadian Media Awareness Network, one of the best media literacy sites. Web site: www.media-awareness.ca/eng/comm/youth/toolkh/index3.htm.

Math, Science, Technology Programs for Girls. Web site: www.aauw.org/2000/models.html.

Melpomene Institute. Studies the link between self-esteem and physical activity in girls and women. Web site: www.melpomene.org.

Me and My Dad. A Web site with weekly tips on strengthening your coparent relationships. Web site: www.extension.iastate.edu/dads/together.html.

Myra Sadker Advocates for Gender Equity. A nonprofit organization dedicated to promoting equity in and beyond schools. Web site: www.sadker.org.

National Association for Girls and Women in Sport. Web site: www.aahperd.org.

National Clearinghouse for Alcohol and Drug Information. Phone: (800) 729-6686. Web site: www.health.org.

National Coalition of Girls' Schools: Great resources for parents from educators specializing in girls. Web site: www.ncgs.org.

National Eating Disorders Association. NEDA is the premier organization for heading off eating disorders before they start. 603 Stewart Street, Suite 803, Seattle, WA 98101 Phone: (206) 382-3587; Referral Hotline: (800) 931-2237. Web site: www.nationaleatingdisorders.org.

National Organization of Men Against Sexism. This small, but national, group holds an interesting annual conference. Web site: www.nomas.org.

The National Women's Health Information Center. Phone: (800) 994-9662. Web site: www.4woman.gov.

The Parents Choice Foundation. The country's oldest and most respected nonprofit guide to children's media and products. Web site: www.parents-choice.org.

Partnership for a Drug–Free America. Phone: (888) 575-3115. Web site: www.drugfreeamerica.org.

Safer Child. Provides great information and resources on a huge range of parenting issues. Web site: www.saferchild.org.

Stop Commercial Exploitation of Children (SCEC). A coalition of health care professionals, parents, educators, and businesses combating escalating corporate marketing directed at children. Web site: www.commercialexploitation.com.

Teaching Tolerance, published twice a year, is a beautiful magazine with great, useful articles—and it's free for teachers! Contact Southern Poverty Law Center, 400 Washington Avenue, Montgomery, AL 36104. Phone: (334) 264-0286. Web site: www.splcenter.org.

Wellesley Centers for Women. Cutting edge research on gender relations and girls' issues. Web site: www.wcwonline.org.

Women's Political Voice. Encourages girls and young women to choose a career in politics. Web site: www.wpvoice.org.

Women's Sports Foundation. The number-one information resource for girls' and women's sports and fitness. Web site: www.womenssportsfoundation.org.

RECOMMENDED READING FOR DAUGHTERS

The Girls' Book of Friendship edited by Catherine Dee (Little, Brown, 2001). Stories and tips on finding and being a good friend.

The Girls' Guide to Life: How to Take Charge of the Issues That Affect You by Catherine Dee (Little, Brown, 1997). Very down to earth guide to taking action personally and in the community.

In Love and in Danger: A Teen's Guide to Breaking Free of Abusive Relationships by Barrie Levy (Seal Press, 1993). An excellent, short look at a hidden and dangerous problem—abusive relationships between young people.

New Moon Friendship (Crown, 1999).

New Moon Money (Crown, 2000).

New Moon Sports (Crown, 1999).

New Moon Writing (Crown, 2000).

This is a jewel of a series edited and written by girls around the United States, with stories, poems, activities, and advice on key issues for young women. Unique books with a great perspective.

No More Frogs to Kiss: 99 Ways to Give Economic Power to Girls by Joline Godfrey (HarperBusiness, 1995). Strategies to help young women become financially savvy.

The Period Book: Everything You Don't Want to Ask (But Need to Know) by Jennifer Gravelle and Karen Gravelle (Walker & Company, 1996). Written by a thirteen-year-old and her aunt.

Real Girl/Real World: Tools for Finding Your True Self by Heather Gray and Samantha Phillips (Seal Press, 1998). Honest and enjoyable to read.

Refuse to Use: A Girl's Guide to Drugs and Alcohol by Ann Kirby-Payne (Rosen, 1999).

Taking Charge of My Mind and Body: A Girl's Guide to Outsmarting Alcohol, Drug, Smoking, and Eating Problems by Gladys Folkers and Jeanne Engleman (Free Spirit, 1997).

Totally Private and Personal: Journaling Ideas for Girls and Young Women by Jessica Wilbur (Free Spirit, 1996).

Webster's Dictionary of American Women (Smithmark, 1996). Over 1,500 brief biographies of U.S. women in history.

You Go Girl! by Kim Doren and Charlie Jones (Stark Books, 2000). Premier athletes like Marion Jones and Chris Evert contributed to this book of lessons aimed at inspiring girls into and in sports.

Organizations, Web Sites, and Other Resources for Daughters

Girl Power. Helps encourage and empower nine- to fourteen-year-old girls. Phone: (800) 729-6686. Web site: www.health.org/gpower.

Girls' Pipeline to Power. Helps girls speak up and take action! Web site: www.girls-pipeline.org.

New Moon: The Magazine for Girls and Their Dreams. This award-winning international magazine is edited by girls ages eight to fourteen and has no advertising. The ultimate alternative publication and one of the best tools to build girls' self-esteem. Phone: (800) 381-4743. Web site: www.newmoon.org.

The School Zone. Office of National Drug Control Policy (ONDCP) information on safety, citizenship, crime prevention, alcohol and drug abuse, HIV/AIDS, labor laws, teen pregnancy. Web site: www.whitehousedrugpolicy.gov/prevent/schoolzone/.

UniverseGirl.com. Encourages girls in math, science, and computer or technology courses. Web site: www.UniverseGirl.com.

www.genderliteracy.com. Women's history as a prevention tool. Building girls' esteem by learning women's heritage.

Web sites for and about Girls. Links to many resources for girls on the Internet. Web site: www.aauw.org/1000/grlsites.html.

Grateful acknowledgment is made to the following for permission to use previously published material:

New Moon Publishing, Inc., for excerpts from the newsletter *New Moon Network: For Adults Who Care About Girls.* Copyright New Moon Publishing, Inc. Used by permission.

Bea Cole, David Glesener, and Bob Whitlow for excerpts from their essays, previously published in *New Moon Network: For Adults Who Care About Girls.* Used by permission of the authors.

Rick Epstein for an excerpt from his book *Rookie Dad: Mediations from the Backyard* (Hyperion, 1992). Used by permission of the author.

Will Glennon for an excerpt from his book *Fathering: Strengthening Connection with Your Children No Matter Where You Are* (Conari Press, 1995). Reprinted by permission of the author.

Kathy Kater for an adaptation of an exercise from her curriculum "Healthy Body Image: Teaching Kids to Eat and Love Their Body, Too!" (NEDA, 1998). Used by permission.

Dads and Daughters for use of "How Well Am I Doing as My Daughter's Father?" quiz, "10 Tips for Fathers and Daughters," and "Ten Tips for Live-Away Dads." Copyright Dads and Daughters, used by permission.

National Eating Disorders Association and Students Against Driving Drunk/Students Against Destructive Decisions for resource materials from their Web sites. Used by permission.

Do you have a story to share about fathering your daughter? E-mail Dads and Daughters at dadsbook@dadsanddaughters.org and tell about your triumphs, struggles, strategies, and joys. Your story may be used in future DADs programs, so please include your full name, address, phone, and e-mail address. Thanks!

Dads and Daughters is the national, nonprofit membership organization of fathers with daughters. DADs provides tools to strengthen father-daughter relationships and to transform the pervasive messages that value daughters more for how they look than who they are.

With a DADs membership, you will:

- get the latest tips and facts on fathering girls.
- receive our biweekly e-mail update, filled with ideas and resources.
- support national actions that influence media, advertisers, and businesses to treat our daughters better.
- learn from dads nationwide—to help your own community and home.

Join DADS today!
Enclosed is my tax-deductible check for:
☐ $35   ☐ $45   ☐ $75   ☐ $100   ☐ $500   ☐ Other

Name _____
Address _____
City _____ State _____ Zip _____
E-mail _____
Phone _____

Mail this form to:
DADs, 2 W. First St. Suite 101, Duluth, MN 55802
Call us at 888-824-3237 for more information.
Visit our Web site www.dadsanddaughters.org to join online.
Send me _____ DADs brochures to give to my friends.

DADS

Discover the trusted resource you'll use right away.
Daughters: For Parents of Girls.
Finally, a newsletter written just for parents of girls!

Daughters gives you:
- Tried and true tips from parents
- Expert opinions and interviews
- "Field-tested" problem-solving strategies
- Practical advice about everyday issues
- Ways to help your daughter grow up as strong and confident as she deserves to be

Get one year, six issues, for only $24.95. Subscribe now!
- Online at www.daughters.com
- By phone at 888-849-8476
- Mail this form and a check to *Daughters*, 2 W. First St. Suite 101, Duluth, MN 55802

Name (please print)_____
Address _____
City _____ State _____ Zip _____
E-mail _____

Please allow 10-12 weeks for delivery of your first issue. Offer valid for U.S. subscriptions only.

Former journalist JOE KELLY is the executive director of Dads and Daughters—the national organization dedicated to improving father-daughter relationships—and father of twin adult daughters. His work has been extensively featured in the media, including NPR, CBS, ABC, *People*, *USA Today*, and the *New York Times*. He was awarded the 1995 Parenting Achievement Award from *Parenting* magazine and helped his wife, Nancy Gruver, launch *New Moon*, the award-winning international magazine edited by girls. He lives in Duluth, Minnesota.